Crossing the River

CROSSING
THE RIVER

A Life in Brazil

Amy Ragsdale

SEAL PRESS

Seal Press
A Member of the Perseus Books Group
1700 Fourth Street
Berkeley, California
sealpress.com

Library of Congress Cataloging-in-Publication Data is pending.
978-1-58005-586-4

10 9 8 7 6 5 4 3 2 1

Cover and interior design by Gopa & Ted2, Inc.
Photos courtesy of the author.
Printed in the United States of America
Distributed by Publishers Group West

For my parents, Jane and Wilmott Ragsdale,
who led the way

For my intrepid family,
Peter, Molly, and Skyler

---

*"As you set out for Ithaca, hope the voyage is a long one,
full of adventure, full of discovery."*

—*C.P. Cavafy*

Contents

Part II: Home
October, November, December

Part III: Widening the Circle
January, February

List of "Characters"

Ada: owner of Pousada da Ada

Adelaide (pronounced *Adeligee*): wife of Yanomami Headman Julio

Ana Licia, Keyla, Larissa, Leila, and **Sara:** Molly's good friends from school

Anderson (*Ahndehsohn*): son of Yanomami Headman Julio and Adelaide

Aniete: our first *empregada* and Katia's cousin

Bentinho: master teacher of the capoeira salon

Berto: son of Yanomami Headman Julio and Adelaide

Breno, Paulinho, Pedro, Ricardo (*Hicardo*), and **Victor** (*Vito*): Skyler's neighborhood gang

Brooke: Molly's friend from Missoula

Dalan, Junior (*Junio*), and **Lu:** soccer teammates of Peter's among many others

Elizia: the bookkeeper at Imaculada Conceiçao and mother of Giovanni

Fabio and **Pirulito:** members of the capoeira salon

Fernando: Molly's ballet teacher

Giovanni: our good friend and Portuguese tutor

Ilda: our landlady

Iracema: family friend and guidance counselor at Imaculada Conceiçao, the kids' school

Irma Francisca: Director of Imaculada Conceiçao

Gel: Aniete's sister

Julio: Yanomami Headman of the village of Ariabu

Kadas-Newells: family friends from Missoula

Karol (*Karau*): Molly's good friend and older sister of Victor

Katia: manager of the Pousada Colonial

Laura (*Lowra*): Katia's aunt

Maria: mom of Italo, Karol, and Victor

Mario: the kids' PE teacher

Molly: our fifteen-turning-sixteen-year-old daughter

Peter: my husband

Robson (*Hobson*): Zeca's uncle

Shirley (*Shelee*): Aniete's cousin and our *empregada* after Aniete

Shirley (*Shelee*): Zeca's aunt and Robson's wife

Skyler: our twelve-turning-thirteen-year-old son

Valdir (*Valdi*): our guide/translator when visiting the Yanomami villages

Vanessa: Skyler's English teacher at Imaculada and homework tutor

Zeca: our good friend

Prologue

STILL JET-LAGGED, I was wakened from my afternoon nap by someone pounding on the door of our third-floor room in an old colonial mansion, which was now a bed-and-breakfast. The person's weight shifted restlessly on the creaking foot-wide floorboards.

"*Eskyloh . . .*"

"Yes? *Oi?*" I flipped off the light coverlet and sat up on the edge of the bed, alone in the cavernous room. My husband Peter had gone for a run, and our kids had already been swept away by newfound friends. I couldn't pick apart the rat's nest of Portuguese coming through the door, but I instantly understood that it was urgent and was something about my son.

Our family of four had arrived three days earlier in this upriver town in northeastern Brazil, a town of brightly colored nineteenth-century row houses, sunny plazas, and spreading flame trees on an expansive stretch of the Rio São Francisco. We would be living here for a year.

I swung the door open to find Breno, our twelve-year-old son Skyler's new acquaintance. Nodding *Okay! Okay! I'm coming*, I fumbled into my flip-flops and followed Breno as he lumbered down the wide dark wood stairs. What could have happened?

Our first night in town, Skyler and his fifteen-year-old sister, Molly, had managed to join a game of soccer. They played barefoot on paving stones, on the lowest tier of a stepped-down plaza. That night, Skyler made two friends, Victor (*Vito* in Portuguese) and Breno. Breno was chunky and light-skinned, with chipmunk cheeks and a way of speaking that always sounded as if his mouth was full of bread. Victor was skinny and dark and almost inaudible. They would turn out to be Skyler's friends till the end. But now, Breno was here and Skyler was nowhere to be seen.

As we spilled out the door of the Pousada Colonial into a blast of sunshine, I saw the long crumbling balustrade bordering the wide river across the plaza and Victor standing by a small, unmarked car. Skyler's orange Crocs dangled from one of his hands. Flip-flops slapping cobblestone, Breno and I panted up to him, sweat popping on my upper lip. Victor's eyes looked worried. He silently handed me Skyler's shoes. I peered into the car. There was Skyler, sitting in front. His blond hair was dark—with blood.

"I was flipping," he choked out shakily, "off a stone wall."

Victor and I scrambled into the backseat, leaving Breno behind, as the car started up a steep hill. I'd learn later that it was an unmarked police car. I had no idea where we were going and had said nothing to the driver, nor he to me. I find when traveling in new places, where I'm not fluent in the language, I frequently trust people I might not as readily trust at home, as though, subconsciously, I recognize I'm not in control.

I reached forward, putting a hand on Skyler's shoulder.

"Sweetie, you're gonna be okay."

"It won't stop bleeding." His voice began to crack as he turned to face me.

Peter and I had noticed that, new to town, knowing no one, and bereft of language, Skyler had been pulling out every trick he knew to find a way into a possible group of friends: juggling oranges, solving Rubik's Cubes, flipping off walls. Five years earlier, when we'd begun our raising "global children" experiment in earnest and lived for a year in Mozambique, Skyler and Molly had attended an international school, where they were taught in English. As a result, though they'd acquired a multinational array of friends, they hadn't really learned the local language, Portuguese, unlike Peter and me, who had come away with some ability to communicate, if only in the present tense. We were all quickly realizing that for this year in Penedo, a small off-the-track town, we would have to figure this language thing out.

"I did two backflips"—he took a big breath—"no problem. Then I decided"—his voice began to sound squeezed—"to try a side flip."

The car skidded under the carport of the tiny hospital's *emergência*. The driver still hadn't said a word. Luckily, early on a Sunday, it wasn't busy. Skyler was whisked onto a gurney, surrounded by what seemed to be the entire staff of ten. They rolled him through the open entrance of the low concrete building, past a reception desk, through swinging double doors, and into a simple room. Its smudged white walls were lined with cupboards, in front of which were a couple of gurneys and an IV stand. Standing at his feet, I watched as a nurse began squeezing water out of a plastic bottle into his wound, cleaning out sand and blood. He looked so small. A deep gash began to emerge, arcing from the crown of his head down to his left ear.

Perhaps I looked more aghast than I realized because I was suddenly ushered out into the hall, where I was asked to *fica um pouco*—wait a little. I sat down in one of the few white plastic chairs scattered along the empty hallway, too dazed to think. I felt as though the little boat cradling our family of four had suddenly been sucked off a calm sea into a whirlpool.

Before long, an older doctor in a long white coat pushed open the door of Skyler's room and walked over to me.

"*É profundo,*" he said softly. I didn't need a dictionary to understand that. "*Sério.*"

Part I: *Crash Course*

JULY, AUGUST, SEPTEMBER

1

The Family of Man

We found ourselves in this predicament largely due to my own childhood. My parents had had a yen for travel, which inspired their approach to child rearing. But this approach had started with my father's early wanderlust. In the early 1930s, he'd repeatedly dropped out of college in Seattle to hop freighters to South America and China. Then, almost by accident, he fell into journalism, perhaps seeing a way to make a career out of adventuring. Working his way up from writing ads for an Arizona radio station to reporting news in Hartford, Connecticut, he found himself, within a few years, in Washington D.C. covering the State Department for the *Wall Street Journal*. He then jumped on the first opportunity he had to transfer abroad, this time to cover World War II for *Time/Life* out of London. After the war, he left journalism to teach and eventually became a professor at the University of Wisconsin, but he continued to finagle work abroad every four years. By this time, he'd married my mom, the daughter of a vaudeville-actor-turned-newspaper-editor and an opera singer. Luckily, she was interested in travel, too.

I spent my first two years in Thailand, second grade in the Philippines, most of middle school in Egypt. After each adventure, our small family of three would settle back into our home base, back into American life, in Madison, Wisconsin. As an adult, I found that despite losing my best friends every time I left to live abroad, I felt grateful for this exotic, wide-ranging childhood, for the curiosity it gave me, and the ease—the feeling that I could comfortably make my home anywhere.

My parents never openly articulated why they went to all that trouble—why they risked taking a five-month-old to live in Bangkok, a city with open sewers and snakes in the yard, where I developed chronic diarrhea; or a six-year-old to Manila, where my mother and I cowered beneath our movie seats, hiding from the gunman who'd disrupted the Saturday-afternoon matinee; or a twelve-year-old to Cairo, when Egypt had reached the height of its tension with Israel and our apartment windows rattled from the bombs taking out planes at the airport. But I suspect that deep down, they knew what they were giving me and that the risks would be worth it.

Those years were exciting and hard. They took work to organize, and they were disruptive, but they pulled us out of our middle-class American lives, and that was good. As a result, I learned to punt when things took unexpected turns. I learned that I didn't have to speak the same language to communicate or to feel what someone very different from me felt. I learned that our way is never the only way. I came to understand that I belong to something much larger than myself, larger than the world of my family or town or class of people or nation. I came to understand in some subliminal, visceral way that I am part of the family of man. I'm convinced those years abroad gave me the best parts of myself—the parts that can adapt, empathize, connect.

Along with my growing love of travel, I was developing another passion. During my high school years in the United States, I began to study dance. In the summer of 1973, I attended a dance camp at Fort Worden in Port Townsend, Washington. We took four sweaty classes a day from teachers brought out from New York and Seattle; we practiced our *tendus* in ballet and spiraling down to the floor in modern on the worn hardwood of the old officer's quarters. In between *pliés* and pirouettes, I explored the overgrown gun emplacements tucked into the fort's rocky bluffs and felt the clammy fog rolling in off the Strait of Juan de Fuca; I mostly did this alone. I felt as though I stood at the edge of the world, at the edge of possibility. The only thing I didn't connect to at camp was my fellow students. It was the summer of Nixon's impeachment hearings. Each night after dinner, I squeezed into the registrar's office where less than a handful of teachers, and I, sat transfixed by the twelve-inch black-and-white TV and listened to Senators Ervin's and Inouye's stern questions. I was fascinated. In the morning, I tromped to breakfast in the old canteen and listened to the other students bemoaning another serving of pancakes and the devastation it would wreak on the size of their thighs. *Is this the world for me?* I wondered.

That fall, when I applied to college, I applied to schools with no dance. I got into Harvard despite my unusual childhood, or maybe because of it. But it wasn't there that I gained the tools I've needed for life. My abilities to get along with people, to stand up for what I believe, to think critically from a wider perspective have come from conversations at my family dinner table and the down-and-dirty trenches of travel.

One Christmas vacation when I was home visiting, my father, then a journalism professor, held one of his graduate seminars at our house in Madison. He pulled me aside.

"I have a student I'd like you to meet." I wondered why. Was my generally reticent father becoming a matchmaker?

Mortified, I disappeared into the other room, but not before I got a look at the student in question. He sat at the other end of the living room in the old Victorian chair by the picture window. Tan and green-eyed, with a shock of thick chestnut hair, he sat with the muscular ease of an athlete, relaxed but alert, like a jaguar draped over a branch.

"He's actually kind of cute," I admitted to my mother, arranging crackers on a plate in the kitchen. I was to learn that he'd grown up not far away on a lake outside of Milwaukee, that he had recently graduated from Dartmouth College and was now a year into a graduate program in journalism.

But what I really wanted to figure out about Peter Stark was whether he had an interest in travel—and I didn't mean a two-week vacation in Venice or Acapulco. I wanted to know if he was of the "hard-traveling" kind; this was one of my make-it-or-break-it criteria for marriageability.

However, that evening in the kitchen of my parents' house in Madison, I didn't have marriage on my mind. After all, I had a boyfriend back at school. I returned to Harvard and completed my degree in art history. But dance had stuck with me. As soon as I graduated, I jumped on an offer to dance with Impulse, a modern-jazz company based in Cambridge. Two years later, my boyfriend and I moved to New York.

There I navigated the juggling world of part-time jobs, dance classes and auditions, and moving from one rental to another. I finally settled in the heart of Greenwich Village in a fifth-floor walk-up with the bathtub in the kitchen. In the meantime, my boyfriend and I split up, and my father quietly returned to matchmaking.

Several years had gone by since my first glimpse of Peter in the Victorian chair. On completing graduate school, Peter's first impulse had been to seek out "someplace remote"—maybe Southeast Asia or Alaska. After finding no openings in the hip, artsy town of Homer, he returned home to Wisconsin, traveling by train through the lower forty-eight. On his way, he passed through Montana. *This looks remote,* he thought. A former Wisconsin editor suggested he check out Missoula, in the mountainous western part of the state. "It's a lot like Madison," he'd said.

It turned out Missoula was a place I knew. I'd spent every summer of my childhood driving four days each way from our home in Madison, Wisconsin, to our summer cabin on an island in the Puget Sound in Washington State. I'd sat happily in the back of our Chrysler station wagon, gazing out the window and tunelessly singing the signs or anything else that presented itself. "Red door, white window frame," I'd croon. I'd looked forward to our stop at the Sugar Shack donut shop on Higgins Avenue in Missoula. That usually came around day three. Other than that, I didn't have much sense of the place.

One summer, my dad, recently separated from my mom, came through New York City to scoop me out of my "struggling-artist, Bohemian life" and make the drive across the country. Forty minutes east of Missoula, Montana, we pulled into a gas station. He mentioned that an old student of his had settled there.

"Why don't you give him a call on that pay phone over there," he said, gesturing to the glass booth in the corner of the overgrown-grass lot. "I'll get gas. Let him know we're close." *Why should I call him? I don't know him.* I wondered. But I followed instructions.

A half hour later, my father bumped the Volkswagen van into the dirt alley next to Peter's tiny house, innocently looked around, and said, "I'm not sure where his house is. Why don't you get out here and knock on some doors while I drive farther down?" I got out, and he disappeared. At the first house, Peter opened the door.

We circled each other tentatively for the next five years, spending time in both New York and Missoula, flying to meet each other all over the country, as Peter pursued his budding career as a freelance magazine writer and I performed and toured with a series of small modern dance companies. It was giddy, but I was being careful. I'd been involved in a few overly enmeshed relationships before, or so I felt. I wanted to be sure this time I could keep a clear sense of myself. As we slowly got to know each other through handwritten letters, heart-thumping phone calls, and occasional trysts, I'd hear about his trips to Isle Royale, or Iceland. I began to think maybe he could be the hard-traveling kind, the adventurous partner I had in mind.

It turned out he was. In fact, he was driven—driven by a fear that the world was so rapidly homogenizing that soon there would be no culturally distinct societies left intact. "We've got to go there before it's too late," he'd say. We got married in 1987. In the first years of our marriage, "there" would be China, Greenland, West Africa, the Tibetan Plateau.

On our five-month honeymoon, we traversed China west to east, on foot, by boat, and by bus, negotiating our way through territory not yet open to foreigners. One night on the Tibetan Plateau, after a day of walking behind a horse cart in the rain, I collapsed onto the straw of a horse stable to sleep. I dreamt of a warm pub in Ireland or a sunny sidewalk café in France. A few days later, as I dragged the horse we'd dubbed "Fat Freddy" over yet another barren fifteen-thousand-foot pass, I hallucinated about breakfast at the International House of Pancakes, picturing waffles with melting scoops of whipped butter, greasy sausage patties, and bottles of sticky syrup. Instead, the next day we sat on sheepskins, sipping warm yak milk outside a yak-wool tent. Our hostess, a nomadic Tibetan, couldn't take her eyes off me. She suddenly erupted in laughter. When it appeared she wasn't going to stop, we asked our Chinese translator what was so funny.

"She says she's never seen blue eyes like yours, except maybe on a wolf."

For far-out travel, in Peter, I'd met my match.

We've been lucky. On settling back into Missoula after our honeymoon, I managed to get the only university dance-teaching job in the state. I was hired to head the dance program at the University of Montana, a job with a huge learning curve, as I'd barely taught and had never been part of a university. For the first three years, I just tried to keep breathing, but it was exhilarating. It was a small program, which meant there was lots of freedom to take it in new directions— nothing was entrenched—and my colleagues were smart, open-minded, and supportive. What there wasn't was lots of money, but no matter; if you were willing to put in the sweat, big things could happen. My cohorts and I created new degrees, added teaching and performance tracks, produced four times as many concerts as had been offered in the past, lobbied for money, and expanded the faculty. Then I began to take stock.

I missed performing. Had I jumped ship too soon? Left New York before I had a chance to really explore its possibilities and my potential? There were no dance companies in Montana, not one. So a colleague and I decided to start a troupe. That's the thing about Montana: If you're willing to put in the work, you can do just about anything. There's no one—and few institutions—to dictate the rules. That's how Montanans like it. Over time, I would come to find that along with that freedom comes little structural support, and that can be taxing.

Peter had moved on to writing books and was working at home, in our three-room railroad apartment perched over the Clark Fork River. He had taken over making dinner, tired of waiting for my late-night arrival. Six years after my start at the university, I was putting in sixty-hour weeks: running a dance program, teaching a full load, producing student concerts, and co-directing a small touring company. I was thirty-five, and it suddenly dawned on me that we might want to have kids.

On a Thanksgiving vacation, I went for a walk in the dank woods behind my family's Puget Sound cabin. I came back to a warm fire in the cast-iron stove, flopped down in a wooden chair, and announced happily to Peter that I'd come to a conclusion: I didn't need to be Martha Graham receiving awards at the Kennedy Center; I wanted to have a more well-rounded life. I told him I thought we should try to have kids. Then I started crying. This was a clue. As I write this, I feel so blessed to have two wonderful children. My heart has expanded in ways I could never have imagined. But I am of the generation that thought that hard-driving career women could, and should, do it all. That struggle for balance, the balance between family and career (an oft-mentioned duo that fails to include time of one's own) is now an epidemic in America. I dove straight into it.

Our first child, Molly, turned two in Irian Jaya, then the name of the Indonesian half of New Guinea. We celebrated with a slice of *Buche de Noel* from a local bakery in Jayapura and gave it to her with a lighted number-two candle and her chopped-up malaria pill. She didn't quite make the twenty-pound minimum for a full dose.

My father, then in his eighties, joined us as we took a small plane from the port of Jayapura up into the Baliem Highlands, home to dozens of rural tribes. Our photo album is filled with pictures of my dad in his lightweight "tropical" suit surrounded by nude men wearing penis gourds; of Molly, her hair a cap of platinum blond, squatting in a circle of black kids; of Molly being toted on the back of a village girl, inside a string bag the women use to carry yams; of Molly (still nursing at the time) squealing with delight at all the bare-breasted women. Just the right start, we thought, for our future child of the world.

Over my twenty years as a dance professor, I've been granted a couple of sabbaticals and have had an understanding dean who was willing to give me additional leaves of absence. And Peter, of course, is a freelance writer. As a result, our lives are more flexible than many. Whenever we've come into any extra money, such as when a family member has died, the money has gone to travel.

I applied for my first sabbatical when our second child, Skyler, was due to be born. We left for southern Spain when he was just five weeks old. Start 'em young. Get 'em hooked. That had been my parents' theory. We chose a place that was not too expensive and had no major diseases.

Those five months in Andalusia, in the ancient Phoenician walled town of Cadiz, went by in a sleep-deprived blur. But it was worth it. While Peter picked up three-year-old Molly and took her to the bar across the street from her preschool to share a bowl of stewed snails, I carted tiny Skyler to the community center, where I'd rented a second-floor studio to choreograph. On the way, I'd stop at the flower market. Inevitably, stern old women would tell me my baby was going to have a deformed back if I kept carrying him around in that hammock-sling thing and would instruct me to take my germ-infested pinky finger out of his mouth.

"Use a pacifier if he cries," they'd say in Spanish I barely understood, but their disapproval was unmistakable.

I like languages, and I'm pretty good at them. So I'd thought that with a little tutoring in Spanish to prepare before we left home, I'd pick it up in no time when immersed. Who was I kidding? With a three-year-old and a newborn, it wasn't like I had time to memorize verbs. And the situation was more desperate than I'd anticipated. It's one thing to figure out how to order at a restaurant and another to try to communicate with your child's teacher when your daughter's having trouble making friends at school or with the doctor when your baby's developing a mysterious rash.

The solo I ended up choreographing was called "First Position." There are five positions for the feet in ballet, and in those days, I felt as if I couldn't even make it to first. In the mornings, in our rooftop apartment, I struggled to persuade Molly to get dressed. The twos had been fine, but the threes, the terrible threes. Are they usually that bad? Or was it worse because of the advent of a baby brother, or because of living abroad? I finally gave up and let her choose her own clothes, clashing reds and purples, let her do her own hair. Who said there was anything wrong with five sprouting pigtails? The Spanish, that's who. The perfectly coiffed children with their perfectly coiffed mothers—in their neat but somehow so sexy business suits, with their matching mother-daughter tucked ponytails clipped with starched bows—looked at us appraisingly, or so I imagined, as I raced up to the school door each morning, dragging my crazily pigtailed child and carrying my about-to-be-deformed baby. Here we are, the Americans, a disheveled heap.

But in the end, Molly zoomed past us in Spanish, spitting out perfect Andalusian *th*'s and ordering lollipops at the ubiquitous candy shops using mysterious local slang. In that astonishing way that kids can subconsciously absorb and sort out language, Molly had found the key and unlocked the door just by osmosis, slipping in and bypassing all those torturous years of masculine/feminine nouns, single and plural agreements, past participles, conditionals, pluperfects and subjunctives.

Skyler became a great travel baby, happily carted onto buses to visit picturesque hill towns, onto boats to cross the Strait of Gibraltar, into oven-hot cars to trek into the dunes of the Sahara, and onto the string of planes to return home five months later.

I returned to my job, heading the dance program at the university, and Peter continued writing. I had happily moved from New York City to Missoula—which turned out to be a vibrant, outdoorsy college town in the mountains—on the understanding that it would be fine as long as, periodically, we could leave.

Looking for a way to keep our family (and myself) traveling and for my dance students to experience a culture that truly integrated the arts into everyone's lives, I developed a three-week winter-session course to take students to Bali in Indonesia. It was in Bali that Skyler learned to walk. The Balinese have a strong sense of spatial hierarchy, which they apply to architecture, geographic location, and even one's own body, meaning you don't ever want your head below your feet—so no handstands, no cartwheels, no falling down for toddlers like Skyler, newly investigating their watery ten-month-old legs. Babysitters snatched him up as soon as his pudgy knees began to buckle.

At four and a half, Molly learned to flick her eyes and angled elbows side to side to the metallic ripple of gamelan music like a Balinese dancer, while I shepherded my mildly culture-shocked American students around town. Three years in a row we arrived, with a new batch of students, in the artsy town of Ubud, always on my birthday. I couldn't think of a better way to celebrate the passing of another year. Then came 9/11 and the terrorist bombings in Bali in 2002, and the program got shot out of the water.

Peter and I began to plot our next adventure. By the time Molly was seven, we'd managed to go to Indonesia four times and live in Spain, but the trips had been short, three weeks to five months. It was time for something bigger. When I had the opportunity to apply for a second sabbatical, we decided to look for a place that met our criteria for raising globally comfortable, globally tolerant kids. This would be the real beginning of our traveling-family experiment.

The criteria were:

: a place where English was not the primary language
: a place where white was not the primary race
: a place where people were less affluent

Well, that left most of the world.

Our theory was that if our kids were to feel at home in that world, they would need to understand that people do not speak English everywhere, but that one can still communicate. They would need to feel comfortable being in the minority, in part so they could understand what that feels like and empathize with those in the minority at home. And it would be good for them to see how much less, materially, most people in the world have.

Molly was at the incipient mall-rat stage. "I need to have . . ." was becoming her standard opening salvo. Every time I heard that opening line, I remembered the ingenuity of the Tibetan nomads in Qinghai, China. They seemed able to glean everything they needed from a yak: wool for tents, dung for fires, milk for yogurt, meat for their bellies. But their needs weren't great. How much do we really "need"?

Looking for a place for our next adventure, Peter and I took the *Times Atlas* and headed for our favorite Missoula oyster bar. We slid onto stools at the counter. Flipping through the atlas, we rapidly ruled out Asia, the continent we'd visited most. We wanted to try something new. Then we practically threw the dice.

"What about Mozambique?" Peter had just been to Mozambique for an *Outside* magazine assignment. "There's a crashing third-world economy, just what we need." He smiled.

Peter and I are well aware of the privileged lives we lead as people able to pick up and move to another country just for the adventure of it, but we can't actually just go anywhere; the reality is that to stay within our budget, we have to find somewhere substantially less expensive than home.

"We could probably afford it then, but wasn't there just a civil war?" I asked with some trepidation.

"Yeah, but it's been over for a few years," he said cheerily. "Things are looking up."

We'd loved our time in West Africa on an earlier trip, before kids; we'd loved the way the vendors in Ghana beat rhythms on their coolers to announce their presence, the way strangers would call out to us, "Hey, Mr. White!" But we'd never been, as a family, farther south.

We finally settled on Mozambique, but reluctantly. As a former colony of Portugal, the country's official language is Portuguese. Between us we spoke Spanish and French, but Portuguese? After six or seven months of finding our minds continually returning to Mozambique, we said, "Okay, Portuguese."

We arrived in June of 2004, deplaning onto broken tarmac. We filed into a single airport building that looked awfully small for the country's capital, a city of millions. In Maputo, Skyler attended first grade and Molly fifth at the American International School of Mozambique. There was nothing very American about it. The teachers were British, South African, and Mozambican, and the system, as far as we could tell, was largely South African. The students came from all over the world—mostly Europe and Africa—and many spoke not one or two, but three or four languages.

"Mom, why do I just speak English?" six-year-old Skyler came home asking. "Mikas"—his Lithuanian/Danish friend—"speaks four languages."

By the end of our year abroad, Peter and I could speak pidgin Portuguese, but the kids could barely speak any.

When we decided to live abroad again, we agreed to continue to pursue Portuguese. That narrowed our choices right down. There are five countries after Mozambique where Portuguese is the official language: Cape Verde, São Tomé and Príncipe, Portugal, Angola, and Brazil. We'd barely traveled in South America despite it being our continental neighbor, and Brazil, as a BRIC country, was poised to make its entrance onto the international stage. We thought it might be good to have a firsthand understanding of this fifth-largest country in the world. Brazil it would be.

My father had recently died and left me a little money. It would go to funding our next year abroad. And this time, the kids had made a request: to find "a small town, with a local school." They wanted to be bilingual. They wanted to be immersed. Peter and I wondered if they understood how challenging that might be.

2

Not Too Big. Not Too Small.

ON NOVEMBER 28, 2009, two days after Thanksgiving, Peter and I stood at the railing of an airport balcony. We looked down at our kids on the other side of the maze of conveyor belts, plastic barriers, and uniformed TSA agents. They were standing with my mother, who had moved to Missoula to be closer to her grandchildren. We waved good-bye, bought a last latte, and boarded a plane. Our sights were set on Brazil. We would have ten days to scout the northeastern coast in search of a town, a place to live for a year.

Our plan was to land in Salvador, Brazil's first colonial capital; rent a car; and drive to the port city of Recife, three states away. We were searching for the perfect spot for round two of raising global children. I don't think Peter and I had spent this much time alone together since Molly had been born, fifteen years earlier.

I've always liked these long airplane trips and, since having children, have come to especially appreciate the enforced time in limbo: the time to read random magazine articles just for fun, the time to let my mind skip as I gaze out the porthole of a window. It seems that, as a working mother, these wiled-away hours sitting on planes are the few hours I've found that are just for me.

For years, I'd felt overwhelmed at work, overwhelmed at home, and my kids had been catching it, from me and from everyone around them. When did we Americans start having to be so good at everything? How many times have you heard someone say that if your kids don't start soccer at age six, they won't be able to play in high school? When did sports seasons start overlapping, because if you don't hit the ice rink while the summer sun is still burning or start indoor soccer training before the snow melts, your team won't win? When did winning become the primary goal?

How many psychotherapists have you heard saying that you need to learn how to just be, that you're not defined by doing. But where does one find the time as an American adult, or now even as a kid, to stop doing, to see what it's like to just "be," when you feel you have to keep your pace on the track or risk losing your spot? When you feel you need to excel in your job, nurture your partner, and provide opportunities for your kids so they can fill their lives with extracurricular activities (chosen for their resume points), get into a top-notch college, stack up those summer internships, and land that dream job, that surefire path to success?

So here I was again, kneeling at the altar of the world, not only hoping to hand down some of the gains from my traveling childhood to my own kids, but also searching for a way out of the hole I'd dug for myself, that limitless hole full of endless striving. Here I was, looking for a way to regain balance and joy. It was time to get myself, and our kids, off the track and into life. I was gambling that living abroad would serve our kids as it had served me, *and* I was hoping it would give me back some of the perspective I'd lost in my scramble to keep up with daily American life. *This* is why Peter and I were taking off for Brazil.

The plane rounded the corner of the tarmac, pointed itself down the runway, and began to pick up speed. I put my hand on Peter's knee.

"This is my favorite part," I said, as I always do at that moment on a plane, exhilarated by the prospect of adventure.

There's no direct way to get from Montana to northeastern Brazil. We were on day two, flight four of our scouting trip, returning north after a long detour south to São Paulo. The plane was following the coastline. To our right, jade-green water deepened into slate gray. On our left, one white-frilled beach followed another, fringed by a line of shaggy palms that morphed into rolling green hills.

Ever since we'd thought of living in Brazil, we'd asked anyone who'd been there, or was from there, where *they* would want to go.

"The northeast," they'd all said.

"It's where all the great music and dance is."

"It's the African part of Brazil."

Later, on a good day, Peter would describe it as "like the American

Deep South. Laid back, slower paced." On a bad day, he'd call it a "backwater."

The ocean suddenly split to the left in a great inland scoop, the Baía de Todos os Santos, All Saints Bay. White buildings were visible ahead on the point. We were coming down into Salvador, a city of two and a half million. Miles of modern high-rises, patchy scabs of tin-roofed shacks, and then sand dunes slid away below us. The tires bumped and skidded onto the runway.

Unlike airports in Africa or Asia, where we'd been funneled into a whirlpool of sweating bodies with something to sell—"Transport?" "A place to stay?"—the airport in Salvador was a breeze. In less than an hour, we'd collected our bags, upgraded our rented Fiat to one with air conditioning, and begun picking our way through knots of highway interchanges onto ever-narrowing streets, from arteries to veins to capillaries, into town.

"Let's try for Barra," I said, perusing our guidebook as we slowed for jaywalking crowds. "The *Lonely Planet* says it's Salvador's new happening neighborhood, good nightlife"—something we hadn't had much of lately—"and close to the Pelourinho. I guess that's the old historic part of town."

Old colonial houses peeked out between jumbled high-rises. Billboards advertised "Shopping Barra," a mall.

"Do you think we can park here?" Peter was leaning on the steering wheel in a tiny cramped street, peering up at a sign with the letter *e* in a crossed-out circle. "What do you think that means?"

We walked along the waterfront under almond trees, their donkey-eared leaves dipping in a quiet breeze, enviously scanning the prone bodies packing city beaches. We checked into the third hotel we found. The first two had been expensive, American prices. The third was cheap, for a reason. Our room was a dim cubicle that looked as though it were rented out by the hour, but it had a window overlooking the bay. I scanned the kaleidoscopic whirl of beach umbrellas, searching for the source of the syncopated drumming.

"Peter! There're some guys doing capoeira!"

I squinted through the window, watching a pair of brown, muscled men, bare-chested in white pants, crouch and spin, fanning their legs high to the sound of the drums and the twang of a single steel string strapped to a stick. My body started to rock and shift, in time with their sweeping legs and diving heads.

As a modern dance professor, I'd wanted to study this Brazilian martial art/dance form for years, knowing its upside-down, acrobatic movements had had a huge influence on break dance and hence the current look of modern dance. Capoeira had begun to appear in bigger American cities in the 1970s, but the closest teacher I could find in Montana was five hundred miles away. This was one reason we were looking for a town in the northeastern part of Brazil. That was where the most famous *quilombo* had been established, a community of escaped slaves, and where capoeira, used by slaves to resist their Portuguese masters, was refined, then banned, then eventually legalized and codified. We wanted to go to the source. I was afraid, however, that at age fifty-two, I might be ten years too late to handle its handstands and head spins.

We spent the next couple of days floating on the warm waves of the South Atlantic, eating seafood and coconut milk stews in outdoor restaurants and downing *caipirinha*s, the local version of a gin and tonic, made with sugarcane alcohol and lime juice. We poked around the hilly cobblestone streets of the Pelourinho, the historic neighborhood that had been home to Jorge Amado. His books had wowed the world with the colorful, if violent, story of the settling of Bahia, this land of sugarcane and coffee plantations. Peter and I thought we'd love to live in this city of millions with its art galleries, nightclubs, and swank high-rises with names like "Da Vinci" and "Warhol." We'd enjoy a chance to be part of its glittering international community. But the kids? We remembered our assignment to find a small town. They wanted to be immersed in Portuguese language and Brazilian life. Maybe they knew what they were talking about. After all, they were no strangers to travel.

Getting out of Salvador is a project, no matter how you work it, whether inland by looping four-lane highways, or through the beach crowds along the water, the way Peter and I did. After only four days in Brazil, we missed our kids but were also enjoying our freedom. We dodged our little Fiat—zippier than our used Subaru back home—through barefoot crowds of bronzed bodies. Then we passed a wrecked taxi: up on the curb, bifurcated by a fallen steel telephone pole. The car looked like a crushed soda pop can.

I flashed back to careening through the streets of Cairo when I was twelve, my fingers clutching the squishy backseat of a cab as my father tersely told the driver the one phrase he had learned in Arabic: "I'm not in a hurry."

Soberer now, we made our way more slowly out of town onto the Linha Verde—the Green Line—the two-lane coastal highway that veers to the northeast and heads out toward the tip of Brazil's bulge. As landlocked Montanans, we had decided, somewhat arbitrarily, that it would be nice to find a town on the ocean.

The road wasn't crowded. There were none of the top-heavy trucks, axles askew, moving diagonally down the highway that we'd seen in other developing countries. Rather, the occasional shiny SUV; maybe an air-conditioned, double-decker luxury bus; a pickup or two. The road, although narrow, looked newly paved. The foliage shifted from palms to bamboo to drier pine. We spent the night in tiny Praia do Forte, home to a sea turtle conservation center and weekend condos overlooking a small harbor. Could this be our town? No. Charming, but too small and too touristy.

We crossed the border into the state of Sergipe, cattle country. The walls of thick foliage thinned and gave way to dry rolling hills, hump-backed white Brahma cows, and stunted inland palms. We swung back out to the coast and pulled into Sergipe's sprawling capital, Aracaju. Though the downtown's five- to six-story buildings were more modern, they looked worn out, tired.

"Arajacu? Aracaja? Why is this name so hard to remember?" we said laughing, wondering if we would ever get a grip on Portuguese.

After driving miles out of town along a sand-swept beach highway, in search of a nonexistent hotel listed in our guidebook, we back-tracked, checked into another, and crossed the busy ocean drive, lit by nighttime stadium lights. Trekking across a deserted beach, narrowing our eyes against gritty, blowing sand, we tumbled down a steep bank and fell into the ocean for a swim in the dark. The verdict: too big, too windy, too soulless. We crossed Aracaju off the list. At breakfast the next day, we pulled out the map.

"Hey, Peter, this looks good. Penedo, in the state of Alagoas. It's a small town. It's not on the ocean, but it's on a big river, and it's only . . . maybe . . . thirty kilometers up from the coast."

We looked it up in the guide.

"'Colonial masterpiece of the state,'" I read, "and you get to it by car ferry. I love that!" When I was growing up, one could only get to my family's cabin on the island in Puget Sound by car ferry.

Leaving Aracaju, we headed inland and poked along the main two-lane highway. It was clogged with earth-moving equipment. The operators seemed to have torn up the road and then left for a permanent coffee break. Finally, we pulled off onto the route that cut down to the Rio São Francisco. The view suddenly improved, as though we'd flipped to a prettier calendar page. The fields were greener. Ample, spreading trees stood alone, blooming white. A hill town rose to the left, its entrance drive lined with geometrically clipped bushes. Fluttering stands of eucalyptus flanked another rise. The road dropped. There was the river.

"Whoa, it's wide," said Peter, a canoeist, eyeing the whitecaps on cobalt blue.

We pulled into the slanted cobblestone ferry slip. Ramshackle buildings squatted on either side. There were no lines, no designated places to park. A couple of men ambled out of the building on the right, a brightly painted yellow bar with the image of a giant beer bottle on its wall. It was labeled *Nova Schin*. We looked out at the river. The ferry was still out in the middle, a matchbox in the distance. Peter walked up to the window to order. "*Um novo shin?*" Months later, we would learn it was pronounced "nova skeen," but the man gave Peter a thumbs-up and cheerfully retrieved a cold, wet bottle of beer.

The little ferry scraped its metal gangplank up over the cobblestones. A truck, a few cars, and several motorcycles inched their way off the boat. No one seemed in a hurry. I watched, mesmerized. What would that be like—to not be in a hurry?

Once on board, we left our car to go stand at the bow. Penedo glim-

mered white across the water, church towers poking up like little excla-
mation points. A big blocky building had been dropped in the middle
of what was otherwise a perfectly preserved nineteenth-century town.
We passed a brushy island on the left and looked upriver, then down,
to open hills spreading away on either side. We were crossing over
from the state of Sergipe into Alagoas. Splashes of red flame trees
and swishing palms came into focus as we drew closer to the far shore.

"This could be it." Peter said, glancing at me. We felt a rev of excitement. "If we live here," he said, pulling himself up a little taller, "I'll
need to bring a rumpled white linen suit."

As the ferry docked, we squeezed back into our little Fiat, and
Peter carefully backed it down onto the cobbles of the landing, which
expanded into a riverside plaza. Despite the lack of signage, we found
the Pousada Colonial, a B and B in an eighteenth-century house on
the far side of the square recommended by our guidebook. Katia, the
pousada's small and bustling manager, led us up a dark wood staircase
and opened a door into an airy, third-floor room. We swung open the
heavy wooden shutters.

"Oh, it's lovely," I sighed, propping my elbows on the two-foot-
thick windowsill. I looked down onto the spreading scarlet of a flame
tree and across the plaza to a broken balustrade rimming a now-
languid Rio São Francisco. It had been a long time since I'd had the
time to just look out a window—fifteen years to be exact, since I'd
moved from twelve-hour days for my teaching career to that plus two
children. We stowed our bags and clumped back down the wide stairs
to interrogate Katia at her old rolltop desk by the front door.

"*O mar é longe daqui?*"—How far is the ocean? Is there a hospital? A
school?

She assured us there were two schools: private, Catholic, one run by
nuns, one by priests.

"I'm not sending Skyler to a school run by priests," Peter said.
Thinking of my cute, blond, eager-to-please little boy, who would be
unable to understand the local language, I had to admit, after all the
scandals, I kind of agreed.

Both schools were K-12, which was a relief; Molly and Skyler could
be in the same building. While I didn't expect supremely social Molly

to have any major problems adjusting, I was more concerned about Skyler. He, too, could be socially adept but was initially more reticent. It would be good for them to pass each other in the hall, especially in the beginning when, without Portuguese, they'd be unable to talk to anyone else.

We ducked through the stone-walled restaurant on the *pousada's* ground floor and headed up the hill to check out the school with the nuns. Half refurbished and half falling apart, Penedo's narrow cobblestone streets were lined with mostly nineteenth- and early-twentieth-century row houses—in oranges, pinks, blues, and greens—which chugged, like strings of sorbet-colored train cars, up fingerlike ridges that stretched away from the river.

Crossing another *praça*, a plaza, at the top of the hill, we rang a buzzer outside tall metal doors and waited to be admitted to the imposing block of building that was Colegio Imaculada Conceiçao. Once in, we peered into the front office through a bank-teller-like barred window. Elizia, the school's bookkeeper and general manager, peered back.

"*Vocês vem de onde?!*" she asked. "You come from where?!"

Tall and black, with 1950s glasses, she wore a form-fitting T-shirt emblazoned with the Virgin Mary—in sequins. We suspected the school might not be what we'd anticipated. Then her stern face unexpectedly exploded into laughter.

"*Vêm por aqui!*"—Come here!—she commanded, and she led us into the cavernous office of the school's director, *Irma*, or Sister, Francisca. Tiny and white, with a broad smile, twinkling eyes, and gray hair poking out from under her habit, Irma Francisca sat behind a broad, immaculately shining desk backed by Christ bleeding on the cross. Peter and I sat down across from her. Peter was beginning to sweat through his shirt, apprehensive about the sure-to-be cryptic conversation ahead. We bore in, trying desperately to understand what she was saying and to make sure she understood us. That she understood that we had two kids who wanted to come to her school; two non-Portuguese-speaking kids who would come sit in class and understand nothing.

I realize one could wonder why we thought this would be a good idea; one might think that from an educational standpoint, the request sounded absurd. But Peter and I hadn't thought twice about it, nor had our kids. After all, my parents had done this to me, and I had been the same age as Skyler. I had attended Franciscan de Marie, a small French school in Cairo. It catered to the kids of diplomats. In those first few months, as I sat blankly listening to the sounds of this foreign language washing over me, one might think I would have been bored, or distressed. But I don't remember being either. I suppose it's like being a toddler, or a dog, trying to figure out what sound or word goes with what, whether the teacher or your fellow students are happy or upset, and whether they're upset with you. I remember walking up, one by one, to stand next to our teacher, Soeur Marguerite, to recite a memorized poem or paragraph out of our science text. I'd deciphered the content from a dictionary and the pictures—this must be about the measurement of liquids; this about solids and gases. The fact is, you begin to ferret out meaning almost immediately with any tools you have, interpreting body language and actions—everyone is getting up and leaving; it must be recess. Peter and I knew our kids would miss some content areas like seventh-grade social studies. But we weren't worried. Whatever they might be missing was likely to be covered again in high school. The one high school course Molly had to take that year in order to graduate was U.S. History. She could take it online. Nothing felt irreplaceable. In our family-value system, the advantages of learning to be fluent in another language, of learning that one could start from scratch and successfully navigate another culture, would far outweigh the disadvantages. But no one said it would be fun or easy. I'm not sure Molly and Skyler quite understood that.

Elizia and Irma Francisca were quite the odd couple. But they seemed curious about us, kind, and, by the end of our conference, open to taking us in.

Penedo seemed to fit the bill: not too big, not too small; not on the ocean, but close to the ocean and on a big river; a charming hill town with colonial architecture, a lively market, friendly people, a possible school. In the end, we chose Penedo largely for its aesthetics.

Well, not only aesthetics. We also wanted a place that felt safe enough for our kids to have some freedom, not like Maputo in Mozambique. There our house had had bars over the windows, walls around the compound, twenty-four-hour guards. Our kids were now teenagers. Our lives would be a lot easier if they could move around on their own.

So far, as a family we'd lived in Cadiz in Spain—also a small town, also in language immersion—but only for five months, and the kids were so young that their regular vocabulary was half sign language anyway. We'd tried Maputo in Mozambique, a big city with a big international community. Although we'd been disconcerted by the underlying class tension and high rate of crime, it had been a blast. Within the ex-pat community, we'd just had to "add water and stir" for a social life; Peter was engrossed in a book project, and I was blissfully taking my first break from my overwhelming work life at home. I could feel, however, that this year in Brazil was going to be different. With older kids and total language immersion in a small town, it was going to be the real test of our resilience and adaptability. But I was already falling in love with Penedo and felt confident we could hack it—maybe too confident.

The scouting trip was great. We were moving fast, laughing a lot, heady with the freedom of choosing a place to live. Brazil was getting into our blood.

Seven months later, we made the jump. We'd cleared our closets; packed away valuables; forwarded the mail; found caretakers for pets; cancelled our Internet service, our recycling and garbage collection, our cell phones and car insurance; submitted ourselves to a raft of vaccinations; turned our house over to renters; and spent hundreds of dollars on visas and thousands on airplane tickets.

Molly, Skyler, and I arrived in Brazil on July 8, 2010—winter in the Southern Hemisphere.

"There's Dad!" the kids chimed in unison.

Peter was in the crowd on the other side of the glass doors as we emerged from customs in the airport in Maceió, the capital of the state of Alagoas. Three hours from Penedo, this was the closest place we could fly into. Craning to see us, he looked tired and hot, but tan and pleased. He'd come a couple of weeks earlier intending to find a place to live (and watch the World Cup with Brazil's soccer-crazed population). On the house front, he'd had no luck. On the soccer front, he was doing better. The doors slid open, and we pushed our luggage cart through. Hugging Peter, I thought he felt thin.

He gestured to two taxi drivers waiting outside by the curb. He'd hired them to take us, and our year's worth of luggage, to an empty lot where we could catch one of the many vans that run every few hours between small towns. This would be the last leg of our two-day journey.

We each had one duffel bag of clothes, a daypack for books and games, and a computer. We were sweating in our jeans. As we sped down a boulevard, I stared out the window at the jumble of boxy shops and tire stores, the nests of electrical lines, and the parade of billboards with words in Portuguese that I didn't understand. It's so disorienting to drop out of the hushed limbo of airplane flight, with its muted light and numbing shot of American movies, into the psychedelic collage of the real world, especially one as kaleidoscopic as Brazil.

We arrived at the van lot early, staked out seats, and crammed in our bags. Now there was nothing to do but wait. Peter left to check out the convenience store at a neighboring gas station. I propped my feet on a duffel and hugged the daypack and computer in my lap. Winter in northeastern Brazil was warm. I wondered if the van's windows would open.

"Want a bag of *Hoofles?*" Peter asked on his return, grinning as he tossed a bag of Ruffles potato chips in to Molly, seated next to me in the back. "In Portuguese, the *r* at the beginning of a word is pronounced like an *h*," he went on. "Like *hestoranchee*. That's *restaurant*. It's really confusing. So, when we get to Penedo, we're going to stay at the Pousada Colonial. We've got two rooms, that great airy one in the front, where you and I stayed"—he nodded to me and smiled, knowing I'd be pleased—"and then one for the kids. We can stay there until we find a place to live. Too bad Ianca has left," he added, glancing over at Skyler, who had squeezed himself into the van's back corner. "She's the eleven-year-old daughter of the family who owns the *pousada*. She's really fun, kind of a live wire. Her classmates were over the other day and whipped themselves into a frenzy when I showed them Skyler's visa photo and told them that he had *blue* eyes." Skyler's face went taut as he tried to swallow his smile. "You'd like that family. The dad's a hot soccer player. But they just left for the Middle East. He got a job as assistant coach for the national team of Dubai."

Over the next half hour, the van filled. Our giant duffels ended up under not only our feet but also everyone else's. No one complained. Finally, the man who collected the money nodded at us and slid the side door shut. We were off, the four of us scrunched, like our bags, into the back row of seats. At home, this would be the moment we'd yell, "One, two, *three!* Hit the road, Jack!" and pull onto the interstate for a long trip. It was a declaration of freedom, of let the adventure begin! This time we sat quietly, looking out the window at our new home. I wondered what our kids were thinking. Did it seem exotic? Or were they already jaded, after living in Mozambique five years earlier? Had we made the right choice?

3

Flies

WE HADN'T EVEN BEEN in Brazil a week!

"Go get your husband," the older doctor in the long white coat at the Penedo emergency room gently suggested in Portuguese.

They would bandage Skyler's head and prepare him for the ambulance trip to the trauma center in Arapiraca, an hour away. He needed a neurosurgeon and a CAT scan, more than they could handle here.

I hustled out the front door to go find Peter and Molly. Skyler's new friend Victor still stood outside, but the unmarked car had left. Piling into a taxi waiting at the end of the block, we were halfway back to the Pousada Colonial when I realized I hadn't even told Skyler I was leaving. I was stricken, imagining him unable to understand what anyone was saying, wondering why they were loading him into an ambulance, and then, why he was all alone.

Back at the *pousada*, Katia told me that both Peter and Molly were still out. Where were they when I needed them?! I threw passports and clothes into a bag and, most important, scrambled to find the English-Portuguese dictionary. This idea of living abroad every few years wasn't starting off quite as planned. In all my years abroad as a child, it had never turned out like this! Peter returned just as I was leaving—someone in the *praça* had intercepted him to tell him something had happened to his son. We agreed that he and Molly would follow in a taxi once Victor had found her.

By ambulance, the hour-long trip took thirty minutes, even over the bucking, shoulderless two-lane road. Sitting in the windowless back of the little van with Skyler stretched on a gurney in front of me, and Cassia, the nurse from Penedo, poised over his head, I would later realize we'd passed ambling villages with plaster houses rimmed in cool verandas, surrounded by the eye-popping green of rolling sugarcane fields. But at the time, I barely looked up from Skyler's face.

Initially, he was talking a lot, frustrated with himself for getting hurt, peeved that he was missing the World Cup soccer finals, which we had planned to watch that afternoon. Portuguese was the first reason we'd decided to spend a year in Brazil. Soccer was the second, at least for Peter and Skyler.

But now Skyler's eyes were beginning to close and his speech to drift. Cassia, with her broad smile and beautifully coiffed poof of black hair, had been deftly changing his blood-soaked head bandage as we jounced through the potholes. She shook her head as he drifted toward sleep, looking worried.

"Skyler, let's do some math problems!" I said urgently. He'd always been good at calculating numbers in his head. "What's, uh, what's thirty-six times . . . times 412? No, maybe that's too hard. Would two digits be better? How about thirty-six times fifty-two?"

He seemed to think. "One thousand, eight hundred . . . and seventy-two?"

"Great. That's great," I said, having no idea what the answer was myself. "How about twenty-three . . ." I continued on. I just wanted to keep him talking, awake, alive.

We were dipping into a gully when the pavement turned to dirt, and we were suddenly caught in a twisting knot of cars slowly picking their way through water-filled ruts. Were we going to put on the siren, flash some lights? But we just slowed down, patiently waiting our turn.

"*É perto agora*"—It's close now—Cassia whispered under her breath, sensing my alarm.

Up the other side of the gully, the boxy, modern buildings of Arapiraca heaved into view, much grimmer than the quaint town we'd left behind.

Within minutes, the ambulance slid into the carport at the trauma center, another nondescript white concrete building. We had arrived. The back door ripped open, and Skyler on his gurney was slid out. I followed as he was whisked through an opening without a door, past rows of chairs with a few waiting people, and through a floor-to-ceiling accordion gate. It clanged shut. He was in. I was out? The gate was manned by men in khaki, their pants tucked into leather boots, machine guns slung casually over their shoulders. One put his arm out and softly motioned me to the side. I watched, my mind beginning to race, as Skyler was rolled away. I had no room to wonder why everyone had guns.

The receptionist was asking me something. ". . . *djefshhhwquwhah . . . ne?*"

Huh? "Skyler Stark-Ragsdale?" I hazarded, hopefully.

He smiled and tried again. I finally managed to give my name and relationship; Skyler's name, age, and nationality; and, throwing my raised arms and head sideways, a mimed description of a side flip, of his accident. They let me through. An armed guard with blue eyes, unusual in northeastern Brazil, led me down the dingy hallway and pointed me through the door of a room on the left.

An intensely bright light was being trained on Skyler's head. As always in Brazil, there was a crowd, most in scrubs, some in masks, some focused on Skyler, others just chatting with their neighbors. Two flies buzzed through the circle of light.

". . . *tem dor?*" Cassia, from our ambulance, was asking me. It sounded kind of like "Nintendo." I flipped through my dictionary but couldn't find it and apologetically shook my head to signal *I don't understand.* Days later, I would figure out that she'd wanted to know if Skyler "has pain," since she had had no way to ask him herself.

"How're you doin', Skyler?" I asked as the surgeon buried another long needle into the thick flap of scalp, squeezing in a three-inch syringe of Novocaine.

"Okay," he rasped.

"Is this almost over?" he asked twenty minutes later, sounding tired but almost matter-of-fact. I was relieved that he seemed so normal.

By the time Peter and Molly got there by high-speed taxi forty-five minutes later, Skyler had gotten seven Novocaine shots and a Frankensteinian stripe of nineteen stitches arcing from the top back of his head down to his left ear. His CAT scan had checked out normal, and I'd been able to give him the running score of the World Cup finals, which, of course, the CAT scan technicians had been watching in between patients.

But it wasn't over. They wanted to keep Skyler for observation, be sure he could keep food down, be sure there was really no brain trauma. As the evening wore on, Skyler and I were transferred from room to room, as space was needed. We watched as the gate clanged open and an increasing number of cases, each more gruesome than the last, were wheeled through. Was this standard Sunday-evening fare, or had things been exacerbated by whipped-up passions surrounding the World Cup? We shared rooms with men who appeared to have been shot, knifed, beaten. We listened to them wheezing into respirators, watched blood clotting their bandages. Privacy was not an option.

I've always dreaded the possibility of ending up in a rural hospital in a developing country, with their mildewed walls, gaping entrances, and flies in the operating room. I remembered my mother talking about a hospital in Cairo when I was twelve. She'd gone in to help a young American woman who'd been turned inside out by the local food. When my mother found her, blood was going up her IV tube rather than the rehydrating solution going down. As an adult, I've heard that's not so uncommon, but as a child, it left a graphic picture of why you should never end up in one of those hospitals yourself. I now know, however, that they can be full of smart, experienced, kind people, capable of saving your son's life.

We met a lot of people at the trauma center, which served the surrounding fifty-two towns. They came to help, to interpret, or just to check in on the *Americanos* (clearly a novelty): Fabiana, a rotund, genial surgeon who spoke good English and gave me restaurant recommendations for her hometown of Maceió; Dr. Lobo, the taciturn neurosurgeon; Lima, the blue-eyed guard who gently ushered us from place to place; Tonya, the whiskey-voiced head nurse; Ivanildo, a lab technician who wanted to practice his English and talk about American music; and of course, Cassia, the ambulance nurse from Penedo, who stayed with us for the next four hours when she could have gone home. She held me tight when my eyes filled with tears, on hearing Skyler's CAT scan was normal.

Being a person who is quick to tears (not necessarily of sadness, but of inspiration, empathy . . .), it was surprising I didn't bawl with relief. But I find in crises like these, my mood drops to calm, like a Ferrari dropping its weight into the pavement getting ready for a high-speed ride through unpredictable curves. Instead of feeling hysterical about Skyler, the emotional intensity of the situation bound me fundamentally and unforgettably to everyone around me. My tears came months later, when I ran into Cassia on the street in Penedo. Then, my gratitude for her companionship and care in this moment came flooding out.

Released too late to go back to Penedo, we spent the night in a small hotel and delivered flowers to the trauma center staff the next day before returning home. Thanks to the Brazilian healthcare system, the entire event, ambulance and all, was free.

When we got back to Penedo, everyone seemed to know what we'd been through.

"*Seu filho?*"—Your son?—strangers stopped to ask.

I knew they were wondering who we were, how, like aliens, we had landed in their town. But no one addressed that now. This was more important. I was a mother with a son, and he had been hurt.

You'd think I might have asked myself at this juncture whether this had all been a mistake—this pulling our kids out of school in the United States, away from friends, putting our jobs on hold, risking our kids' lives (or so thought some of our friends). But as a person who tends to keep moving forward once I've taken a step, it didn't even occur to me.

4

We Make a Friend: Zeca

SWEET SIXTEEN. In Brazil, the significant birthday for girls is fifteen, perhaps because some start getting pregnant then. But Molly was about to turn sixteen, and it seemed especially significant to me, in part because I'd been preparing myself for months for the sexual onslaught from macho Brazilian men that Molly might attract, as a young, beautiful blond—at least from the "Brazilian Man" I'd imagined: charming, handsome, and thinking about nothing but SEX. I'd been wondering whether a girl from small-town Montana was going to be equipped to handle it.

Molly's birthday has always been a production, starting with the three-day event (the family party, the friend party, and the slumber party) through her elementary school years and gradually tapering to the family dinner and a night out with friends by the time she was in high school. Even so, there we were in a town where she knew no one, and I knew that for her, her birthday mattered. I wanted it to feel special. We were still living at the *pousada*. That morning, Antonio, the *pousada*'s cook, secretively called me into the kitchen. He wanted to show off the sausage and massive slab of beef that he'd bought for Molly's birthday *feijoada*, the traditional celebratory Brazilian bean stew. Katia, who worked the desk and would turn out to be our rock—providing us with a seemingly infinite supply of family members to help us over the course of the year—had ordered an incredibly gooey chocolate cake. She was small and neat in her uniform of brown pants, yellow blouse, and wedge heels on tiny feet. She exuded efficiency.

"*Dona Amy, não se preocupe*"—don't worry—she would say, listening intently. *I will handle everything* was the subtext. And she did. Periodically, she would roll her doe-brown eyes and sigh, "Oh my gawd," her one phrase in English. But she'd just laugh and shrug at the latest mishap.

Elizia, the firecracker of an office manager from the school the kids would be attending, had sent Molly a huge bouquet of roses, though school wouldn't start until the next day and they'd never met. (How did she even know it was Molly's birthday?)

Amazingly, considering we'd only been in Penedo for a bit over a week, Molly's birthday had attracted a crowd. Victor and Breno were hanging with Skyler—who was wearing his newly purchased "Brasil" baseball cap to hide his Frankensteinian arc of stitches. Karol (which they pronounced *Karau*), Victor's older sister, who would become one of Molly's best friends; Katia and her Aunt Laura (Aunt *Lowra*); Antonio's daughters Amanda and Ananda; and a handful of others I didn't recognize were there as well, including Zeca.

A week earlier, the day before Skyler split his scalp open and took the harrowing ride to the trauma center, we'd been invited by a new acquaintance to the Penedo Clube de Ténis. I'd been asking if there was a pool anywhere in town, and Dr. Fernando, a family friend of the owners of the *pousada*, came to our rescue. He invited us to the tennis club. Dr. Fernando was one of the few people who spoke Portuguese slowly enough that I could actually follow it. I liked him immediately.

The next morning, Peter, Skyler, Molly, and I left the Pousada Colonial, trooped up the ridge, and found the club, with its bright white walls and turquoise blue trim. We opened the iron gate and wandered in. It had a commanding view of the *lagoa*, a "lake" that no longer existed but had left a huge grass-and-sand basin in the valley below.

A door popped open in a building on the left.

"*Ahh*—blankety, blankety, blank—*Americanos!*—blankety, blankety, blank—*música.*" A jovial man in heavy rectangular glasses above bulldog jowls was motioning us to come in. Where was Dr. Fernando with his slow speech and clear enunciation? (Peter would soon devise a helpful phrase in Portuguese: "When you talk to me, imagine you're talking to a six-year-old.")

Dr. Fernando was nowhere to be seen, but we'd just met Eduardo, the club president. He marched us onto a glassed-in porch, sat us down at the end of a long table, and ordered up some Coke and beer.

Around the table were a dozen other mostly graying men, who at 10:00 AM were drinking beer and shots of honey-colored *cachaça*, sugarcane rum. Eduardo picked up a guitar. A large songbook was open in the middle of the table. One man leafed through it.

"*Aqui o.*" Here.

They began crooning a bossa nova—all except the young man at the far end, with the ebony hair; a long, chiseled jaw; dark, intense eyes; and a smile that revealed a slight gap between his front teeth. Zeca. He was the first of three twenty-six-year-olds I would come to think of as our "guides."

When I'm traveling in a strange place where I don't speak the language, I observe much more than at home, where I've come to take things for granted. But I know so little and understand even less. I find myself making up stories about the places and people I meet. It's easy to start confusing the stories with reality.

I also find myself relying on sources I might not under normal circumstances, either because they present themselves or because they're the only ones I can communicate with. I trust people I might not if I knew more, because I have no choice. Often these are young men. It's not that they're necessarily bad characters; they're just not the experts one might seek out given more choice, though in fact they are often experts in their own ways.

In our travels before we had kids, Peter and I were continually picked up by teenage boys. I suppose they had time and curiosity. We'd hire them to be our guides. On a story assignment of Peter's in northern Greenland, we camped on the tundra outside the village of Qaanaaq and were found by Akiak, a seventeen-year-old. He became our translator. When Peter commissioned an Inuit hunter to take us by dog sled out onto the frozen sea ice, it was Akiak who translated when we got stranded, the ice unexpectedly breaking up; or when I needed somewhere in all that white to change a tampon; or when we camped for two days on an ice floe, waiting for the huffing snort of surfacing narwhal.

In Ghana, it was again teenage boys, two this time, who offered to take us hunting for "bush meat" in the jungle outside a town in the province of Brong Ahafo. We looked for hollow fallen logs and stood back when they shot randomly into their dark holes, pulverizing whatever was inside. I guess this was amusement, not dinner. They generously shared their lunch, stewed we-didn't-ask-what (because it looked an awful lot like rat), transported in a gym bag.

In Indonesia, it was Ari who took us to his village to stay with his mom, where we were housed in one of the many cubby rooms kept for visiting males, invited in solely for a one-night stand, in that matrilineal Minangkabau society.

Once we had kids, this stopped. The teenage boys dropped us.

But the twenty-somethings picked us up. At the tennis club, Zeca ambled over, in his long, loose shorts, soft T-shirt, and lazy flip-flops, and sat down.

"I don' really like this music," he confided in English that came out like a dotted line. "You know . . . Alison Chase? I like . . . Alison Chase. Thaz . . . good music!" He dropped his chin emphatically as he said it. It would be months before I realized he'd said "Alice in Chains."

Over the guitar music Zeca told us he was the son of a lawyer and had become a lawyer himself, a labor lawyer defending the "little guy," the laborer.

"Labor law is good . . ." he paused, "for making money. Because the law here in Brazil protects the worker, so if they get money from the company, then I get part of it." He puffed his chest and did that *yo, check me out* head bob, grinning and making it sound like he was just in it for the money.

Over time, we'd learn otherwise. Over time, we'd hear that he hadn't really wanted to go into law, but now he felt stuck. His unmarried sister had just had a baby boy, whom he adored. "I have to be able to buy him milk." We urged him to think about pursuing something he really loved. After all, his large extended family was happily helping his sister raise her son.

That day at the club, he handed me a plastic straw filled with *cachaça* and honey. "You should try these. They're really good."

By the end of a couple of hours, Molly had sung a solo, "The Girl from Ipanema," which she had learned at home in Portuguese without understanding any of the words; I had sung "Ten Thousand Miles" in English, accompanied by the club president's wife, who, like Molly, clearly didn't understand any of the words; Skyler had wowed everyone with some fleet-fingered classical guitar; and Peter had dutifully tossed back several shots of the high-octane *cachaça*. Life was feeling good, really good.

The sky was intensely blue, the river sparkled far below, these people seemed so happy, and we were part of the family. Just like that, or so it seemed.

The next time we would see Zeca was a week later, when he showed up at Molly's birthday party at the stone-walled restaurant in the Pousada Colonial. In clothes that hung loosely on his taut body, he hovered by the room's open French doors, downing beers and chain smoking.

Lots of people smoked in Penedo, both men and women. I'd seen a Health Department sign over a grocery store register telling men, "*Fumando é ruim para sua ereção*"—Smoking is bad for your erection. Talk about targeting your audience. But then Zeca, with his mahogany skin and easy smile under silver-rimmed sunglasses, oozed a playboy's invincibility.

Zeca declined the stew: "I don' actually like it that much," he said confidentially (echoes of his opinion of the bossa nova). I was beginning to get the impression he was a bit of a maverick.

Katia appeared out of the kitchen with the giant cake, Molly blew out the candles, and everyone sang, "*Parabéns a você . . .*" We gathered it was "Happy Birthday."

Like the stew, Zeca refused the cake: "I don' really eat sweets, but it look good."

It would be some time before I'd understand why it felt like we were forcing our guests to eat the cake.

"It's weird, or just different," Skyler would say months later, after he'd attended several birthday parties. "They don't share the cake. It's there, but no one eats it."

A few hours later, people began to drift away.

"Do you like fishing?" Zeca asked before he left. "Good. I gonna take you fishing. My uncle, he has a fishpond."

It seemed we were making a friend; a friend who would become one of our primary guides.

5

A Tenuous Foothold

"Oooh, those are a little long," I said, eyeing Molly's navy-blue polyester pants, the bottom half of her new school uniform. It was six in the morning, the day after her birthday. Up on the third floor of the *pousada*, we were getting ready for the kids' first day of school.

"I can hem them, but will they be okay for today?"

"Yeah. It's fine. Skyler!" she shouted across the hall to where her brother was still in bed. "We need to get going!" He pulled the sheet up higher, not at all sure now about this local-school thing.

"Peter, can you go down and see if Antonio's making breakfast?" I asked as I scrambled to stuff new notebooks into their backpacks. "Antonio said he'd open early so the kids can have some breakfast before they take off."

Molly would be taking thirteen subjects, including four sciences, religion, sociology, philosophy, and Brazilian literature—all in Portuguese. Skyler had nine. School was slated to start at seven. The Brazilian school year starts in February, so now, in mid-July, they would be entering into the second semester.

Nothing about this was sounding easy. Though we had hired a Portuguese tutor back in the States, the reality of what it might be like to not understand anything was just too distant to grasp. Despite repeated urgings to do the homework the tutor assigned—"You'll be thankful later"—at twelve and fifteen, their I'm-sure-it-will-be-fine outlook on life had won out. Now reality had arrived, like a semi ready to accelerate down a hill in the wrong lane.

I'd attended Catholic schools twice as a child, always when we'd lived abroad, first in Manila, at age six, and then in Cairo, when I was eleven and twelve. In Manila, I remember begging my mother not to send me to school. At Assumption, they were fond of telling you that you were going to be punished tomorrow, the better to let you wallow overnight in miserable anticipation. I'd sat in front of my second-grade class in a dunce cap; stayed after school more than once to fill the chalkboard with *I will not talk*; and stood, humiliated, a second grader in the corner of the kindergarten classroom, face to the wall. All this for doing things like playing "stomp on your toes" with my partner while waiting in line to come in from recess, two-by-two like Madeline.

You'd think I would have done anything to prevent our kids from having to go through the experiences I'd been through. But I found myself laughing and saying, "Well, everybody should go to a Catholic school at least once in their life."

It gives you entrée to that special club—the CSSC—Catholic School Survivors' Club. And since it appears that the private schools in developing countries, the schools where the local elites send their kids and where all the Brazilians we'd met in the United States said we must send ours, are frequently Catholic, I wasn't surprised that in Penedo there was no other choice. This would all be part of the experience.

After a hasty breakfast of buttery fried eggs, dry chocolate cake, and *graviola* juice, I headed out the door in front of them, wanting to snap a picture of their first walk to school. They looked preoccupied.

"How're you doing?" I asked anxiously.

"Okay," they both said quietly.

The Brazilian school day is short. Skyler would be there for four hours each day, Molly for five. The number of kids in blue pants and white knit shirts, the standard uniform no matter which school you went to, was growing as we made our way over the broken sidewalks and up the ridge. Colegio Imaculada Conceiçao, or Imaculada, as we would come to call it, was at one end of the pleasant *praça* at the top. It was strikingly unadorned and institutional compared to the surrounding houses, with their baroque frippery or angular art deco embellishments.

Cars blocked the street at odd angles as parents dropped off kids in front. We squeezed our way in. Irma Joanna, the nun from whom I'd bought the kids' uniforms, waved us over.

"*Tudo bem?*" Her smile shone white in her dark face.

Iracema, the *coordenador* of the middle school, walked up and asked us how we were as well.

It was only a week after Skyler's trip to the trauma center. Sweat trickled down the small of my back as I struggled to explain, in pieced-together Portuguese, why Skyler was wearing a hat and that I hoped the teachers wouldn't ask him to take it off. I'd made sure I knew the word for *stitches* and tried to emphasize that he had nineteen.

The students gathered in the courtyard to sing a song painted on the wall with lots of references to *Deus*, the only word I could catch. Then Molly and Skyler were swept away. *Well*, I thought, *here goes.*

Four hours later, Peter and I waited for them under the voluptuous red lips painted on a hanging sign that advertised Boca Cheia, "The Full Mouth," a *lanchonete* across the street from Imaculada, where we'd agreed to meet for lunch. Kids were beginning to spill out of the blocky yellow building. My eyes rapidly sifted through the flood of blue and white to find Molly and Skyler.

Then I spotted them, in separate groups. They seemed to have friends! Before leaving for Brazil, I'd laid out colored sheets of construction paper around our dinner table one night. "We're going to make a mobile," I'd announced, trying to imitate the hands-on approach of the kids' small, progressive Missoula school. "You can do whatever you want with the paper, but on each piece, you're going to write what you hope to get out of this year in Brazil. Things you want to do or learn."

Twenty minutes later, the table was covered with orange and lime-green triangles, rectangles, and Matisse-like squiggles, and Skyler had made an origami canoe. Both kids had said they hoped to "make friends."

Now they crossed the cobbled street to where we stood.

"Molly, you're out early. How was it?"

"Mom, it was crazy! It's totally chaotic," she started, bubbling over as usual.

We had been braced for the strict, banished-to-corners, writing-*I will not talk*-1,500-times Catholic schools of my traveling childhood. But it turned out this was the chaotic, talk-anytime, move-your-desk-anywhere, apply-nail-polish-during-class, leave-the-room-to-answer-your-cell-phone, write-*Fuck*-on-the-board kind of Catholic school. Brazilians are all about fun.

"Skyman, what about you? How was it?"

"Fine," he said, eyes down, tugging on the brim of his cap. He didn't offer any more.

Imaculada would become the center of Molly's social life and Skyler's nemesis. It didn't help that he was starting out the year defying the dress code by wearing a hat. And it didn't help that we'd been advised by the school's director to put him in the *Sétimo Ano*, thereby skipping the first semester of seventh grade, because they thought it would be better for him to stay with his age group. Molly dropped back to the *Primeiro Ano*, a repeat of the end of her sophomore year in high school, so that she could focus on learning Portuguese. That turned out to be a better fit in every way.

After weeks of living out of duffel bags at the Pousada Colonial, we suddenly found a house to rent for $350 a month. A professor of pedagogy at a community college down the backside of the ridge had introduced himself to us when we were catching lunch one day at Boca Cheia.

"*Vocês são os Americanos,*" he said—You're the Americans. "It's a pleasure . . . you can call me the Professor. I know of a house for rent, and I know the owner. I will talk with her for you." The house was just across the plaza, four doors down from Imaculada, on the Praça Jácome Calheiros. How had we missed it?

"Be careful how you say *Jácome,*" Peter later noted. "My soccer buddies laughed hysterically when I said *Jacomé*. If you put the accent on the third syllable, it means, 'I've already eaten,' or, more specifically, 'I've already eaten *her*.' Get it?"

We crossed the *praça* to check it out. The house sat on one edge of the town's main ridge and was structured the way all the old houses were, like a railroad apartment, attached to buildings on either side. There were only two windows—one in the front and one in the back.

"I'm afraid it's going to be dark." Peter was worried.

And the noise! You'd think a small upriver town might be quiet. But huge buses, cars, and motorbikes rumbled over cobblestones three feet from the front door. It felt as though the onslaught of sound might raze the house to the ground, sound waves zapping concrete walls into nothingness. It made us wonder about taking the place at all, and, if we did, whether we could ever open the front window or, even more, the front door.

"Ohhhh! You guys! Come look out the back." I'd just unlatched the large square of a back window and swung it open. My eyes were filling with tears.

The yard sloped steeply away into flouncy mango trees, shaggy as big-hipped English sheep dogs; coconut palms like skinny 1960s rock stars, one-legged in skintight jeans with spiky, long-haired wigs on top; and papayas, leaves like crinolines, spreading in frilly layers, spotted yellow on green. Beyond this, the view dropped away, like a Renaissance painting, to the street below, then dipped into a velvety green field, dotted with humpbacked cows and white egrets. Across the field, Bairro Vermelho, one of the poorer neighborhoods, rose up the next ridge, a wall hanging of box houses in oranges and pinks, pistachio greens and robin's-egg blues. Horses galloped down its vertical cobbled streets, their riders expertly glued to the saddle. Beyond, palm trees were silhouetted against the molten ribbon of river. Sliding off to the northwest, it split and rejoined around overgrown islands, disappearing into the hazy hills of the interior. Clumps of water hyacinths floated down, along with brightly painted motorized canoes. Most of the canoes carried fisherman standing in pairs, one throwing a net off the bow, the other steering the long-handled motor in the stern. The back-window view was a Leonardo, with its foreground, midground, and background in rich, oiled hues.

The back was the reason we decided to take the house, despite Peter's concerns that the four rooms would feel small, despite the fact that we would have to furnish it from scratch—stove, medicine cabinets, closets, and all.

One week and $3,000 worth of furniture later, we were in. I'd bought an upholstered bench just the right size to fit into the nook by the back window. The view made me gasp, right up until the end.

The front door opened onto the *praça*, with some ragtag grass and flame trees, one of many such plazas. Once a month, the glass-and-metal door would rattle open, and we'd hear a whiskey-voiced *"Oi!"* It was Ilda, our landlady, with her small, round face in dark-rimmed glasses and a head of thinning jet-black hair. A retired mathematics professor, she was small but commanding.

"Tudo bem?"—All is well? Dark eyes sparkling, she would stride into our house, her jean-clad hips slung forward, her feet sluffing along in low pumps. She always had the air of a lord surveying his estate. Of course, it was hers; but, still, her unannounced entrances were a little disconcerting.

Out in the square was a central gazebo, which was pretty despite its chipping paint and the balustrades peeling away on one side. Over time, Skyler would discover that he could climb the trees trimmed in geometric cubes and stand—"Look, Ma, no hands!"—with his head poking out the very top. He would persuade his friends Victor and Breno, and eventually feisty Ricardo, to climb into the bigger of the trees to make a fort out of hammocks and a boogie board.

It turned out that when the hot months came, the straight shot from front door to back window sucked in a welcome breeze, and the small dark bedrooms, especially with our newly installed air conditioning, were ideal retreats. Peter and I nicknamed ours "the cooler."

We hesitated to open the windows in our front door, however. The first day we moved in, a crowd of children were looking through and shouting, *"Mohlly! Mohlly!"* How they knew her name, I don't know. When I went out to introduce myself, they asked, *"Cadê Eskyloh?"*—Where is Skyler? "Victor's?" They already knew.

One day, early on, Katia's Aunt Laura intercepted me at the market. She immediately introduced me to a cousin who ran a vegetable stand. "You must buy your vegetables from her." And she promptly told her, and everyone else we met, that we were living at No. 52 Praça Jácome Calheiros. There would be no secrets.

We would find ourselves using "the cooler" to escape more than just the heat.

In Penedo, I found that the simple act of speaking took a lot of thought. It was like doing a math problem every time you wanted to open your mouth.

"They just know which words are masculine and which are feminine," Peter said incredulously one day. "They don't even have to think about it!"

Every day in Brazil, I'd realize—after the fact—that I'd just said something ridiculous; and every day, I'd think how kind Brazilians are. They didn't laugh. They didn't deride. They might look momentarily confused, but it would pass as I blundered on and they teased out my meaning.

How many times did I ask Iago, the ten-year-old boy next door, to return our cake, instead of the ball? How often did I tell Bentinho, our newfound capoeira teacher, that I needed to sit and rot, instead of stretch? Funnier still, Peter, early in his Penedo soccer career, got hit with a ball in the groin and groaned, *"Minhas castanhas!"*—My cashews!—thinking *castanhas* was the word for *nuts*. Who knows if they even use that slang?

It turns out they use a number of English words, but with a Portuguese twist. They add a long *e* at the end, and in Portuguese, an *r* at the beginning of a word is pronounced like an *h*. Together this results in great transformations, like *hockey ee holy*: rock and roll.

In Portuguese, when you say, "I am," you need to distinguish between "I (temporarily) am" and "I (permanently) am," because you use different words depending on your state of being. Thus, "I am—*eu sou*—(permanently) a woman," but "I am—*eu estou*—(temporarily) tired." I could never think fast enough which one I needed, so I unconsciously settled on always using the temporary. I was temporarily Molly and Skyler's mother; I was temporarily American; and my house was temporarily there, i.e., tomorrow it might be gone. This choice was probably a reflection of just how tenuous our life there felt to me in general.

By the end of August, two months into our time in Penedo, we were wondering if it was worth it.

One day, I was sitting at my little corner desk in our front room, which we'd dubbed "the garden room" for its wicker couches and giant plants, finally getting down to work. I'd given myself the first months to get situated in this new place, but now I needed to turn at least some of my focus back to my work from home. After twenty years of teaching, I'd retired from the university two years before. I had wanted to focus on running my dance company, Headwaters Dance Co., which I'd separated from the university several years earlier, and I had wanted more flexibility in my days for the last years before Molly left for college.

While I'd founded the dance company with a colleague under the auspices of the university, when my partner decided she no longer wanted to share in directing the troupe, I pulled it off campus. I thought that if I were going to continue to direct it on my own, it would be more efficient to run it as a nonprofit. When I announced my intention to separate the company from the university, the university's legal advisor threatened me, saying, "You'll never last a year out there," as though I were heading out into the jungle without food or shelter. *I'll show you*, I'd thought. It had been five years, and while the company was surviving, it had begun to suck the air out of my lungs. I loved my volunteer board, but despite their enthusiasm and generosity, in the end, I was the grant writer, fundraiser, marketer, company manager, choreographer, and rehearsal director—and, don't forget, someone had to launder the costumes and paint the sets. And through it all, we weren't making enough for me to really get paid. Something needed to change. My intention was to use this year of hiatus to shore up the company's finances by continuing to write grants and send out fundraising appeals, things I could do long distance, over the Internet. Perhaps I could build up a cushion, reduce some of the stress of gambling every year that I'd be able to pull off another season. I admit on that day in August in Penedo, fundraising was the last thing I wanted to think about. I really just wanted a total break.

I was pulled out of my reverie when Skyler slammed open our metal front door, slumped in, and silently disappeared into the bedroom he and Molly shared. Molly dragged through the same door a half hour later, looking hot and exhausted. One more day of school down. School that Skyler hated, with its interminable hours of sitting and

understanding nothing. Of greater concern, he seemed to be developing an alarming self-loathing.

"I can't do anything I used to. I can't run fast anymore. I suck at
math." Each time he made a misstep on the *futsal* court, he was convinced anew that "they hate me now." This was not shaping up to be
the confidence-building, look-how-I-can-cope-with-challenges experience that Peter and I had hoped for. We tried to reassure him that
it would surely get better, as soon as he could speak a little more
Portuguese.

"Well, since I have no friends, I might as well find a hobby," Molly
announced as she rounded the corner and collapsed into the orange-
and-green hammock hitched to the wall behind my desk. The circle
of girls that had picked her up in class were great while at school, but
Molly's lack of language made it hard to include her in their after-
school social life. "I've always wanted to bake. I like to paint. I'm not
very good at it, but I like it."

I dug some money out of my bedside table, and we promptly
crossed the *praça* and spent sixty dollars for art supplies at the *papelaria*.
At least she had a plan.

Peter's agent had just emailed to say that a book proposal of Peter's,
which had been making the rounds of New York publishing houses
when we left, had been roundly rejected. It was the project he'd planned
to work on while we were in Brazil. He began to wonder what he was
doing there, began to have a hard time getting up in the morning. He
was losing weight.

Though I was struggling with my career, I seemed to be the only
one in our family who wasn't struggling with Brazil, and watching the
rest of them was shaking my convictions.

6

"I Hate Brazil"

WE WERE AN ANOMALY in this town and, as such, became instant celebrities, *Os Americanos*. No one, on meeting us, guessed we were American. Maybe Argentinean? French? Italian? Southern Brazilian? Anything that would explain our white skin in this largely darker-skinned place. Right away, people we barely knew told us they'd seen us: "in the morning in the market," or "in the *praça* with your daughter," or "you traveled to Carrapichu yesterday" (the town across the river). They frequently warned us about *ladrão*—robbers. "You shouldn't carry that bag, there are *ladrão*."

"*Por quê Penedo?*" everyone wanted to know.

Clearly, people found it curious that we would choose this town, but they were pleased, too. They liked their home and were flattered that *Os Americanos* had chosen it, out of all the possible places in Brazil.

Peter and I weren't so sure. We were questioning whether we'd chosen the right place after all; wondering how well life in this town— with no bookstore, no movie theater, no stoplight, no lane lines—was going to hold up; wondering whether we should not have listened to the kids, knowing as we did that total, unrelieved immersion could be hard, that it might mean no friends for them and surely none for us, that after the initial novelty wore off, it could be a year of spinning our wheels, lonely and tired of each other's company. In short, it could be a disaster.

Two months in, "I hate Brazil" had become Skyler's mantra.

This was not what parents who had just moved to a foreign country for a year of cultural immersion wanted to hear. There we were, six thousand miles away from home, on a different continent, in an upriver town in rural Brazil. Peter and I were not thrilled about bagging it all just because the place wasn't to Skyler's taste. On the other hand . . .

"Why do you hate it?" I asked, trying not to sound frustrated. The kids and I were crossing the *praça* in front of our house on our way to a *sorveteria*, an ice cream shop. A tinny, cavernous bus rattled over the cobblestones in front of us as we were about to step off the curb. It passed, and the little *sorveteria* reappeared across the street, bright blue with white art deco trim.

"They're mean. Brazilians are mean. They tease you, they say mean things, they taunt." Skyler's voice was rising in pitch.

"I know what you're saying, Skyler," Molly chimed in. We'd entered the small shop, with its cluster of ironwork café tables. Molly was balancing a self-serve scoop in her right hand as she surveyed the bins of ice cream. "But I think it's just their culture. They do it to everybody."

"How do they taunt?" I pursued as I scanned the names, wondering what they were—*graviola*, *maracujá*. I hadn't experienced anything like taunting. I'd received nothing from the people of this small town but "*Qualquér precisa*"—Whatever you need. Was this just the difference between adult and kid lives anywhere?

Skyler had become more tongue-tied, whether because of incipient adolescent hormones or the effort to straddle two languages, Portuguese and English, I didn't know.

Molly shrugged. "They're just really direct. Like, they just say it, if they think someone is *feio*"—ugly—"or fat. They say it right in front of them. Like the other day, when I was walking with Ryan,"— *Heon*—"and Helene, she just said, 'Molly, don't you think Ryan is fat?' What was I supposed to say?" She offered her bowl of ice cream to the woman at the counter to be weighed.

"They just laugh at you if something bad happens, like if you fall down." Skyler was warming up. "When you do something wrong in *futsal*"—Brazilian small-court soccer—"everybody yells at you. Everybody! I hate Brazilians."

Peter and I had carefully chosen Penedo because the kids—note, *the kids*—had requested immersion in a small town. Now, for better or worse, we were immersed. No international schools, no foreigners, no English.

We finished our ice cream and headed back out into the eye-squinting sun. In August in Penedo, daily torrential rains alternated with cerulean skies. Given the humidity, one could see why plaster mildewed so fast and plants grew straight out of the walls.

"Well, we don't have to stay, you know. We can see how it goes," I offered, wondering how readily we would really pull up stakes. "I think it'll be easier when we can speak a little more."

"I doubt it," Skyler mumbled, eyes downcast.

"It's hard when you don't know what people are saying," I continued, as we stepped off the high curb onto the cobblestones. "It's easy to think they're making fun of you when probably they're not even talking about you at all."

In retrospect, for Skyler, this year was terrible timing; not the opportune moment to drop an increasingly self-conscious, prepubescent boy into a competitive, macho culture where he didn't understand the social cues and couldn't speak the language. How had we not foreseen it? I *had* thought about it, but I'd concluded it would be fine. After all, I had been twelve when my parents dropped me into a French school in Cairo, where I, too, couldn't speak the language. But just because it turned out well for me didn't mean it would for him. A twelve-year-old girl is not a twelve-year-old boy. Penedo is not Cairo.

7

Finding Our Guides

GIOVANNI WOULD BECOME another of our guides, along with Zeca. Also twenty-six, he was the eldest son of Elizia, the school's office manager, and when we asked for a Portuguese-language coach, the school's director, Irma Francisca, recommended her assistant's son.

Giovanni had graduated from the school some years earlier and was now dismally working his way through law school in Arapiraca, the town with the trauma center, while also working as a technology specialist for a college there. Given his commuting schedule, it was no wonder that he was perpetually yawning. We set up private lessons. Peter, Molly, and I would each have an hour with him once a week in the courtyard at Imaculada. "Don't you think I'm getting enough Portuguese, sitting in school four hours a day?" Skyler had said, exasperated, when we suggested extra lessons. I didn't think we could push him any more than he was already being pushed. He was excused.

Tall and burly, Giovanni was a light-skinned black man. "My great-grandfather was white," he told me right after he'd said he was proud of his "people." I had presumed his "people" were black, so I was interested he felt a need to tell me his great-grandfather had been white. We'd just been talking about race in Brazil, all the different terms, as I was trying to understand which were politically correct and which insulting: *mulato, moreno, pardo, preto, amarelo, asiático* . . . he hadn't mentioned *espânico*, which is how I would have classified almost everyone I saw. Brazil is an amazing melting pot, but, as in the United States, the issue of racial prejudice continues to be troubling, and blacks and native Brazilians seem to be disproportionately denigrated. The kids and I, especially Skyler, would continue to try to sort it out over the coming months.

I came to like Giovanni a lot. At first he seemed like Eeyore. He would sit across from me at the small stone table, perpetually rubbing his eyes, gaze down, consistently cynical. But after a few months, I found he could tell a very animated story, eyes alight, pausing for emphasis, laughing with delight at my surprise or indignation, and he was suddenly able to meet my eyes, looking for the reaction. He'd been transformed from Eeyore into a round-faced, laughing Buddha.

"Really! Alagoas is at the *very* bottom?" I asked, having found that Giovanni was a great source for political, social, and economic statistics.

He nodded emphatically. "We have the worst numbers in Brazil. Lowest income, highest poverty, highest unemployment, and highest illiteracy, although that's improving." (And this was the place we'd chosen for its old-world charm.)

Eventually, however, I learned that Giovanni had a number of passionate interests: *futebol*—soccer—politics, social justice, and cars. One day, he brought a Matchbox car to my lesson. "These are my passion, and this is my favorite." He gave the little white Mustang with the blue racing stripe a push with his index finger.

He didn't have much good to say about Brazil. I wondered if he felt ashamed of it, especially in comparison to the United States, at least the "United States" he knew from American TV and films. He'd watched more of those than I had, learning to speak most of his English that way.

"I was born in the wrong place," he sighed one day, although later he admitted anywhere would have its problems.

I remembered the teenage boys in the village in Ghana, one of whom had bragged about a brother who, "born in the wrong place," had "made it out"—to the South Bronx. I'd asked if the brother was happy. "Well . . ." he'd hesitated, and then he'd caught himself and listed all the things his brother had: a car, a job that paid ten dollars an hour. "A lot for Ghana," I'd said, though it was not a lot for New York. "But is he happy?" I'd asked again. He'd conceded maybe he was a little lonely. *Hmmm, and experiencing a little racism for the first time in his life,* I'd thought. But his brother was adamant.

One morning, I ran into Katia, the manager from the Pousada Colonial, on my daily trip down to the market. She mentioned that she had spoken to her cousin. "Aniete is worried about you, Dona Amy," she said, looking concerned. "She says you were crying on your bench by the window."

How could I explain to Katia in my stilted Portuguese that Peter (whose book contract had not materialized) was depressed, Skyler hated school, and even Molly, usually a stalwart, was demoralized? How could I explain that this had all been my idea and I wasn't sure I could hold everyone up? How could I explain my growing feelings of resentment, vying with guilt, vying with sympathy for my struggling family—and my confusion about what to do? How could I explain this to Aniete? Although, given that she was privy to our every move, she could probably explain it to herself.

Aniete completed our trio of guides. Like Zeca and Giovanni, she, too, was twenty-six and, conveniently for us, was in need of a job. We'd housed a Brazilian exchange student back home in Montana the previous spring, and she'd told us, "In Brazil, *everybody* has an *empregada*—a household helper."

Everybody with money, that is. Katia and her Aunt Laura clearly thought we belonged in that category. We agreed that Aniete would come in five days a week from seven in the morning until three and clean, wash clothes, and cook. It would cost us a mere $200 a month.

Aniete had moved to the "city" from the family farm at sixteen, first to live with Katia and then Aunt Laura, with whom she still shared a bedroom. Under five feet tall, pretty and petite, she had a wide face and zipped lips that turned down whenever she felt uncertain, as when Peter was describing how to make something new for dinner.

"*Hoje, vamos fazer comida italiana . . . de China . . . de Tailândia . . . França . . . Americana,*" he would say, flamboyantly waving his arms in our white-tiled kitchen as if to say, *The world is at our fingertips!* Aniete would look increasingly incredulous, raise a skeptical eyebrow, and turn her zipped lips down, but continue to listen.

"*É diferente,*" she'd say, doubtfully eyeing another concoction of Peter's, something exotic, like the pork chops in red cabbage he was holding out in the frying pan. How *estranho!* It became a daily what-wild-thing-are-we-going-to-make-next joke between them.

When we said her cooking had been good, she'd light up with pleasure.

"*Sim? É bom?*"—Yes? It's good? her voice almost squeaking with relief.

It would take months, but in time, adrenaline rushing, she would hold up yet another condensed milk pudding, just out of the oven. "*Já invento,*" she would say with pride. "I just invented it!" The "invention" would consist of something like the addition of a tablespoon of raisins. It seemed we'd opened up a whole new world of culinary improvisation, something that reached beyond northeastern Brazil's staples of rice and beans, barely.

Aniete slipped silently about the house, like smoke on the white-tile floor. The tile floors might not have creaked like our wood ones at home, but when *I* walked, my cartilage crackled; I guessed that was the difference between twenty-six and fifty-two.

"*É um pouco tranquilo aqui,*" she let on one day in the first week or two of her time with us. "It's a little quiet here." A little too quiet.

So we bought her a radio, one that picked up international stations, so that she could listen to music during the day and we could pick up the BBC at night and make up for our world-news blackout, as our best source was the state paper, the *Alagoas Gazette*, with its litany of local robberies—exploding ATMs, gunmen shaking down buses—and tales of political corruption. We'd hear Aniete singing to the radio while kneading our clothes on the plastic washboard that came with the washroom one floor below. Always a little flat, she crooned away with oblivious abandon.

8

Time to Watch and Listen

It WAS RARELY QUIET in Penedo, at least by our standards. The sounds were layered like a complex symphony, from the Doppleresque crescendo and decrescendo of the buses rumbling past our front door, to the soft sound of rain on leaves in the back, to the distant patchwork of village sounds from Bairro Vermelho across the valley. Those varied depending on the time of day.

At five, daybreak, we mostly heard animals: hoarse roosters, staccato dogs, whistling monkeys, and rasping crows. But by midday, the music started, an infinite variety of scraps on the wind, floating out of windows without glass whose wooden shutters had been thrown open. Then there was the insistent cheerfulness of the pop that blared, at deafening volume, from speaker systems mounted on passing motorcycles and vans. When we first arrived, these nomadic speakers were advertising political candidates, as elections were just four months away. Each candidate had his or her own song with earnest lyrics about jobs and education dressed up in pop rock. (A good way to reach a population with a high rate of illiteracy.) After two months, they almost drove us out of our house.

Then there were the itinerant vendors, each with an identifying rhythm or melody, announcing the sale of coconut water, bread, tapioca cakes, or popsicles and ice cream—that last with a pitch that rhythmically rose and fell like cursive, *"Picolé e Sorvete, Caicó!"* By nightfall, the music was overlaid by a blanket of pulsating insect sounds.

Punctuating the symphony was the daily, startling pop and crackle of firecrackers—or were they small sticks of dynamite? At first I thought it was just party-time-all-the-time in Penedo, but then I started to think the jangling pops might have announced things like "time to go to church." Finally, I began to think Penedenses just like noise.

Walking down our street one evening, I heard, then saw, a man leaning on his windowsill, pumping away on a whistle. I thought he was trying to get someone's attention or signaling something; then I decided he was just making noise for the hell of it: a piercing declaration of *Hi, I'm here.*

This was just another of many events, inexplicable to an outsider, for which I would invent an explanation. It reminded me of walking down a main street in Maputo, in Mozambique, and hearing the watchful young men emit erratic whistles. I'd spy them hidden in the shadows and wonder if they had some code, a way of alerting someone down the block, *Here comes fresh meat, Big unzipped purse,* or *Wallet in back left pocket, partially exposed . . .* It took months before I figured out that they were the same guys who, pointing two fingers to their eyes and then one to your parked car, would offer to watch it for a few coins. They helped each other out, letting a sleeping compatriot know, with a quick set of whistles, that their car's owner was about to return.

Some years ago, one of the things that made me realize I would choose Montana over other places to live was my growing understanding that I valued living in a place with little or no manmade sound. Penedo was not such a place. Manmade sound seemed to be prized— the louder, the better. By the end, I found I rather admired this insistent celebration of life, especially since, recalling Giovanni's statistics, I knew life there could be hard. Brazil has the ninth-highest homicide rate in the world—and our peaceful town of Penedo turned out to be right in there with the best of them. Giovanni once said, shaking his head in resignation, "We just live in fear, fear, fear."

But he laughed as he said it.

"Ana Licia says Brazilians are the happiest people on earth," Molly announced one night, quoting one of her classmates, as we lounged around our dinner table.

"Are they?" I mused.

Or are they "HwH," "Happy with Help"? Was it that with a little beer—okay, a lot of beer—a little pot, or a little crack, the not-very-promising world looks a lot better? Of course, we have a lot of people on the HwH plan in the United States—drinking, using antidepressants—and we still don't claim to be the happiest people on earth. What's the difference? I wondered what role ambition—the pursuit of achievement—and the resulting workaholism might play in keeping us in the States from being the happiest people on earth. Ambition and workaholism were two things I'd been dealing with a lot. I suspected they were at the root of my struggle to maintain balance and joy.

In the United States, it feels to me as though our poor brains are addled, overwhelmed by the complexities of our world (as are the computers that are taking over for us, addled by the sheer volume they're expected to handle). In the United States, we say the addling is caused by the pace, too much, too fast—stimulation, information, options. What's driving the pace? In the States, we like to think we thrive on stimulation; we want options—who wouldn't? But when is the pace too fast, and the options so many that they're consuming us? Would we actually be happier with less? In northeastern Brazil, the pace definitely isn't too fast, and there often aren't a lot of options.

It must be baffling to the vast Brazilian poor how the few rich can so readily steal the food right out of their mouths, over and over and over again, century after century. It's not like the rich can't see the effects of what they're doing; it's right in front of you—in the rows of tiny houses with no water on dirt streets, their roofs leaking and dengue fever flying through their unglazed windows. Those poor don't have a lot of options. Their lives aren't focused on achieving their potentials. But then, somehow, the inhabitants of those houses are still singing, still rocking their hips to the *frevo* music—until the young men get drunk and shoot each other.

Sometimes my type-A American self has felt frustrated with people in other countries, usually the poor in developing countries who, understandably in their feelings of powerlessness, attribute their situations to fate. I've found myself harboring conservative-American pick-yourself-up-by-your-bootstraps thoughts: *Come on! Where's your get-up-and-go?* But when it comes to producing *happiness*, I find myself wondering which approach might be the more successful—the resignation to fate or the pursuit of achievement?

Fate had nothing to do with my family's worldview. My father, raised on Horatio Alger and existentialism, and my mother, an early feminist, passed down the belief that I could create my own future. I was in control—though they were the first to acknowledge that my educational privilege and middle-class finances had everything to do with my greater chances for success. As a result, I have forged ahead on the theory that if I just work hard enough, things I hope for will happen; there are no forces greater than myself. That's a lot of pressure. I watch middle-class Americans furiously striving as though the power is all theirs, if only they put in another night or weekend at the office, squeeze in another hour at the gym. But now, I wonder, when it comes to happiness as opposed to "success," whether we might be better off in the end, have less existential angst, if we found a balance between fate and self-determination. Perhaps rather than "resigning" ourselves to our circumstances, we could "relax" into our situations, stop pushing so hard—for what? We could find a few friends to hang out with and sing, rock our hips, blow a few whistles—just for the hell of it. Just to say, *Hi, I'm alive! And I'm thankful for that.*

In Penedo, there was a lot that was alive. If you thought something might be crawling on you, something probably was. One's connection to life in general is much closer in tropical places, where critters ooze out of the pores, and the houses aren't quite so sealed and screened as ours at home. The trick in a tropical place seems to be how to keep the outside out.

It took a few weeks before I began to notice the ants.

"Peter?" I queried, staring at the white tile wall above the kitchen sink. "Can you see where they're coming from?"

He was lost in thought at his computer at the dining table.

"*Hmmm?*"

"These tiny ants. They just seem to materialize out of nowhere." I perused the white caulking, which was now dotted black and in motion, snagged a dishtowel, wet it, and gave a few unlucky ants a cursory swipe, knowing that really it would make no difference.

The next morning, I made what had become our standard breakfast—fried bananas, sliced mangoes, scrambled eggs, and fried bread (toasters seemed not to exist). I packed the kids out the front door for school: first Molly, anxious not to be late, and fifteen minutes later Skyler, pleading, "Do I have to go?" This, too, had become standard. Shortly afterward, Aniete arrived, disappeared downstairs into her washroom, and reappeared in her "work clothes," tight pedal-pusher jeans and a fitted T-shirt.

I had settled onto the bench by the back window, cup of coffee and Portuguese dictionary in hand, for my morning language drill, when I heard a high-pitched whistle. I looked out and, to my delight, saw something like a hybrid of a koala and a lemur in miniature, deftly running along the barbed wire fence that separated our long strip of yard from the neighbor's. It had a flat nose, tufts of white hair sprouting around small, circular ears, and a long, ringed tail.

"Aniete, *o que é?*" I called out, pointing. "What's that?"

She walked over from the kitchen sink, wiping her hands on her pants.

"*Um sanguin,*" she stated matter-of-factly.

"*Um quê?*" It would be months before I could sling around that special nasal *ng* that gives Portuguese its resonance. "*Sahngweeng?*" I said, trying to make my nose buzz. Aniete smiled ever so slightly.

This *sanguin* had all the amazing agility and manual dexterity of the squirrel-like monkey that it is. It scampered up the barbed wire fence to the neighbor's papaya tree, shinnied up the trunk, and gutted the pendulous fruit from the bottom up. Its six-inch body eventually disappeared inside, so that it looked like a papaya with a tail.

For the next several months, I watched them from my morning perch, up to seven or eight at a time, lying spread-eagle on a palm frond, letting others pick through their fur; smaller ones played tag, running out to the ends of precariously dipping fronds, dropping four feet to one below, then spiraling around the trunk and leaping into a nearby mango tree.

"*Eles vao vir na janela . . .*"—They'll come to the window if you put out a banana. Aniete was smart and patient and quickly became our coach for many things.

Along with the *sanguin* were gray lizards that darted up the garden walls, stopping to knock their heads side to side, like East Indian dancers, or pump their front legs like leathery-skinned old men doing pushups on speed.

"Hey, Peter, there're three cows in our yard. I wonder whose they are," I remarked a few days later. Peter was back in his place at the dining table.

Then, a week later, "Hey, Peter, there're two guys with machetes in our yard. They're hacking away down there."

Whether they were hinting that we might hire them to clear the weeds or just helping themselves (to what, I'm not sure) was never quite clear. There were a lot of things that never became clear, such as how our neighbor could come over into our yard and just dig up a bush and take it without saying a word. (It turned out its leaves cured coughs.) There was something kind of renegade about this, kind of Wild West.

Above our yard, in the air, the birdlife was kaleidoscopic in black and white, rust and yellow, iridescent blue. Flocks of long-necked white egrets flashed as they circled over the field below us, banking in the morning sun. Above, huge buzzards rose on afternoon thermals, silhouetted wings spread wide and still. In the evening, bats came out, swooping in so close you could see the scalloped points on their wings.

That bench by the back window soon became my favorite spot. I noticed all these things because I had time—time to sit and watch. Time that I never seem to have in the States. Why do I have to leave the country to slow down enough to observe, to reflect? I'd wondered whether I could find the same thing by staying in the United States but moving to a smaller town. When I moved from New York City, where I was working three jobs to supplement my meager income as a dancer, to Missoula, Montana, to check out this guy Peter, I thought I'd found the answer, a way to slow down. But soon after we'd married and returned from our honeymoon in China, I was hired to run the dance program at the university, and there I was in a basement studio, twelve hours a day. I could have been anywhere.

When Peter and I decided to move to Mozambique, I'd reached my limit. Ever since the births of Molly and Skyler, I'd been trying to fig-ure out how to downsize my job. I'd sat in a parent-teacher conference at Molly's Missoula preschool, feeling totally inadequate. Her teacher looked at me sympathetically and suggested I buy a book called *The Good Enough Parent*. I felt relieved, for a while. But in the end, it didn't sit well. Just good enough? These are my kids we're talking about. I felt I couldn't do anything well. "C'mon, we need to go," I was constantly urging my kids. "I'm sorry I'm late" had become my opening line.

I felt exasperated with my inability to curb my ambition to be great at work, great at home, great . . . We've all heard it. You can't run away from yourself. But for me, crossing an ocean helps. There I can grant myself the time to gaze out a window, to really see where I am, to reflect. The trick is how to hang onto that when returning home.

9

A Gringo Befriended

By THE END of August, the rains were subsiding. Peter came home from his Sunday soccer game by the river, limbs limp and shirt soaked, looking dragged out, but also softened somehow. He'd been at loose ends since the failure of his book to sell, was combating an incipient depression, and was only slowly starting to think about other possible writing projects. I'd been worried about him and was relieved he was finding a source of exercise and camaraderie. The endorphins were good for him. The game had started at three. It was now seven. I was serving dinner.

"I must have danced with fifteen men," he said. I was puzzled. I thought he'd been playing soccer.

Peter, an old high school soccer player who'd picked up the game again in his forties, had, like Skyler, been looking forward to honing his skills among the world's best in Brazil. Of course, it became immediately clear on our arrival in Penedo that the "world's best" don't play past age thirty. Until then, Brazilian men are among the most amazing specimens of manhood on the planet, capable of any imaginable physical feat. After that, they grow paunchy and bald and start losing their teeth. I tried to make sure all the teens and twenty-somethings with whom Peter was playing understood that he was *fifty-seven*. But I don't think they quite believed this tan, muscled man with the full head of chestnut hair was really that old. I was lobbying for his preservation. We didn't need any more head injuries like Skyler's.

Lu, the owner—*o dono*—of this slung-together team wasn't your American sports team's high roller. He had a business, with a bucket and sponge, washing cars down by the ferry slip. As owner, his job seemed to be to organize the games against similar teams in other towns, to gather money from the players to rent the city bus for transport, to raise the money for uniforms. Now paunchy and snaggletoothed—old for Brazilian soccer but younger than Peter—Lu took Peter under his wing. Peter, the over-the-hill player, could come play with them if he wanted to. "We'll have the only *time internacio- nal*"—international team—"in Penedo," Lu had said, beaming.

Peter was delighted to have been asked. Not all of his teammates' arms, however, were quite as open as Lu's. Little Frankie, black hair streaked with blond, glittery studs in his ears, was always yelling at Peter as they played.

"*Toca a bola!*"—Pass the ball! Peter, playing a more American game, i.e., a passing game, rather than the glittering, footwork-heavy Bra- zilian game of keep-away, rarely *had* the ball. This was just Frankie's habitual cry, and Peter offered a good target.

Junior, however, at twenty-two a little older than Frankie, was curi- ous about this *Americano*. With a quick smile and easy manner, Junior didn't seem to flaunt his skill quite as much as the others, though he was among the best goal scorers on the team. Peter found the tutor he'd been looking for. He asked if Junior would come to games early, give him some pointers, help him develop a "powerful shot." (This had been one of Peter's wishes on the mobile we'd made at home.) Junior, unemployed like many of the other players, seemed flattered and pleased both for the money Peter offered and the chance to get to know the gringo.

After this particular Sunday game, they'd gone to Janelas, the night- club across the street from the field, to suck beers and dance. "I think it was their way of saying they like having me on the team," Peter mused. "To pay for drinks"—he looked a little rueful—"but also just to be on the team. Junior said he's never had a gringo friend before. He said, 'Usually the gringos are afraid of us. They think we're going to rob them.'" Peter mused some more. "Of course they do, one way or the other." He smiled.

"But that's not the same; you pay because you want to," I said, hand- ing him a plate of stewed chicken on rice that Aniete had made earlier.

"*Hmm.* Ever since the road trip to Bom Conselho, Junior has been teaching me how to dance. He shows me, and I try to do it." Peter raised his arms over his head and knocked his ribs side to side. "He thinks it's funny. So today he said, 'Every time we make a goal, Peter's going to lead the dance.' I didn't realize he meant in front of the fans."

"Did you?" Molly asked, aghast.

"Yeah. We'd run over to that balustrade to do it, you know, where people are leaning on the railing. He'd also said if we had a penalty kick, I'd take it, and if I made it, Lu would buy everyone beers afterward, and if I missed, I'd buy."

"Sounds like he figured that one out," I said, laughing.

Dalan—or *Ninguém*, "Nobody," as he'd been nicknamed by the team—was another one who had figured some things out.

"I'm just a walking ATM machine," Peter would snort some time later.

He soon became the regular funder for a number of people around town, usually men who, shy with me, were unabashedly open with Peter. There was Magrinho down the block, who appeared at the door asking for five *reais* (pronounced *heyice*), about three dollars, for medicine for his daughter. There was Iago's dad, next door, who started out saying he'd pay back the tidbits he borrowed, supposedly for their *energia* bill—though his habitual lurching walk and reek of *cachaça* belied that—then shifted to saying he would trade us cheese for the money, then dropped all pretense. Peter finally dropped him. But he hung onto the frail white-haired man with the dapper black felt hat who would rap on the glass panes of our front door with his cane. He wore the same blue-striped shirt, soft from hand-washing, and always asked for money for his wife's eye drops. And Peter kept Dalan.

"I went down to the *baixa* to find my watch today," Peter said as he settled back into his spot one morning at the dining table, his office. (*Baixa* literally means *low* and is a common name for both the geographically lower part of a town and the commercial part of town, at least in water-based places where the commercial life develops around rivers or oceans.) "I'd left it with the guys at soccer last night so they could keep timing for *dez ou dois*." *Dez ou dois* means *ten or two*. When they played pickup games, they frequently played for either ten minutes or two goals, whichever came first. Then they'd rotate in a new team of two to four players. Peter was the only one with a digital watch to keep track.

"Dalan said he'd take care of my watch. He helps out somehow at Gordo's *lanchonete*, doing odd jobs, so I looked there, and they just pointed. He was asleep on the concrete floor behind the Coke machine with my watch on his wrist. I think maybe he doesn't have a home."

I once identified Dalan's lean body miraculously asleep on the hard cobbles of the ferry slip, unbothered by the loading of cars, trucks, and backfiring motorcycles. Coach Lu had moved on to running a video game business out of the front room of his house, and Dalan had taken over washing cars. He was dark-skinned, with the sharper nose and small eyes of an African Arab. His speech was barely audible, and he moved like a cat burglar, silent on callused feet. I liked him despite the fact that I didn't trust him (not because he wasn't a good person, but because he had some of the do-whatever-you-need-to-do-to-survive desperation of the really poor).

Over time, you begin to sort out those who attach themselves to you because you have something they want (money, soccer balls, some amorphous potential for a better life), and those who hang around because they're genuinely interested in you. Dalan was probably a little of both.

One morning, Peter and I were sitting at Menezes, an open-air *lanchonete* near the river, and Dalan sauntered over and sat down. He barely talked. He just sat next to us, which I rather appreciated. It made me feel included. I had the feeling, however, that his body never fully relaxed into the chair, that he was always on alert. That day, one of the "Gypsy" women, in their trademark long, diaphanous dresses, lime green this time, asked to read our palms. I'd asked who these people were, and all anyone could say was, "They're not from here." I wondered if they were distrusted the way I'd heard Gypsies were in Europe. As she went on and on, tracing one line, then another in our palms, intoning incomprehensibly, I began to wonder what Dalan, sitting across from us in his muscle shirt and surf shorts, thought about all this.

"*É tudo verdade. Elas sabem tudo,*" he whispered when she was finished, barely moving his lips. "It's all true. They know everything." Too bad we hadn't been able to understand any of it. In retrospect, we could have used a heads-up.

Sometime later, Peter was musing about Brazilian character. "They have an almost-animal quality. They're always watching; they see everything." That was certainly true of Dalan. He never missed a beat. When Peter was open in soccer and no one passed him the ball, Dalan did. When I struggled to swing my baskets of groceries onto the city bus, Dalan appeared to help. Our first week in town, that man who'd run across the *praça* to tell Peter his son had split his head open? That was Dalan.

Somehow I could never bring myself to call him "Nobody."

10

"Quer Ficar Comigo?"

LIFE SEEMED TO BE settling down, if more easily for some of us than others. Before leaving the States, I'd had my share of anxious visions about what could happen to our kids in a small town in Brazil. Among them, I'd wondered whether our beautiful blond teenage daughter would fall prey to sexually predatory men. Would her inherent celebrity status as an outsider protect her, or would she be seen as a special prize, a conquest, a target?

My mind had been filled with the stereotypes one can have before getting to know a place. For Brazil, I'd imagined macho cruising men and scantily clad women. We would find that while the women were scantily clad, they, at least Molly's friends, were much *less* likely to hop into bed than her sixteen-year-old American counterparts; that while a Brazilian woman might wear a "dental-floss" bikini, she would never go topless. The statistics on rape and the demoralizing debate about whether a woman, through her dress or behavior, "asked for it" are just as disheartening and confusing in Brazil as they are in the United States, but not any more so. Ultimately, we would get to know many protective, respectful men to whom I would gladly have entrusted my daughter.

Nevertheless, Molly and I had been warned by a Brazilian friend in Missoula that it was a common practice at parties to be asked by someone you'd just met if you wanted to make out. "*Quer ficar comigo?*" No strings attached. It turns out this is not a prelude for anything more, as it can be in the United States. But still, with a stranger?

So when Molly came home from school one day jubilantly announcing that she'd been invited to her new friend Keyla's fifteenth birthday party, we thought we were prepared. Molly was excited. She barely spoke Portuguese and, so far, only two people we'd met spoke English, but she could dance, and, at a party in Brazil, dancing would get you a long way.

"Mom, what should I wear?"

"What do you have?"

At ten that night, another new friend, Leila, came to pick Molly up. Molly was wearing jeans, a T-shirt, and her favorite multicolored flat sandals. She opened the door. There was Leila—in a beige satin minidress and four-inch heels, beautifully showcasing her mahogany skin and long legs. Molly rushed back into her room.

"Mom, what can I wear?"

She re-emerged in a short black dress and the only heels she owned, two-inches high with a tame strap.

"Have fun," I called as she slipped out the door. I doubted she'd heard me, or the trepidation in my tone. Molly has never been one to look back, when friends are involved. I remember dropping her off for her first day of preschool in Missoula, age three. I couldn't get her attention to wave good-bye; nor at the next preschool in Spain, age three and a half; nor for fifth grade in Mozambique, age ten. She faces forward.

Parties in Penedo start at ten or eleven, after our bedtime. We had no car. We'd considered finding a taxi driver to bring Molly home in the wee hours but had thought better of it. After midnight, *if* they were willing to work, chances are they would be doing it under the influence. In Brazil, the parties are intergenerational, so I knew Leila's mom was there and would drive them home when the party ended. But if Molly wanted to leave earlier, she was stranded with no way to bail. We kept our cell phones by our bed, figuring maybe we could call Zeca, one of our trio of guides, if she was really in trouble. It turned out Zeca was often at the same parties.

That first time, I woke up at 3:00 AM. It was still dark. No sign of Molly. I'm naturally optimistic and I really trusted her; even so, I wished she were home. I was less anxious, however, than I would have been in Montana. Perhaps because in Brazil I didn't know enough to know what to worry about. She'd been told to keep her eyes on her drink (in Brazil the legal drinking age is eighteen, but it's not enforced) and stick with friends, but the U.S. bogeyman, drunk driving, didn't exist. Lots of people were drunk, but almost no one was driving.

I went to lie down on the living room couch. Not long after, Molly quietly opened the front door.

"How was it?" I asked blearily.

"Oh, Mom, it was really fun, but . . ."

"But what?"

"It was kind of overwhelming, too. There was lots of dancing. It was really cool. Everyone dances. They love to dance. But these guys—"

"How old were they?"

"Oh, I dunno. Twenty . . . ish? But they made a big circle around me and they were shouting, 'Mohly, Mohly, I love *you. I love you.*'"

"In English?"

"Yeah. In English. For a long time. It was really loud. And they wanted me to dance. And they kept asking me to *fica"*—to make out—"with them."

"Wow, Molly. What did you do?"

"Well, my friends were trying to protect me. But finally, I gave in. I told Felipe, you know, the guy who worked at the desk at the *pousada,* that I would, cuz at least I kinda knew him."

"What did you tell him?"

"I said, 'Okay, one.'" She brandished her index finger. "One quick one. Then he stuck his tongue down my throat."

"Oooh, yuck. What did you do then?"

"I retreated into the kitchen. They were really nice to me. Everyone was *so* nice to me."

Well, we'd been warned this would happen to Molly. But to Skyler? It turned out that at age twelve, our tan, blond, blue-eyed son had an impassioned female following, both his age and older, acquaintances and total strangers. Brazilians aren't shy, and they start young. They'd regularly ask him to kiss them, at school or on the street. Anywhere would do.

"Mom, what do I do? I want to go play tennis, but there're all those girls out there!" And there were—a little tittering clutch eagerly watching our front door from the concrete benches in the *praça*. He was trapped in our house.

"Can you just say we don't do this in the States? That we don't kiss strangers?"

"I've tried that. They just say, 'But this is Brazil.'"

In Skyler's first few months in school, we received several love notes a week, surreptitiously slipped under our front door. Once I heard it and whipped the door open, mischievously hoping to catch the author. She'd vanished. On purple or pink paper, with heart or rainbow stickers, in a combination of Portuguese and broken English, they ranged from the fairly innocent (and somewhat inscrutable), "Never get out of Brazil that is a rock. I'll die," to the racy, "Just want your baby well," or "I'am Prostitute and you is my Bum," or better yet, "Fuck! *Te Amo!*"

One Saturday, Skyler took part in a capoeira demonstration at a school. He and I had recently begun to take lessons in this Brazilian martial art/dance form. As soon as Skyler and the other *capoeiristas* arrived at the school, he was swamped by girls wanting to pose for pictures with him, which he dutifully did. The California surfer: shaggy blond hair, clear blue eyes, a big white smile painfully frozen on his face. Theoretically, this should be a boy's dream, but it wasn't.

11

The Table Goes Silent, Time for a Break

WE DECIDED it was time to blow town, at least for the weekend; our fishbowl existence was becoming a little wearing—okay, somewhat exhausting . . . all right, just plain frustrating, at least for some of us. I was feeling guilty. Compared to Peace Corps workers or anthropologists out in the bush, what did we have to complain about? A clean house with tile floors and windows, kitchen help, lots of friendly people with arms wide. What was so hard?

A lot. The effort to express myself clearly in a new language, speaking at a kindergarten level when I had fifty-two-year-old thoughts, was surprisingly exhausting, as was the need to have all antenna fully extended all the time, so I could have a shot at understanding the response.

Every morning, I'd visit the dictionary before I made the day's foray into the world and build up my armament for some anticipated conversation. *Prego, massa, cabo*—nail, plaster, computer cable—and my favorite, *liquidificador*, blender. Then there was the constantly being caught off guard because it turned out that though I thought I'd been understood, I hadn't, or I'd said something I hadn't meant to.

Even our minimal social life was wearing. Early one Sunday morning, Zeca's uncle Robson (they say *Hobson*) had showed up unannounced, his family peering out the windows of their sleek gray sedan, inviting us to come out to the family farm, *para andar os cavalos*—to ride horses—around the fishpond.

Zeca would come pick us up, he said. I asked what time.

"*Meio-dia*"—Midday.

Good, that would still give us part of the day to ourselves. So I was confused when Zeca arrived half an hour later.

"But it's only ten. Robson said midday." I was quite sure. I persuaded Zeca, accommodating as always, to come back later.

By the time we bumped down the rutted mud road to the fishpond, the horses were grazing listlessly.

"*Meia hora, Amy, não meio-dia! Meia hora!*" Robson laughed. "Not mid-day, half an hour!"

He and his wife, Shirley (pronounced *Shelee*), and their two kids, Julia and Mateus, had been waiting for us, out of cell phone reach, for two hours. But they graciously served us olives and urged *cachaça* on Peter. The kids in their swimsuits rode the pokey slow horses, skinny legs dangling toward stirrups out of reach. Eventually Shirley asked, "*Já almoçado?*"—Have you already eaten lunch? Lunch is the big meal in Brazil. Dinner is more like a snack. We drove the few miles back into town to a local sports club, where another couple, friends of Robson and Shirley's, joined us. You might think that I'd already dispensed with my language mishap for the day, but no.

That was when I thought I heard the fat-bellied, bare-chested husband in the other couple use a word I'd heard and wondered about before.

"*Que significa* arrobar?" I asked the table, repeating the word I thought I'd heard.

It went silent. Then, slowly, Zeca, said, "Well, it can be like a, what is this?" he was miming wrenching at something.

"A crowbar?"

"Yeah, but more, it's . . ." He'd been choosing his words carefully and had now come to a complete halt. "Not a good word. When you are angry at someone, maybe you say this."

"Oh, *asshole?*" I asked.

Zeca nodded his head vigorously, seeming relieved that I'd gotten it on my own. The wife of the man who had said it—or at least I thought he had—watched me intently, her painted eyebrows raised, her wilted smile unmoving.

It was definitely time for a break, for a little time on our own, for some *English*-language immersion. We'd chosen Penedo partly because it was only thirty minutes from hundreds of miles of ocean beaches. That weekend, our destination was Pontal do Coruripe, a deserted stretch of sand with a funky *pousada* we'd read about in the *Lonely*

Planet guide. This B and B was run by Ada, an Italian woman who spoke English and had a library of books in multiple languages. Heaven.

We'd been told we could flag down the little vans that provided daily transportation to towns around the state of Alagoas. So we were leaning against the iron bars that surrounded the baroque pink mansion across the *praça* from our house, our motley collection of umbrellas, backpacks, soccer ball, and boogie board arrayed at our feet. As it turned out, we had lots of time to look through the bars and study the bulging presence of the pink Peixoto family house, with its curving lines and romantic murals in blue tile of sailing ships from another era. Of Portuguese descent, the Peixotos remained one of Penedo's premier families. In the early 1900s, they had built the textile factory we could still see, shining picturesquely white, across the river. In the 1950s, they'd built the Hotel São Francisco, the "modern," anvil-like block plopped down in the middle of the tiny commercial district.

"Skyler, just kiss Mariana. Then maybe we can get into that house!" Molly pleaded, only half joking. Mariana Peixoto was a tall girl who'd just beaten Skyler at arm wrestling. Skyler had been under pressure from his classmate Mateus, Mariana's annoyingly pushy cousin, to kiss her.

Mateus was Skyler's nemesis. He was one big mixed message, solicitous one moment, taunting the next. "It's not even that he's so mean to me," Skyler had said one day. "But he's mean to others. It makes me uncomfortable." When it came to sex, Mateus was claiming king of the hill.

"He says he's done it with girls," Skyler said one day, sounding dismayed.

"Do you believe him?"

"Yeah. I bet he has." Skyler was beginning to sound desperate. "He's always pushing me to kiss girls. When I say I don't want to, he says it's because I'm afraid."

Mateus had settled on Mariana for Skyler's proving ground. Mariana lived in the pink house. If only Skyler would kiss Mariana . . .

More vans passed, but not the one to Pontal. Either because of our sketchy understanding of Portuguese or general Brazilian vagaries about time, we hadn't been able to get a clear sense of the schedule, and now it was getting dark. We decided we'd better schlep our gear down the hill and find a taxi. We found a willing driver down by the ferry slip.

"This is a seatbelt situation," I said. But the belts were missing parts. This is when you let go of all the precautions you'd take at home and just hope your guardian angels aren't asleep on the job.

In minutes, it would be dark. We sped off over the cobbles, houses and shops on the left like some kind of dimly lit cubist jumble, and weedy, open fields meandering down to the river on the right. Lighted shops gaped through raised garage doors. Already people along the side of the road were difficult to see, their dark skins blending into the blackness.

Night driving in foreign countries is like getting ready for a race— part adrenalized excitement, part dread. I try to relax into what seems to be an inevitably wild ride and quell the anxious anticipation of what could go wrong. It was easier when I was younger. I remember, when I lived in Cairo as a child, loving this feeling of speeding through the darkness, the temperate breeze washing over my face through open windows. In Cairo, the only time a car *could* fly was in the predawn, when we'd be racing for the airport. Then the otherwise perpetually crowded streets were surprisingly empty.

Later, just before Molly was born, Peter and I had flown by airplane from morning till night in a great looping arc from Cairo, near the Mediterranean, to Ghana, in West Africa. By the time we approached the airport in Accra, we'd been sucked into an ocean of darkness. This great city appeared to have no lights. On the trip into town, the airport taxi driver opted to use his headlights sparingly, suddenly flipping them on at inexplicable moments, for example, just in time to blind an oncoming car.

That same strange combination of exhilaration and anxiety came back when we lived in Mozambique and would find ourselves racing for the South African border, a couple of hours away from our house in Maputo, for a wild-game-viewing weekend in Kruger Park. We'd been warned that we did not want to be out on the roads after dark. We'd quickly gotten the picture from Maputo's expat community. Lock your doors when you're *in* your car, so people don't reach in and pull your purse—or you—out. Travel in convoys. Travel in daytime. And *don't* break down, especially in South Africa. "There," we were told, "they don't just rob."

Ten-year-old Molly had been pressuring us to go to the South African town of Nelspruit, just across the border, a three-and-a-half-hour drive. She wanted to go to the mall.

"We didn't come to Africa to go to a mall!" was Peter's response.

But I caved. All her friends went. It was important for her to fit in. I started asking around, looking for a convoy. No? Okay, let's get a grip on the statistics, confront this amorphous fear. How many people have really been hijacked on the road? No one knew. I was aware of how easily fear can take hold without much actual grounding. So—conscious that I didn't want unsubstantiated fear to dominate my decisions and as it appeared there were no statistics and few personal stories—I decided to go for it. The claptrap Suzuki jeep we'd bought a couple of months earlier from a Pakistani used-car salesman was already in the garage for repairs. In the meantime, we'd been given a loaner.

Early on a Saturday morning, Molly and I backed through our gate in our borrowed white sedan, passports and a reservation for a recommended guesthouse in hand. An hour later, we were at the hilltop border crossing, an unassuming clapboard building. Passport control was its usual confusing jumble of people pressing forward to get the required stamps, but we made it through. We began the descent into South Africa. The countryside was bucolic, rolling hills with orange orchards, rock outcroppings, and trout streams—somehow immediately lusher than dry, hardscrabble Mozambique. But I was on the alert.

And then it happened. The steering wheel jerked. The rubber slapped. I swerved to the side of the road. We had a flat tire.

I pulled over and jumped out, hoping for a spare and a jack. Within a minute, a white pickup truck with two black men pulled over in front of us.

"Molly, get out of the car!" I shouted as I raced around to the back and opened the trunk. I wanted her to have a chance to run.

I was screened by the raised trunk. Should I pick up the crowbar lying in front of me?

And then the man appeared next to me.

"May we help you?" he asked.

Before I could answer, they were fishing out tools and had the tire changed. It turned out one was an English-speaking South African. They were returning from a visit to the home and family of the other, a Mozambican man, and were headed back to their jobs in a South African toilet paper factory. Before I could offer to pay them for their help, they'd gotten back into their truck, where they waited for us to take off, then followed to be sure we were all right.

So much for getting killed by the side of the road.

I felt chagrined at my susceptibility to prejudice and relieved to be reminded of the real goodness of most people. Constant distrust is exhausting, but it's so easy to fall prey to fear, especially if the safety of one's children might be at stake. On the other hand, over the course of our year in Mozambique, a family we knew did get hijacked on this same South African road and escorted at gunpoint into the bush; robbers tied up the French teacher from our kids' school and her children in their house in Maputo; and a Belgian acquaintance of friends was shot in her car. So maybe we were just lucky.

I was hoping we would have the same luck here in Brazil as our taxi picked up speed on leaving the cobbles and hitting asphalt. The stretch paralleling the Rio São Francisco was long and straight and unusually free of potholes. The headlights of an occasional oncoming vehicle would start as a distant glow, then tree trunks would pop into silhouette as it rounded the soft curves, until finally its lights appeared head on; each time it seemed we were about to collide, but somehow the car would skim past. Occasional clumps of people would appear by the roadside, evanescent visions in sudden Technicolor, flashing up on a screen and as rapidly disintegrating back into nothingness.

Once we hit the coast, the terrain changed. Now spindly coconut palms in orderly rows reared up into the headlights, marching along like fence posts—plantations extending for miles. The land began to dip and rise, diving into tangled draws and cresting into the sudden openness of sugarcane fields, their densely packed spiky grasses forming a canyon that our little car sped through under a wide, moon-shot, cloud-filled sky.

As we approached the town of Coruripe, traffic picked up, and we began the high-speed game of "tailgate, duck out, and dash." Soon after, we cleared town and reached Pontal, a small oceanside village on a point.

We arrived just in time for dinner at Pousada da Ada, after flying down a steep hill through a gauntlet of small houses, turning left at the *praça*, then right at the *Frango Vivo e Abatido* sign, and right again where the arrow dimly painted on the side of a house pointed the way.

The warm eating room glowed through open windows overgrown with hibiscus, oleander, and bougainvillea. From inside, we could hear the clink of glasses and silverware. Ada appeared in the doorway.

"Ahh!" Her voice was low and rasping. "You made it!" she said in English. "Excellent. How was the ride? Not too fast?" She chuckled. "These drivers, they are crazy here in Brazil. Come."

She ushered us along the veranda—past casually scattered conch shells, a low-slung hammock, and a windowsill lined with empty blue and green bottles. Skyler brushed a coconut-shell chime, setting off its lackadaisical, hollow clatter. We crossed a walkway to a white stucco bungalow. It was partitioned into several rooms, each without a ceiling, open to the clay roof tiles. Someone perched on a beam could spy into each room, as if looking down into a dollhouse. We threw our bags onto the gray stone floor and returned to the main house, where we joined the other guests at one large table.

A couple, both social workers from Germany, two young Austrian architecture students, and a ruddy-cheeked, white-haired Austrian banker greeted us jovially. The table-wide conversation meandered along pleasantly in English, German, and Portuguese. (Italian-born, Portuguese-raised Ada could speak all of these and more.) Ada zipped in and out, cigarette in hand. Petite, tan, and wrinkled, with short salt-and-pepper hair and alert dark eyes, she monitored the continual flow of dishes: creamy yam soup, fried fish dumplings with salsa, buttery vegetable stir-fry, and scalloped potatoes. I gratefully slugged down the *caipirinha* waiting at my place, decompressing from the high-speed ride and the daily strains of trying to speak Portuguese. It was such a relief to finally feel I didn't have to be "on," as we all did in our spot-lighted existence in Penedo.

Finishing off our guava ice cream, the kids and I retired to our bungalow to settle in for our nightly ritual of listening to *Harry Potter* on an audiobook. Peter stayed to talk to the other guests, basking in the chance to have a more complex conversation, to use words that just spill off your lips.

I stared up through the sweeping white folds of the mosquito net into the underside of the clay roof tiles and watched a white rat run the length of the central beam. In my newly relaxed state, a state I hadn't experienced in months, the rat seemed magical. I wanted to believe it brought good tidings. I felt very content.

We would eventually discover that our state of Alagoas has three kinds of beaches: highway beaches, where people drive their cars into the shallows, unfold chairs, and sit in the ankle-deep water; party beaches, where no cars are allowed but the sand is studded with umbrella-shaded flesh and a parade of vendors; and classic postcard stretches of deserted, palm-lined white sand. Pontal is the latter.

Our first morning, we picked our way through an empty lot, climbing down a rock bulwark to drop onto a vast arc of sun-soaked sand. A luminescent jade ocean broke white over rock reefs. On our left, a sandy bank rose to an airy coconut plantation, trees aligned in rows like elegant couples engaged in some aristocratic dance, fronds bowing and curtseying in the light breeze.

"Do you think I could flip off that?" Skyler asked, pointing to a dip in the sand bank. After splitting his head on the stone wall in Penedo, he'd been plagued by doubts. "I'm never going to be able to flip again," he'd mumble periodically, a remark that half wanted a response and half didn't, sure that the verdict could only be bad.

Peter and I, both physically oriented people, had consciously let our kids to take some physical risks as part of our child-rearing strategy.

By *risk*, I mean things like walking on a railing a few feet off the ground, jumping off a wall, climbing trees. We felt that ultimately, our kids would be safer if they developed their physical abilities and had practice calculating the risks. Our guideline for risks was: A broken leg is tolerable. Paralysis is not.

Peter studied the bank. "Yeah. I think you could." We knew it would be good for Skyler's confidence if he could "get back on the horse."

Skyler climbed the bank, adjusted his feet, looked back over his shoulder, threw his arms a couple of times overhead, then jumped and landed. He ran over to us, talking fast now.

"How high was my head? Do you have your camera? Did you get a picture? I'm going to do it again. Are you ready?"

It was so good to see him excited about something. I had that same feeling of relief I get when a nagging background sound—a generator, an air conditioner—suddenly disappears. In perpetual coping mode, I hadn't allowed myself to recognize how much tension I'd been carrying around, like a lead weight in my pocket.

Molly, Skyler, and Peter are much gutsier body surfers than I am. They look eagerly out to sea, watching for good waves to catch. They don't seem to mind the smashing and grinding on the sand when the wave deposits them on the beach.

"Mom," Skyler suggested, always eager to include me, "if you feel yourself starting to roll forward, just do this"—he covered his face with his forearms—"so you don't break your neck."

"Whoa, did you see that one?" said Molly, head popping up through warm foam. "I flipped all the way over!"

"I almost lost my suit," Peter laughed.

I, too, stood chest-deep and faced the great waves, rolling milky green, a smooth wall rising five or six feet in front of me. But inevitably, I chickened out and dove through rather than surfing in. Miraculously, no matter how big they were, even if I was late and the wave was already crashing, I popped out the other side unscathed. If I timed it just right and dove through the glass wall, my body would ripple out behind with a luscious, almost disembodied feeling, as though I were a paper doll fluttering, head toward a fan.

I loved the feeling of just floating on my back, out beyond where the waves broke; of feeling my body, so light, being carried high on a swell and then sliding down the back side; or of letting my legs dangle down, the wave gently lifting me off the sandy bottom before setting me lightly down again. Sometimes I tried leaping toward shore with the wave as it rose and was lofted up, suspended on a cushion of water, better than dancing with any human partner.

I loved the feeling of being so connected through my senses. For once, my mind was in storage. I wasn't worrying about my family trying to adapt to a foreign country; I wasn't in hyperdrive, preparing for a dance performance; I wasn't plotting out the next step, checking things off the list.

As an academic, I'd had long vacations and always marveled that, even then, I could never completely relax. The first time I'd managed to, it had required leaving the country—setting up house in Maputo; establishing a simple, daily routine of coffee on the balustrade-rimmed terrace of an old colonial hotel; gazing blankly for hours at the turquoise pool and the vastness of the Indian Ocean beyond—before my mind would release its grip. This was the second time, finally, at the end of September, almost into month four. It made me wonder how one lets down in the States when one doesn't have so much time and what happens to a body that's continually revved.

We'd been caressed by this all-encompassing warmth on other visits to the tropics. Chubby-legged Molly had run naked on the beaches of Bali; baby Skyler had nestled into a soft Spanish breeze; waves had launched our bodies off the shores of Mozambique. It's easy to understand why, in these climates, the drive to "do" just slips away, why the faces of people in these places look so relaxed, so soft. They have none of the pinched tension, the clenched muscles I see in most of the places I've lived—Wisconsin, Massachusetts, New York, Montana—the frigid north, where people have to "do" just to stay warm.

An afternoon passed, and the next morning; then we had to catch the van back to Penedo. We'd thought of nothing but crashing waves, the great spread of sky, the gentle swivel of palm fronds, the amniotic warmth of the water. We slipped back into Penedo, skins crusted with salt, muscles warm with sun, limp and relaxed.

12

Running the Race

Two weeks later, the distress was back.

"Why do I have to go to school?" Skyler wanted to know again. Clearly the question was rhetorical, the vent through which blew his general anxiety and frustration.

It was late September. Both Molly and Skyler had been chosen to play on Imaculada's *futsal* teams and had just returned from a five-day competition in Bahia, ten hours and two states away. Hoping that a few months of language immersion would improve Skyler's school situation, we'd asked him to stick it out at Imaculada until the Bahia trip, after which we would reconsider his options; maybe homeschooling would be better.

When they'd left for Bahia, we had watched them standing alone amid the swarm of classmates and teachers. They'd bravely marched forward, their small bags (Skyler's old Missoula soccer bag and Molly's carpet bag from Bali) looking unlike anyone else's, and handed their luggage over to be loaded into the belly of the bus. Skyler was armed with Rubik's Cubes, number puzzles, and Uno cards. Molly had a book. Many of the guys had brought drums. Skyler's math teacher had a guitar. I was so proud of my kids. If I'd had to spend five days in nonstop, Portuguese-speaking company, I would have bolted.

During their trip, Peter and I scored a much-needed date, our own five-day trip, to Salvador, for a dose of fine dining, English-language bookstores, big-city museums, and art—a chance to check in with each other, assess our situation.

What I mostly remember from that trip was the evening we spent on the deck of a yacht club restaurant on the Baía de Todos os Santos, sipping a cold Riesling and eating artisan cheeses under the overhanging arm of an enormous plane tree. The light shifted from pale blue to aquamarine to cobalt as the boats—two-masted schooners, enormous motor cruisers—gentled into their slips. It was even romantic—a feeling that had become sadly alien during the logistics-filled years of work and parenting.

In Salvador, I felt I was floating on the cushion that comes with money and international sophistication. I sank into the lushness of it all, thinking it doesn't take much. I was reminded of the time during our honeymoon crossing China, when Peter and I had emerged from weeks of walking across Qinghai Province, into the polished gold lobby of a twelve-story hotel in Chengdu. That evening, we'd sat in the rooftop garden, savoring a gin and tonic imported from England. It had seemed the ultimate luxury.

There in Salvador, Peter kept saying, "Penedo is so small," as though he were wondering what to do with it. I was afraid to pursue the remark, afraid to delve into what I feared I'd find—that he was feeling purposeless and unhappy, that he wanted to go home. To me, turning around now felt daunting and like admitting defeat; and what would that do for the kids, for building their confidence?

I was also beginning to wonder if there was a gender divide. I had noticed before, among older retired friends, that the women often began to travel, sometimes almost obsessively trying to see the rest of the world in the time they had left, while the men tended to stay home. I was beginning to see the same divide in our family. While no one was finding it easy, Molly and I were more readily embracing the experience. Granted, our experience as females was different than Peter's and Skyler's as males, not just because of who we were but also because of the difference in male and female worlds in Brazil. Molly's friends weren't yelling at her when she made a mistake or pushing her to do things socially that made her uncomfortable. I didn't have to prove myself on a soccer field the way Peter did. But I did seem to be trying to prove that we could do this, live immersed in a very different culture than our own. I didn't want to feel I was forcing everyone else in my family into my experiment, however, so when Peter repeated, "Penedo seems so small," I let the observation hang.

We made sure we got back to our little ridgetop house the evening before the kids' midnight return. When they fell through the front door, dropping their duffels onto the floor, exhausted, Molly's universe had flipped. "It was sooooo fun! I'm really glad I went. It was craaazy. The two girls I roomed with were great."

But Skyler's had not.

"It was okay. I didn't get to play very much."

"But Skyler, you made a goal!" said Molly, trying to buck him up.

"Yeah. But you made two."

"Yeah, but we lost. But that was okay. I just felt bad 'cause my team depends on me so much. But your team was great."

"Oh, yeah, and there was this guy, he did a rainbow *and* a bicycle kick. He was amazing." Skyler's bad mood was gone, just like that. Pubescent hormones?

"On the bus home, they improvised songs that were about all of us," Molly continued. "At first, I was sort of mad about the one they made up about me, but then it was okay. The whole bus was singing, *'Não, não, não, não quero ficar com ninguem,'*"—No, no, no, I don't want to kiss with anyone—"because I'd said I didn't want to *fica* at this dance they had."

"Did you guys sing or play guitar?"

"Skyler played a little guitar. It was really fun."

"Fantastic."

Progress!

My hopes raised, I was especially disheartened when Skyler woke up feeling down again. It was Friday morning, two weeks after Pontal, one week after Bahia and time for the big discussion with Skyler about school. Round One.

We'd been trying to walk the line between letting Skyler make the decision—either recommit to Imaculada or change to homeschooling—and making it ourselves. I'd been wondering whether we were copping out as parents by putting the decision too much on him. Part of our dilemma was that we weren't feeling clear about what would be best ourselves; there was the social/psychological situation, which was clearly tough at Imaculada, and then there was also the education.

While, as teachers and writers, Peter and I felt we could design writing projects about a variety of subjects, we had no formal training in age-appropriate curriculum. On the other hand, we weren't too worried, as we believed much of the education he was getting, and that we valued, had nothing to do with school.

That Friday morning, thinking a change of scene might make the discussion easier, Peter and I nudged Skyler out of the house. We were silent for the ten-minute walk down the ridge. After Skyler plowed through two chocolate-and-vanilla swirls, we caught a *lancha*. This brightly painted cigar-shaped passenger ferry would carry us across the river, a twenty-minute trip, to Carrapichu, a hill town that specialized in making ceramics. We'd thought it would be fun to be on the water, but it wasn't. Skyler sat across from us on the long bench that rimmed the wall, the coming conversation hunkered down on the floorboards between us. The boat had turned upriver, hugging the far shore of an island to take advantage of the weaker current. I looked past Skyler, through the square openings in the wall, and concertedly examined the water hyacinths caught in the eddy, with their round, juicy leaves and conical lavender flowers.

As we came abreast of the town, the captain ferried the little tube across the current and nosed it up onto the shore. The fare collector hopped out and slid the gangplank down onto the sand. Hunched under the ferry's low ceiling, we made our way to the stairs and climbed up into the sunlight. We began the slog up the steep main street.

Ceramics spilled out of every house—garishly painted vases, cookie-cutter figurines of drunken cowboys, placid farm animals—all laid out on the sidewalk to dry. Our destination was a small plaza with a bougainvillea-draped arbor where we could order a soda pop and sit down at a yellow plastic table. After ordering a couple of Cokes, we sat, stiffly, looking out over the river to the slip of island across the channel. I suddenly realized we'd inadvertently trapped Skyler, literally up the river without a paddle. It didn't go well.

"Skyler, you have the power to make a change in your life," I started. Peter stood by listening. "You've been saying it's *your* life, so it should be *your* choice. So now you have a chance to make a choice to change something, probably for the better."

"I don't want to be homeschooled!"

"Well, that's not the only option. Let's talk about all the options. Should we make a list of pros and cons?"

No answer.

"Okay. Let's make a list of pros and cons. What would be the pros of staying at Imaculada?"

No answer.

"So does that mean there are no pros?"

No answer.

"Okay, what about the cons?"

"It sucks."

"Okay, it sucks. I'm writing down *It sucks*. Why does it suck?"

"I don't know. It just does." A pause. "I hate Brazil."

The conversation went on like this until Skyler, who had already walked off once to jump over the retaining wall onto the grassy hill below, said he needed to take a walk, by himself. "Okay, but come back with some thoughts about what you want to change," I said. As usual, this wasn't turning out to be the neat, rational conversation I'd envisioned.

He stalked off across the street. I felt the town was small and quite safe. Peter wasn't so sure. "I feel like following him."

"I think he'll be okay."

"But it could be hours. The next *lancha* is at eleven thirty. I don't think we should do this all day." He left to follow Skyler up the side street.

A couple of young men riding bareback came galloping down the hill past me. Earlier, there had been a number of small horse-drawn carts laden with hunks of gray clay. Today must be clay-delivery day. I liked the horsiness of this town; the day we'd come here to pick up our commission of ceramic dinner plates, six horses had been tied up in front of the town library, like horses in the old American West tied up in front of the saloon.

On our way up, looking at some of the newly fashioned wares drying outside people's houses, Peter had noted, "They make the ugliest statues."

"I don't think they're so bad," Skyler had retorted, eager to oppose.

"I rather like the one-eared goat," I said.

"I think that's an accident," Skyler had said.

"Sometimes accidents turn into the best things. Somehow, with the one ear, he's more . . ." I searched for the word.

"Appealing," Skyler tried, suddenly caught up in the question rather than the fight.

"Yes, more appealing. More expressive."

In the midst of all our turmoil, amid the heels-dug-in resistance, we'd have good moments like these: as long as we didn't talk about school—about the hours of struggling to understand in Portuguese or of spacing out, crazy with boredom; about the castigations on the *futsal* court, which no local seemed to take personally but which Skyler had a hard time shaking off; about the unrelenting pressure to kiss girls.

I had my back to Skyler and Peter when they returned, Peter in the street, Skyler hugging the wall of houses. But I knew they were coming because the woman facing me at another table made that slight lift of the chin that says, "Over there."

We walked back to the landing, Skyler ahead of us. Round One: stalemate.

Watching Skyler struggle with adapting to life in Penedo, and hearing Molly's realization that it would not be as easy to make friends here as it had been in their English-speaking school in Mozambique, I was filled with awe at what we were doing in Brazil and also wondering how I'd managed not to analyze the situation better before we'd committed to it. We were not as far "out" as some, like missionaries or anthropologists, but we were definitely out there, more than my family had ever been when I was growing up.

I thought I knew everything there was to know about living abroad as a child, being a three-timer myself as a kid—in Thailand, the Philippines, and Egypt—and having already done it twice with our own children, in Spain and Mozambique. I was convinced that although the experience was not always fun, one would definitely come out richer for it. I, too, had been dropped, cold, into a school in another language—at the same age as Skyler was now. But there were small differences that may have made all the difference between an experience that was difficult but also fun, and one that was just difficult.

My family always lived in big cities—Bangkok, Manila, Cairo—which had international communities from which to draw one's friends. My parents had access to a circle of intellectually stimulating, internationally sophisticated, *English-speaking* locals. We didn't have that in Penedo. Though I went to a French school in Cairo, two other students there were native English speakers. They were my friends; in retrospect, they were my only friends. There were no kids like this for Molly and Skyler in Penedo.

So at the end of September, the kids' third month in school, Peter and I were asking ourselves: Do we stick this out because we set out to do it, by God, or do we bail? If we're willing to bail, how long do we wait to see if it gets better? How much better is enough? Do we resign ourselves to a hard year on the theory that in the end it will be a "growth" year? How much do we subject our children to suffering, so that they can learn from it? How much are they suffering? Not only were we in the unknown culturally, we were also in the unknown of our own psyches and, more agonizing for Peter and me, meddling with the unknown of our children's psyches. Just because living abroad turned out well for me, I couldn't assume it would for them.

So then came Saturday. It was the first day of the *Jogos da Primavera* —the spring games, spring starting in October in the Southern Hemisphere. As we understood it, all the schools from town and the surrounding communities would participate in fifteen days of sports competition, including *futsal, vôlei, handebol,* swimming, and running races. And there were some big competitors, like the public school down the street with its student body of six thousand (three five-hour shifts daily of two thousand students each, morning, afternoon, and evening). Being good all-around athletes, Molly and Skyler had been invited to do just about everything.

I woke up at six, unlocked the padlock on the back window, and swung it wide, always an elating moment. They'd started the post-harvest burning of sugarcane stubble, so the air had been notably hazier, but that morning, it was clear to the far hills, and a cool breeze slid in that brought welcome relief from the increasingly sweaty nights. Eventually Peter emerged, followed by the kids. Our breakfast of scrambled eggs and *linguiça* was relaxed; at least I think it was. It's hard for me to remember now because most of the day was eventually obliterated in my mind by the explosion.

Skyler's first event would be that afternoon, a one-kilometer foot-race over the cobblestones through the middle of town. He had been matter-of-fact about it when he announced it on Friday, but by some-time Saturday morning, he was saying, "I don't want to run."

Skyler actually loves to run. He'd surprised us when in third grade he ran not only the one-mile Fun Run in a hometown Missoula race but also spontaneously joined the 5K and then the 10K, becoming the youngest that morning to participate in the trifecta.

"Well, you probably don't have to," Peter mused, barely looking up from his *Alagoas Gazette*, "but you need to go tell Mario"—Imaculada's PE teacher. "He's specially coming to the school at three, to give you a ride to the starting line."

The morning dragged on, each of us doing our own thing, which meant Skyler was mostly on Facebook or watching reruns of *Friends*, Molly was reading on the iPad, I was writing on my computer, and Peter was writing on his.

At 2:40 PM, I called out, "Skyler, it's time to get dressed. I've pulled out your shoes."

"I don't want to go. Why do I have to?" The tired litany.

"Out of consideration for other people who are nice enough to help you."

"Molly doesn't have to."

"Molly doesn't have the chance to. Girls here don't get to do all the things that boys do. She'd love to participate more." It turned out there would be girls running, but none from Molly's school.

I was moving faster now—pulling open his drawers, looking for shorts—not because we were late, but because I was getting frustrated. He was lying on the bed, barely watching the computer screen.

"Turn that off, now. Skyler, it's quarter to three."

"I don't want to do this."

"Get up, now!"

He slumped off down the hall to the bathroom and came back, slamming the gate to the downstairs laundry room on the way. I walked over to it.

"Come back and close the gate quietly. I'm going to count to five. One, two . . ." My voice had that low, menacing quality it gets when I'm done negotiating. There is something about slamming doors that has always sent me. ". . . five."

He didn't come. I sped down the hall, lifted him under the armpits, and shoved him toward the gate.

"I don't know how to close the gate," he protested.

"Watch very carefully, and maybe you'll learn something." My voice was louder and more clipped now. "Lift, push, pull, and then this will fit over the top."

It was ten to three.

"I'm not going."

Peter chimed in. "Skyler, you have to at least go talk to Mario. Get your shorts on."

Skyler left his room, walked to the back, and started climbing out the second-story window. I ran after him, grabbed him under the arms, and jerked him back in, dumping him on the tile floor, furious now (and alarmed). "Get in here!"

Molly slipped by. "I'm going for a walk."

Three o'clock. Peter looked out the front door. "Okay, Skyler, Mario is there. He's waiting for you."

"I'm . . . getting . . . dressed," Skyler said miserably.

I crossed the *praça* to go talk to Mario and keep him there until Skyler and Peter arrived. As always, there was really no hurry at all. We Americans can build up a lot of tension around time. Mario was explaining something to me, most of which I couldn't absorb; my mind didn't have the energy to ferret out meaning. Peter and Skyler crossed the *praça*, Skyler dragging behind. Apparently he'd decided to "think" about the race. A *colega* of Mario's came with a car and ferried Peter, Skyler, and me down the street to Diocesano, the other private school in town. The kids would run from one school to the other.

The race that was scheduled to start at three thirty started at four thirty. Kids gathered under a banyan tree in their school pinnies, and eventually someone arrived with numbers. The two other boys from Skyler's class who'd been selected to run showed up in their Imaculada royal blue. Skyler and Peter went off into a field of banana trees so Skyler could change into the running shorts he hadn't put on. I left with the camera to walk back to the finish line.

What would I be taking a picture of, I wondered, Skyler in his misery? Or would I take a happy picture that would join the other happy pictures in the photo album of our year in Brazil, belying how hard it had really been? Or would he not run at all, leaving me waiting with my camera, wondering what had happened?

Our *praça* was transformed. There were escort police on motorcycles, an announcer extolling the virtues of the spring games for the health of our youth, and the ubiquitous music blaring. Then, as we saw the first runner crest the hill, a man in a lime-green jersey extended a mortar high and shot the deafening firecracker. I squinted to find Skyler.

The first boy wore pink and white, not Imaculada's colors. Then a barefoot boy in light blue, an Amazonian-Indian-looking girl in yellow, and then Skyler.

"Go, Skyler! Go!" I shouted, trying hard to keep the tears out of my voice. "*Eskyloh, Eskyloh!*" chanted some other Imaculada parents, beginning to clap.

By the time he crossed the finish line, first for his school, tears streamed down my cheeks.

Sweaty and exhausted, Skyler seemed pleased. He even smiled for the picture. *Skyler with Carlos and Mario, after the 1 km race,* the album caption would read. They guzzled water from cups handed around by volunteers and poured it on their heads. Lots of other boys from the race, boys Skyler didn't know, were coming up to him and patting him on the back.

"*Obrigado, obrigado,*" he said shyly, nodding. "Thank you."

The next morning, when we brought up Skyler's school situation, he readily agreed to a compromise—three days each week at Imaculada, two days at home with Peter and me. He'd found the courage to make a change, to get off the track, that peer-created treadmill that dictates what's right for everyone, except perhaps for you.

13

On Learning to Be a Man

SKYLER AND I attended the capoeira salon three nights a week. I don't know why I want to call it a *salon*, except that somehow it wasn't exactly like a class, more like a place of sharing—a place to learn a sport, an art, but also a place to celebrate Afro-Brazilian identity, to play, to compete, and to grow into a man with the guidance of elders. (Women practicing capoeira is a new twist. But there were usually at least a couple of us.)

"*Quer jogar?*"—Want to play?—they'd say gently as they invited you into the *roda*, the sparring ring.

Capoeira, a martial art, was brought to Brazil five centuries ago by black slaves imported to the Portuguese colony from Africa. As it is clearly a powerful training tool for fighting, the Portuguese slave masters outlawed the practice. At this point, it went underground. The *capoeiristas* disguised it by transforming it into an "innocuous" dance accompanied by music, so they could continue to train. But even after Brazil gained independence from the Portuguese in 1822 and slavery was abolished in 1888, it continued to be illegal under the new regime. As a form that had been developed to enable an escaped slave to fight, one against many, unarmed against armed, capoeira continued to scare those in power, now that it was in the hands of the newly freed slaves, newly unemployed and marginalized. Hundreds of *capoeiristas* were arrested and imprisoned on Fernando de Noronha, an archipelago of islands 220 miles off the coast, and thrown into jail in the new urban centers like Rio de Janeiro. Now their own people found it threatening. No wonder. The power of the form is palpable.

Skyler and I would leave our house at the "blue hour," as my father used to call it, when the sky becomes deep and, in Penedo, the mystery planet appeared. (None of the constellations in that Southern sky looked familiar.) We'd saunter down the narrow sidewalk, hugging the wall of houses, the lumbering buses passing so close they'd raise the hair on your arm. The old were leaning on their windowsills; the young were in doorways or paired in the shadows.

We reached the open door of the capoeira salon, housed in a peeling pink building dating from 1843. Along the roofline sat busts of bearded, European-looking men. Below the busts, the pink paint peeled to reveal successive layers. Black graffiti tied it all together. The salon's huge blue shutters would be closed, but the door would be open, and often Pirulito would be standing there, surveying the street. He was small, with pale, pocked skin and a curl of brown hair on his forehead. His ready laugh revealed braces. I guessed he was about eighteen.

"*Boa noite. Quer jogar?*"—Want to play?—he'd ask, twirling his pants cord.

"*Talvez hoje*"—Maybe today. I smiled.

I especially appreciated him because he was one of the first to invite me to spar, hesitant and clumsy as I was. We entered the high-ceilinged room and removed our flip-flops before going up the short set of stairs. A bat swooped through. The room's wooden ceiling was beginning to cave in.

"*Salve,*" we shouted.

"*Salve,*" we heard back.

I could never get a grip on what this meant, but I gathered it was important to announce one's arrival and for those already there to acknowledge it. Maybe it was a throwback to times when the newcomer might not have been so friendly.

Skyler crossed the room to exit into the open-air courtyard, where the players change into the capoeira uniform: white polyester pants held up with a cord, and a white shirt with the blue logo of Pura Ginga (the name of the local group, which has since changed to Mandingueiro). I asked Skyler if that felt awkward.

"Well, it did the first time when I didn't know what I was supposed to be doing there and all of a sudden these guys start dropping their pants! But now it's okay."

The cord's colors (there are sometimes two) indicate the level of the player. Skyler immediately tuned into the hierarchy and figured out which colors meant what.

Often when we arrived, there were already people working on something in a more or less organized fashion. But people would continue to arrive, and leave, over the next hour and a half. As a result, we never really knew when the class started or when it ended.

The sessions did have a teacher, Mestre Bentinho, the man from whom we also bought chickens, which he'd freshly slaughtered behind his house. Tall, slender-hipped, his arms bulging with muscle, he had a quick, charismatic smile, bright in his chocolate-brown skin. He made us warm up with jumping jacks, bouncing stretches, repetitive lunges, and abdominal crunches. He then moved into teaching us combinations of lunges, squatting spins, and kicks, which jab, fan, and whack, all linked together with the glue of the *ginga*, a triangular step—side, rock back, rock front—used as a brief moment to reassess before the next attack.

Or this was mostly how it went. Frequently people would walk through the open door behind us, and Bentinho would begin a long, shouted conversation, finally sauntering away altogether to sit down and chat. Either someone else took over, so that we'd repeat whatever we'd been working on, over and over and over, until Bentinho noticed, or things gradually dissolved. This is when Skyler and his pals would start practicing aerial flips and slow-motion cartwheels (moves you were just supposed to pick up by osmosis), the older guys would start sparring in pairs, and I'd flop down on the floor to rest. I could feel my fifty-two-year-old legs getting sore right in front of me.

As a dancer, I could pick up the sequences, the order of movements, easily, which is different from being able to actually do them. I had no problem figuring out which way to turn or which leg was threading through what, and I could swing my legs higher than anyone there, which I did with gusto, mortified that I might accidentally hit someone ducking underneath me. But when it came to supporting myself upside down on my arms and, more significantly, knowing which way to dodge, I was lame. I seemed to have no instinct for self-defense, continually dropping my head *toward* a fanning leg rather than away.

And this was not a lackadaisical, summer-afternoon fan; this was a slashing blade ready to lop my head off.

Those were Mondays and Wednesdays. On Fridays, the instruments came out—the *berimbau, atabaque,* and *pandeiro*—to be played in rotation by anyone who volunteered; the *roda,* the circle of participants, twenty or so, was formed to contain the energy, and two by two, we'd enter and spar. My stomach always tightened in nervous anticipation, but this was clearly Skyler's and the other young men's favorite part.

The *berimbau* is like an archer's bow with a gourd attached near the bottom. It's not easy to play. The first problem is balancing the string where the gourd connects to the bow, which is heavy, on your pinky finger, then pinching a round, flat stone between your thumb and index finger with that same hand, to tamp and untamp the string, in order to change the pitch. In the other hand, you hold a delicate stick, which you tap on the string to beat out various rhythms. It makes a twangy, metallic sound with a two-pitch range. When you've managed to coordinate all of this, you learn to dampen the gourd by bouncing it on your stomach. By the time we left Brazil, I was still trying to get the stone to hit the string.

The *atabaque* is a long drum on a stand, and while the rhythms the others played on it seemed fairly simple, I could see in their faces that when I tried them, something didn't sound right. It seemed I couldn't even master the *pandeiro,* a sort of tambourine. I had rather hoped I could play an instrument as a way to contribute and avoid having to go into the ring. But I found I could also happily just stand and clap, helping to hold the energy of the circle. I could barely understand the improvised singing but would try to join in the call-and-response, desperately catching up to the gooey mass of vowels I could make out only after they'd been sung. Bentinho usually led these, with that driving, semi-singing, semi-shouting sound—a style that lends itself to singing outdoors, where capoeira would have originated.

At first the tempo was slow. Two players knelt, facing each other, below the musicians. Often they crossed themselves. Then they slowly cartwheeled into the circle, never losing eye contact. That was important. They moved in mesmerizing slow motion, prowling. This "Angolan" style was low to the ground and molasses-like—a continuous dreamy morphing of forward lunge into retreating crouch, slow headstand-cartwheel, long hooking leg reaching between the other's ankles. The eyes never lost contact as the two players circled, moving forward and apart, upside down and right side up, panthers looking for their moment to attack. I never noticed when the next pair knelt under the musicians, but eventually, the initial pair touched hands and ceded the ground. It was the older men in the group who usually practiced this style, and there was nothing that looked old about them. Their lithe power was totally intimidating.

As the tempo increased, the young bucks started to enter the ring, and the style changed radically, into the *regional* (pronounced *hehgee-own-ow*), a newer, faster form. This was where Pirulito excelled. In this more upright form, legs started to flash through the air in a blur, each player's feet aimed at his opponent's head. The players began to handspring and flip. Feet skimmed by ears, given extra speed and force by spinning or jumping into the kick, but never made contact. That was the point: to have the power to destroy but also the control and judgment to use it only when absolutely necessary. The salon was the place to learn this and how to apply it to life. Needless to say, I tried to get into the circle early, before the tempo sped up. Skyler, however, liked the speed and, to my amazement, was there kneeling by the musicians within our first week.

Another small, eighteenish guy also liked this part, and he often sparred with Pirulito. Both, not even five feet tall, one white, one black, danced nimbly around each other, legs fanning faster and faster, feet skimming by heads, forearms protecting their faces as they got progressively closer. Even though the goal was never to touch, one could still see when one player got the better of another. Usually everyone laughed and the sparring continued or passed to the next pair. But with Pirulito and his dark partner, who seemed to seek each other in the ring, the laughter seemed inevitably to disappear and the tension to rise, like mercury in a thermometer. The intensity of their eyes and the force of their kicks shot upward, until one Friday, they broke the space between them. Just as they started grappling hand to hand, Bentinho and other elders intervened with words and bodies sliding between. The fiery eighteen-year-olds were separated and pulled to opposite sides of the circle. The sparring stopped. The magic was broken. Bentinho said something about *"Capoeira é respeito"*—Capoeira is respect. The young men started to protest, but not much. They knew they'd lost control.

The *roda* ended early that night, but before it did, the pair was made to shake hands and enter the ring once more. Everyone was careful it didn't go on too long, and the thermometer was not allowed to rise. Afterward, we stood in the circle, feet tightly together, right hands to our hearts, left palms flexed and extended in front of us, chanting a call-and-response after Bentinho: *"Capoeira é . . ." "Capoeira é . . ." "Capoeira é . . ."* As we gathered up our clothes, the elders gathered in conversation. No cheerful *tchaus* were offered as we left.

That night, Skyler and I walked back up the ridge, enjoying the cool air of the evening, but quieter than usual. He had his capoeira uniform cinched in his cord and strapped to his back like a true *capoeirista.*

"Do you think they have something going on outside capoeira, those two guys?" Skyler asked. "It just seems like every time they get together, there's a problem."

After that night, Pirulito came back, but his dark partner never did. I was sorry. I missed his elfin presence. "He's like a deer," Skyler had said once.

I had hoped somehow that the world of capoeira could have helped the two of them overcome whatever their differences were. But maybe that was asking a lot.

I hoped that the capoeira salon might be a place where Skyler could find a gateway into a supportive world of men. Initially, our lack of language was a handicap. I suspected that Bentinho had good things to say about learning to develop and control one's power, about perfecting one's skill but taking care of one's partner, about what it means to become a man and work for the greater good rather than one's own glorification. These would be timely things for Skyler to hear and learn to practice in a safe place at this point in his life. But even without the language, there was a lot one could feel from the aura of the place and the way the *jogadores* "played" with each other—the way they could play hard but still be gentle, the way their concern for the other came first, even with an adversary, the way respect for each other as humans was at the core.

One night, a Wednesday, an unexpected *roda* was held at the end of class. I was struck by the fact that everyone in the circle cut in to spar with a particular boy. I wondered why they were singling him out. When he was clearly exhausted, they let him stop, and the *roda* ended shortly afterward. We stood, feet together, and Bentinho spoke for a long time. I could pick out "... *este rapaz de treze*"—this boy of thirteen. Then he asked a couple I'd never seen before if they wished to speak. The woman had that tight-throat sound as though she were struggling not to cry, but she managed to say, "*Ele é um bom filho*"—he's a good son.

Then the seriousness of the moment—this step through the first of those mirror-multiplied doorways into manhood—broke. Everyone dispersed into the room and we were given slices of cake and guarana-flavored soda pop.

Skyler, too, would soon turn thirteen. I hoped we'd stick it out that long in Brazil so that he, too, could have the chance to be tested and pass through such a doorway, to experience a rite of passage that doesn't exist for many young people in the United States. I hoped that here in Brazil, Skyler wouldn't have to make his way alone but would have instead the comfort of a group to help him understand who he is, as an individual, and what his role might be as part of something larger than himself.

14

Relax

BY THE END of September, our third month, we'd survived an ambulance trip to Arapiraca (and Skyler's next five visits to the emergency room—for stitch removal, dehydration, and spreading foot infections); we'd found a house and furnished it from scratch; the kids had started school; Peter was generating new writing projects; and I'd established a pleasant daily routine of market shopping and work for my dance company back home. We'd accomplished a lot.

I made a list:

In three months, I have learned:

* to pick out the good juice oranges with the small pores.
* to stop the grizzled old man in the bent felt hat with the street cart and buy a warm cup of coconut-milk-and-corn soup.
* to drink chilled *água de coco* out of a green coconut with a straw, while waiting for a *lancha* to take us across the river.
* to get to the bank at 7:00 AM, before the lines form and the ATMs start to break down.
* to be sure I have "small money" for the market because vendors rarely have change.
* to hide my money in multiple places, the way the market women hide cash in their bras, in the folds of the stall's black plastic roofing, or in the microwave, as at the snack stand at the sand-soccer court.
* to say *"Né?"*—Isn't that right?—at the end of most sentences, and, if in doubt, to just use the verb *ficar*—to become, to stay, to make out: it works for most things.

⁑ to shout *"Salve"* and take off my flip-flops when entering the capoeira salon.

⁑ to kneel down, touch the *berimbau,* and cross myself (the first situation in which I've ever felt the need) before entering the capoeira ring to spar.

⁑ to throw toilet paper into the wastepaper bin, not down the toilet.

⁑ to never eat with my fingers—to eat French fries with toothpicks, cake with a napkin, pizza with a fork.

⁑ to knock on the door of the blue house advertising *"Trufas"* and wait while the shirtless man in shorts gets up off the couch and disappears into the back room to reappear with delicious, homemade chocolate truffles.

⁑ to sit down by our back window at five thirty to enjoy the sunset over the river with a *caipirinha* and watch the feasting swallows give way to bats as the land darkens and the warm lights of Bairro Vermelho appear against a still pale sky.

⁑ to relax.

PART II: *Home*

15

A New Start

WHAT IS IT about rainstorms that's so exhilarating? I stood at our back window, watching the distant hills fade to white, then become obliterated, the bright patchwork of houses across the valley muting before my eyes. The cows in the valley bottom didn't seem to notice, but the egrets didn't fly. Is it hard for a bird to fly in a downpour? The monkeys, however, were fleeing: running the obstacle course of jagged-glass-tipped walls, barbed wire fence, and bouncing banana and palm fronds to dive under the teased wig of a mango tree. All the usual sounds—the scraps of music, the passing buses, Aniete's radio—were gone, drowned out by the deluge.

Standing there by the window, I remembered all the other rainstorms, the ones I got caught in, and that exhilarating liberation from convention that somehow came with getting totally soaked.

The one when, as a college freshman, I had gone with my boyfriend to a Cambridge grocery store to buy snacks and got caught in a downpour carrying them home. Getting soaked sent us into a leprechaunish dance in a campus courtyard, oblivious to grocery bags dissolving into the pavement.

The one, thirty years later, when my ninety-three-year-old father had left our house in Mozambique for a walk. A half hour later, the rain came. I set off in our old Suzuki jeep searching, windshield wipers unable to clear the flood even when I set them on high, imagining pneumonia seeping through his lightweight suit. I found him, calm and happy, in the library of the American consulate—a wonderful library that I hadn't bothered to find in the ten months I'd lived there.

The one in my first month in Penedo that sent the skin peeling back on my cheap umbrella. Hopping the river streaming down the cobblestone street, I ducked into the nearest doorway and hastened down a dingy corridor to pop out into the open air of Eliason's back-patio restaurant. (Eliason, round and grounded like John Belushi, but with the compassionate demeanor of a Benedictine monk, had befriended Peter during his first days in Penedo, helping him look for a house.) I found the one dry table under a leaking thatch overhang. Eliason brought me a thermos of *cafezinho*, a thick, sweet espresso served in a tiny cup. When I left an hour later, he wouldn't let me pay and handed me a takeaway tin of beef and pork kebabs.

"*Para seu almoço. Peter me emprestou dinheiro*"—For your lunch. Peter lent me money.

Somehow every time it rains, something magical happens. Maybe it's that wholesale washing of the world, the chance for a clean slate.

Rain makes you stop, makes you dive for cover and stand panting, hair wet like a dog's, in the church door, or the artist's studio, or under the plastic of a stall. It makes you stop and take the time to watch.

"Skyler, come see the rain. It's amazing!" I called out then from the back window. I put my arms around him, and we stood a foot from where the rain streamed off the rounded roof tiles in strings of crystalline beads.

This was the second day of our experiment to teach Skyler at home two days a week. The first day hadn't gone well. But this morning, when he'd asked if he could stay and I'd said he could *if* he did his work without resistance, he'd affably agreed.

A new start. Every day, there was a new start; it all seemed so tenuous, both our perch and the place itself. We watched a lizard run out from behind a vine on the backyard wall, the rain causing the vine to collapse behind him as he ran, finally leaving him with nowhere to hide. The vine had just grown in the last couple of weeks. Easy come, easy go.

The sun and the rain insidiously wore everything down, remelding it into the earth. Even the people. As soon as I got there, my walking pace slowed. That quick New York clip I'd never lost, even after moving to the mountain West? I lost it in Penedo—just like that.

The passing of seasons was subtle there, the differences so subtle that they dawned on you as bodily cravings. We arrived in winter, and I found myself gravitating toward the churro cart for that skinny donut filled with gooey, burnt-sugar *doce de leite*. Imperceptibly that craving ended, and I began guzzling cold *água de coco* or cans of Coca-Cola wet with perspiration, and finally I was simply in desperate need of ice, in everything—juice, coffee, or straight into the mouth in cubes.

The rain was supposed to have stopped at the end of August. It was October. I was glad the rain was still there, for the sudden gusts of cool breeze, the extra burst of energy, and the chance to take a break from life, to get soaked.

16

Forró Dancing with Zeca

I heard Peter on the phone in the other room.

"I'm going to give you to Amy. This is her territory. Maybe I will, too, but I might be in bed. I have a game tomorrow."

Oh, dear. I knew it was probably Zeca with another invitation to a late-night party. We'd consistently turned them down because it was so hard to *start* to party at ten at night. We were beginning to feel rude.

"Amy? Hello." Zeca spoke in considered spurts. "Can you go to *forró*—tonight? If you want—I can come. I was going to ask-ed Skyler today; but since I know you have—the veto power"—I could hear the smile in his voice—"I thought maybe it is better to ask-ed to you."

I laughed. I'd been startled when, soon after we'd met him, Zeca had invited Skyler to go out to the *forró* clubs with him. A twelve-year-old? Knowing that they didn't start until at least ten at night, and having just heard from Zeca how he started decanting tequila into super-sized pop bottles at age twelve, I'd let him know that I had "veto power." Zeca loved to put newly learned English phrases to use.

Forró music and dance is famous in Brazil (and is showing up in the States as well). There I was, a dance professor, at the source, and I still hadn't seen this rapid-fire partner dance, with its twitching hips and jitterbug-like turns. I was beginning to feel guilty.

"That sounds great. Molly," I shouted down the hall, "do you want to go out to *forró* with Zeca tonight?" She'd recently been complaining that we did everything unfashionably early.

"Well, there'll be at least three of us," I said, returning to the phone. "What time would be good?"

"Maybe . . . ten? Or . . . nine? I don' like this kind of music, but you can see. After twenty-six years, I still can't do this dancing, but maybe you will see it and you can teach me." By this time, I'd realized that

Zeca could actually do almost anything, but underlying his playboy bravura was this streak of self-deprecation.

I hoped I would be able to stay awake.

Zeca's knock came around 9:30 PM. Anticipating the style of night-club dress I'd seen on Molly's friends and their mothers, I'd gotten as dressed up as I could—black pants, a slinkyish (by my standards) black top, dangling earrings, and, well, flip-flops. If I could have been vacuum-packed into my pants and had some teetering high heels, I might almost have fit in. Molly was managing better in her recent purchase of skinny jeans, racer-back silk top, and strappy four-inch heels. Skyler, to my surprise, had selected his orange button-up shirt. I think he'd worn a buttoning shirt maybe four times in his life.

"Okay, aaare you rehhhhdy?" Zeca's tipsy speech was slurred.

As a labor lawyer, Zeca had just been to the house of a client of his, a former security guard. The man had been shot on the job, then fired, and now the company was refusing to pay workmen's comp. The judge had sided with the company.

"This man, his house is very poor, an' he has a little child, by him-self, an' he can't buy milk for him. It's very bad." Zeca looked like he was about to cry.

It occurred to me then that Zeca was in labor law for more than the money, especially as it appeared that while the law might protect the worker, the judge might protect the company, so Zeca's share prob-ably rarely came through. His decision to advocate for the little guy would fit his family's history of taking the high road: the grandfather he admired, who successfully ran for mayor of Penedo entirely on his own money so he would owe no one; his uncle who had become an accountant to expose government fraud.

At the last minute, Peter rallied and came along after all. We piled into Zeca's little black Fiat, the bright blue lights of the dash shining in the darkness, and sped off over the cobblestones, tires shuddering, rock music on high. We think a lot about drinking and driving in the United States, but it didn't even occur to me that taking off with Zeca in his semi-inebriated state might be a bad idea. I knew we didn't have far to go, there weren't many cars in Penedo, and frankly it's hard to go very fast on cobblestones.

Arriving in a neighborhood a little farther out the ridge, we could hear the scene before we saw it. We parked at the end of a long row of cars and walked toward the bright lights and sound. There was the inside party, at the club, and then there was also an outside party. Two small cars bristled with speakers. This was not about fine listening. It was about a shot of adrenaline straight to the chest.

"At *carnaval* [Brazil's famous pre-Lent, blowout celebration], there are ten cars like these *equip som* cars with the big speakers. You can't hear anyting," Zeca was shouting.

Zeca waved his hand at the street-side food stalls. "We call these *caga já*. 'Crap, now.'"

The Filharmonica, an outsized club in the middle of a quiet, residential neighborhood, stood before us. Closed gates barred the entrance. At ten, they hadn't started selling tickets. I watched a man in a red shirt buy beer from a vendor. Cracking it open, he spilled its foaming contents down the front of his jeans. It turned out he worked for the club and had started partying ahead of time. A few minutes later, he let us in.

The place was cavernous and empty, like a one-story parking garage with a maze of dingy indoor/outdoor spaces. In one, banks of speakers flanked a stage. We wandered out into a back courtyard. The proprietress was starting up a grill. Molly and Skyler went over to check out the club's other facilities, two pools and a large indoor *futsal quadra*—part sports club, part nightclub. How many drunks had fallen into the pool?

Peter dutifully accepted the beer Zeca offered, with a fleeting look of dread as he anticipated the next day's hangover.

We killed time. Zeca would not have called it that. "Killing time" implies a hierarchical valuing, implies that some time is worth more than other time. Here, all time was equal. "Productive" time was not more valuable than "nonproductive" time. I think for many Americans, "hanging out" falls into the sometimes necessary but irksome category of *stalled, waiting*. We want to be doing, not just being.

The conversation turned to Zeca's family history.

In the sixteenth century, the Portuguese had divided their newly colonized land into long strips leading back from the ocean and handed them over to select nobles from Portugal. Here, in Alagoas, we were living in one of the first strips to have been claimed.

"Yah, so just a few families had all the land. My grand-grandfahdder?" Zeca looked at me for confirmation.

"*Great*-grandfather."

"Yah, great-grandfahdder, had a ranch. It was half of Sergipe"—the neighboring state across the river.

"We've read that it's still true that there are only a few families who control all the wealth and political power of Alagoas. Who are they?" Peter asked.

"Oh, I dunno, now. Before—people paid attention to dese tings. But now . . ." Zeca flapped the ends of his fingertips back and forth past each other, like swinging saloon doors, a gesture indicating something was finished.

I wondered if he were glossing things over. Peter and I had run into two professors from the local branch of the University of Alagoas ordering kebabs at a joint down in the *baixa* and had asked them the same thing. Taking a quick scan of the room, they leaned into our table and whispered, "Yeah, the . . ." their voices disappeared ". . . they each have their part of Alagoas. People would be killed for running for office against them."

It was now eleven, and two women, very big women, in heels, hot pants, and sequined bras strutted in. Both had exceptionally long curly hair, one platinum blond on her large-boned black face. They had a couple of guys in tow.

"Are they transvestites?" I asked, curious what macho Zeca thought of the obviously gay guys I'd seen around town.

"Yah . . . probably."

"They are?" Skyler looked disbelieving. "Do those other guys know?"

"Probably they are gay, too." Zeca thought. "Or maybe they are just drunk. Yah. I had some friends, some gay friends in school. They were nice guys. It's not a problem if they don't hit on you. They have many women friends—and that is good, too. They can introduce you."

Zeca smiled knowingly at Skyler. I was pleasantly surprised. I wasn't sure we'd find the same tolerance in all sectors of our Montana town.

The tall blond was starting to dance now, swinging her hips in a lazy figure eight as her fingers stirred the hair of the man sitting down next to her. Finally, the *forró* music had started. A man was crooning with an electronic piano and hand drums.

"What is he singing about?" I asked.

Zeca held out his right hand, middle fingers tucked, index and pinky fingers extended like horns. "You know this? We do this when a man's wife has shitted on him."

"Cheated on him?"

"Yah. Shitted on him."

"No, cheeeeted," I laughed.

"Yah, cheeeeted," Zeca nodded.

"How would you describe Brazilian humor?" Peter asked, changing the subject.

"Humor? Here I can talk about anybody, if they are white or black or brown or red or yellow or gay or have some problem. People outside, sometimes they think we are mean. But I don't think so. You know, we had this friend in school—he was in a . . ." He mimed pushing wheels.

"A wheelchair."

"Yah, a wheelchair. He would ask to borrow a pencil, and we would say, 'Yah, if you walk over and get it.' He didn't mind. I think it is better."

This was what we'd been hearing from Molly and Skyler. They hadn't found it so amusing.

Zeca laughed. "There's a joke about black people. There's a black man, and he carries around a parrot, here—on his shoulder. An' he runs into some . . . other person . . . an' that person asks, 'Where does that animal come from?' An' the parrot says, 'I dunno, from Africa somewhere.'"

I laughed, but I felt uncomfortable, thinking of all my black capoeira friends.

"Are there any jokes about the Portuguese?" I asked.

"Oh, yah! We say they're dumb." He stood up, pulling his chair back. "You know what we say?" He put one foot up on the chair. "The

Portuguese tie their shoes like this." He leaned down and reached for the foot on the ground.

It reminded me of Giovanni, our tutor, saying that he wished the Portuguese had not managed to expel the Dutch who had invaded what is now Alagoas in 1630 "because the Dutch took what the Portuguese did—raising sugarcane and cotton—and did it so much better. We would be a different country," he'd sighed.

I glanced at my watch—midnight. Peter was flagging. Skyler was slumping lower in his plastic chair. Molly, however, was looking ready for anything. I knew she'd been yearning for more nightlife. ("I'm a teenager. I'm not supposed to be going to bed at nine!")

"I have a game tomorrow," Peter began.

"Oh?" Zeca looked curious.

"With the guys down by the river. Maybe I will play; maybe half the time, in the second half. Maybe I will be on the side the whole time." He shrugged his shoulders.

We made our way back through the dim rooms. Out on the street, the scene was hopping. The "outside" party, of people who can't afford the ten-*reais* (seven-dollar) cover, was rocking out to the *equip som* cars mixed with the *forró* music, which was by then easily jumping the club's walls—one big, pulsing soup of sound. I felt bad because the bouncers were saying they wouldn't let Zeca back in. We flopped into the little black car, Skyler in front, in the privileged "guys-hanging-out-and-listening-to-rock" spot. Although I was disappointed to miss the dancing, it had felt good just to get out—a reminder not to withdraw. The next day, Peter found a text message from Zeca sent at 1:39 AM: *All is good. I'm back in.*

17

Why Are All the Poor People Black
and the Rich People White?

BY OCTOBER, each of us had begun to develop a social niche. Mine centered largely around a widening network of acquaintances made in the course of daily chores focused on household needs and the kids' school. Peter was a regular at pickup soccer games down in the *baixa*. Molly, rapidly finding her way into the maze of Portuguese, had been pulled into a tight group of five girls from school, and she had Karol, Victor's sister, from the neighborhood. Karol had started to drop by regularly for dinner, and afterward, she would disappear giggling with Molly into the kids' room to listen to music, look up Brazilian and American singers on the Internet, and teach Molly Portuguese.

Skyler's classmates were good about inviting him to special after-school events, like birthday parties (though he'd missed the first few because the last-minute invitations directed us to places like "Igor's house," no address, no phone). But on most afternoons, the kids' classmates seemed to evaporate. During school hours, Skyler's classmates' primary interest in him seemed to be in whom he was or wasn't kissing.

Finally, one day after school in early October, Skyler dragged himself through our front door, dumped his backpack by the shoe basket, passed me at my desk in the corner, and slumped into the dining room. I overheard him asking Peter, installed at his place at the dining table, "What should I do? I'm so tired of Mateus bugging me to kiss Mariana."

"Ohhh," Peter started slowly. "I guess what you're wanting is some fatherly advice." He stalled. My ears lengthened. "Maybe you should just kiss her and get it over with."

"Really?" Skyler sounded shocked.

Molly reported later that day that Skyler had done it, before an audience of seven at the *clube de ténis*.

"How did it go? What did he say?" I asked her.

"He just said it was gross and wet."

I burst out laughing. But I didn't really think it was funny. What a way to enter puberty, on stage.

At school, Skyler had finally let it be known that he liked the looks of a girl in the class below his, Ingridi. The next day, sitting in their antiseptic white classroom, a schoolmate handed him a questionnaire, in English, that had been carefully designed on a computer. At the top in shadow box font, it commanded: *ANSWER*. Then five questions followed:

> 1 – What do you think of Ingridi?
> 2 – You flirt with her? Yes [ ] No [ ]
> 3 – What is the prettiest? Mariana [ ] Ingridi [ ]
> 4 – What has Ingridi what other girls do not have?
> 5 – What is needed for a girl to have your heart?

Questionnaires seemed to be a popular form. Molly had been the subject of one designed by her friends and handed around to the boys in her class:

> Who do you think is prettier? Molly [ ] Ana Flavia [ ]

"Why do you think they chose Ana Flavia as the other girl?" I asked.

"Because she was the girl the boys thought was the prettiest before I showed up. It's funny. She's the other white girl with blond hair, dyed . . . I think Leila's beautiful, but she's black."

Black. At my weekly Portuguese lesson with Giovanni, we'd taken to talking about Brazilian culture and politics. We'd meet in the court-yard at Imaculada, looking down into the green valley and Bairro Vermelho, the largely black neighborhood rising up the opposite side. It was nicknamed Powder Hill, for gunpowder. One day, he said with his usual cynicism, "We have a saying here, that the only people who go to jail are the three *P*s: the poor, the prostitutes, and the *preto* [blacks]."

"I'm glad we live in the poor neighborhood," Skyler said out of the blue one day. We were threading our way, single file, along the narrow sidewalk on our way down the ridge to the capoeira salon. I was surprised he thought our neighborhood was poor. Historic neighborhoods tend to have cachet in the United States, so I'd been feeling we were living in one of the more desirable parts of town. But most of his privileged schoolmates lived about a half mile farther out the ridge, in a newer neighborhood, where there were individual houses in walled compounds with yards.

"Why?"

"I just feel like kids here appreciate things more."

During the previous few weeks, he'd been invited to several birthday parties, to the houses of kids whose parents were doctors, lawyers, and successful business people—Penedo's moneyed class.

"Natalia Maria's was pretty cool; it had a huge yard and a baby crocodile in a pen. But you should have seen Isabella's. She has the most *awe*some house, with a pool and a sand court with a volleyball net, and soccer goals at each end and a place for *forró* dancing . . . Their houses are bigger than even our house at home! They all have computers. Junio has a Wii. They probably think we're poor."

A few weeks later, he brought it up again. He was really trying to figure this class thing out.

I remembered that in first grade in Mozambique, he'd asked, "Why are all the poor people black and all the rich people white?" At six, he was sussing out possible connections between class and race. A few months later in Maputo, I'd picked him up after school in our claptrap jeep. "Mom, would you love me if I was black?" he asked as he climbed in. I wondered if the question was connected to his observation that Tunji, a black West African boy in his class, was the fastest runner. Skyler had always been a fan of speed. Whether by land, sea, or air, maximum speed had been the unifying characteristic of each of his favorite animals—the cheetah, the sailfish, the falcon. So if being black meant speed, it might be worth it.

Soon after our arrival in Penedo, we'd been invited to join the tennis club, where we'd first met Zeca. It wasn't cheap, by local standards, but we were happy to join. It was just a block from our house, on the other side of the ridge, and had a pool. When we joined in August, it was still winter and was considered by the other members far too cold to swim, so I had the pool to myself. Sometimes Molly would join me and we'd swim our laps, then climb our elbows over the pool's edge and, legs dangling, soak in the expansive view, our eyes tracing it down into the lime-green valley below and across the Rio São Francisco to the white, tumbling hill town of Neópolis and the glimmering Peixoto-family textile factory.

I loved taking tennis lessons. This was the second time in my life that I had. The first was as a twelve-year-old at the Gezira Club in Cairo. I still remember crossing the open expanse of golf course to reach the tennis courts, early Saturday morning mist rising out of coarse crabgrass. I felt then that this grassy opening was like a special wet, green secret in the middle of Cairo's dusty maelstrom. The *clube de ténis* in Penedo offered a similar feeling of retreat, at least for me.

For Skyler, it was different. As it turned out, a bunch of his schoolmates also belonged. Initially I thought this would be great, a way for him to connect outside school. But it was immediately awkward.

"Mom, do you think we can go swimming at the pool?" Skyler was standing in our front hallway and swept his arm over Victor, Breno, and Ricardo. The three neighborhood boys had become Skyler's primary friends, his gang. Ricardo was ten, short and brown, with the muscled back and arms of a grown man. He had a lot of energy and a short fuse. Like Victor, he was part of the capoeira salon. The boys were faithful regulars, appearing unfailingly at our door every day after lunch. I'd come to recognize Victor's stretched silhouette through the frosted glass, as he leaned there waiting. There were no doorbells, and they rarely knocked; instead they shouted, *"Eskyloh!"* a system that worked well in a place where houses were small and windows usually open.

"Well, I don't know," I replied, contemplating the pool question. "Maybe. I think you can bring guests. Let's go ask."

The answer was no. Skyler was in; they were out. Despite this first rejection, Skyler's neighborhood friends continued to come find him at the club, sending the pool cleaner to pull Skyler out of the water or off the tennis court. It couldn't have been much blacker and whiter. Them or us?

While the population of northeastern Brazil is primarily darker skinned, especially compared to southern Brazil, where most of the white European immigrants settled, there are still class distinctions based on race, and blacks are clearly at the bottom of the economic scale. There has been so much intermarrying that ferreting out classifications is complicated on the ground. Nevertheless, there are racially based cultural practices that separate groups and create hierarchy. Two of the ones I was most interested in—capoeira and Candomblé—were clearly connected to Africa and blacks and as a result tended to be looked down on by those who didn't want to be associated with those groups. The upper classes in Brazil would play soccer or tennis or practice an imported martial art like taekwondo.

When you're traveling, you're more likely than at home to mix with economic classes lower than your own. You don't know which neighborhoods are rich and which poor, so you blindly stumble into ones you might normally avoid, and the residents of those poorer neighborhoods don't question why you're there because your foreign appearance immediately excuses you.

Or maybe when you travel, you automatically change your frame of mind; you're traveling because you want to see how other people live, so *everyone's* interesting. In fact, the more different, the poorer, the better; whereas in comparable situations at home, you feel guilty or somehow threatened. At home, that means crossing the street when you see that "strung-out guy in the hoody." That guy you actually know nothing about but think you do.

I'm not as afraid when I'm traveling—maybe because in my ignorance of my surroundings, I'm freed of the assumptions I might otherwise make. I find I'm more willing to jump the class barrier, despite knowing that I'm vulnerable—I know I have things others could want, and I'm particularly obtrusive so maybe more of a target, though maybe less, too, protected by my celebrity. I realize that vulnerability may make others feel *more* afraid when traveling, precisely because they don't understand the cues. But for me, my childhood abroad reinforced my confidence in basic human kindness and the feeling that we have more in common than not.

When living abroad, on one's own without job connections, one is totally dependent on the knowledge and kindness of strangers. The power table is turned. Suddenly one's cleaning woman, or that fruit seller, or the man who drives a taxi are enabling me to feed my children, find them healthcare, and are giving me a community, a feeling of belonging. It doesn't matter what socioeconomic class they come from. I'm grateful.

When I'm abroad, I want people to like me, in a different way than I do at home; I want them to like me *and* to like Americans. In Penedo, I wanted to imagine them saying, "The *Americana*, she's a nice lady. Those *Americanos*, they're so friendly." So I smiled. "See, she's not stuck up. She smiles at everyone." I smiled more. Maybe I thought smiling would help erase our differences.

One day, Molly had folded herself into the wicker couch by my desk and said we needed to find some service work for Brooke. Brooke, an American friend of Molly's who was going to join us for Christmas, needed to fulfill the community service hours required of all seniors in their Missoula high school.

"You know, it's not that easy. It's not like she can just show up, find an orphanage, and help out. She doesn't speak Portuguese; she may not have any particularly helpful skills. There's no *school* to build, you know." I was feeling a little resentful of this seemingly popular answer to American do-gooder impulses.

It's hard to know how to help, to know what is actually helpful. Of course, this is true in the United States, too, but there I can at least give money to my chosen charities. In Brazil, there are no solicitations in the mail—at least there weren't for us.

In Mozambique, the company of a German friend had built a well for a village that had no water. The women of the village had been walking twenty kilometers, roundtrip, to a river each day, toting water on their heads. Who wouldn't be grateful for a well near home? The village women, as it turned out. They enjoyed the social life that revolved around the walk to the river. And what productive things were they going to do with the time saved? Make things for sale to raise their income? To buy what? Time? Time with friends? They already had that. The Germans were confounded when the well went unused.

While we were in Mozambique, we'd purchased land, with help from our relatives, dug a well, and bought building materials for a house for Sarah, our cook. She'd been living in two rooms with her two daughters and six grandchildren, with no electricity and no running water. But two years later, though the house had been built, she still hadn't moved in. We didn't know why. Figuring out what's really helpful just isn't that easy.

18

My People: The Butcher, the Baker, the Furniture Maker

MOST MORNINGS, I pulled out my straw bag, with its stash of plastic bags inside, and headed down the ridge to the market.

One day, I passed the woodcarver whose shop was under the radio station at the near corner of our *praça*. Sitting on a stump in his doorway, American pop music throbbing behind him, he whittled, exuding a smiling contentment with life. He waved to me, and I gave him the thumbs-up (a ubiquitous gesture here) and moved on down the hill.

Around the corner, I raised my thumb, a hopeful question, to the man across the street in front of the unmarked garage door that was our bakery. I was too late. The bread was usually sold out by nine. The bread, of which there were two types, leavened and unleavened, was disappointing in its bland squishiness but was better when fresh.

We briefly tried the home-delivery option, buying from the man who would randomly show up with bread in a cloth-covered rack on the back of his bike, squeezing his turkey-baster horn to announce his coming. But our needs and his schedule were too unpredictable. He brought back good memories, however, of the conveyor belt of fresh ingredients that used to pass by our walled house in Mozambique, of the way Peter used to bargain with the woman who'd come by with squid in a bucket one day and random vegetables in a cardboard box the next.

"*Pode encontrar um peixe vermelho?*"—Can you find a red fish? Peter would ask. Sure enough, the next day she'd show up with one, which she'd probably bought from the fishermen who would stand by the side of the road like hitchhikers, holding out their thumbs, sporting a dazzling silver fish dangling there by its gills.

Then of course there were all the other itinerant Mozambican vendors whistling to pull someone out from the inner recesses of the house, their dark faces looking hopefully through the barred gate. They bore carts of fruit, handfuls of brooms, armfuls of shirts or woven baskets. The brooms and baskets now sit unused in our Missoula basement because the buying was about supporting the vendor, not about the need for the goods. About saying, "Thanks for giving me a way to have a relationship with someone local."

In Penedo, I was grateful for my relationships with the market vendors. They provided a window into local lives and helped me feel part of the community. They were my social life.

Beyond the bakery were the rows of rickety stalls, temporary structures made out of one-by-twos with a shelf for wares. Black plastic stretched over the top for a roof. The vendors had been out on the street for two years while the 1890s market building was renovated. By October, they were painting its scalloping arcade and high-ceilinged rooms peach and white. I hoped it would be finished before we left.

"*Quando vai estar pronto?*"—When is it going to be ready?—I'd ask Celia, my favorite fruit woman, a rotund mother of eleven who looked like she was melting into her fraying wicker chair.

She'd laugh and roll her eyes. "*Ninguém sabe*"—No one knows.

Among the stalls, there were the specialists, with eggs or cheese or grains or fruit and vegetables, medicinals and spices, or nonperishables like watches and clothing. Then there were the generalists. Stands that carried everything from batteries and joysticks for video games to stickers of Jesus and Mary, pet collars, and cigarettes.

That day, I bought eggs (you counted them out at ten cents apiece into a custom-made carton), butter (ladled out of a bin by the half kilo with a wooden spatula), a pineapple, a papaya, and a bunch of mini-bananas. I happened to look down, as I was disentangling the bananas, to see a live goat, lying in a wheelbarrow at the level of my right thigh. Live animals were a common sight. Earlier, I'd passed a man pushing his bike, his right hand holding a live chicken dangling by its red feet and a bunch of writhing green crabs, bound in a plastic net bag. Next to Celia was Edivaldo, a medicinals and spices man. I counted eight types of sticks or bark, for making tea.

I continued on to my favorite butcher. His corrugated garage door was rolled up to reveal a row of succulently plump chickens on a marble counter and great hunks of red meat hanging on huge hooks above them. My butcher often had a whole pig's head, very white, hanging there as well, with its severed feet on the counter below. Brazil is definitely a meat-oriented country, with numerous cuts we could never identify. The one thing we figured out was that you could get your *carne* either *mole* (soft) or *duro* (hard). That day, I was looking for pork tenderloin. Nené, the assistant butcher and a member of Peter's soccer team, said they were out.

I continued down a small side street toward the main *praça* by the river, passing metal wheelbarrows full of fish, shining silver and gold, slender and wide, smooth and scaly, river fish and ocean fish, many with numerous parallel incisions, for marinating.

Reaching the *praça*, I headed for one of the many food kiosks. As I sat in one of the white plastic chairs sipping Coke from an old-fashioned glass bottle, a woman dropped a small political flier in my lap. It was a list of candidates to vote for in the upcoming state and federal election. But it didn't list the candidates' names. Instead it just listed their numbers, the numbers that the voters would enter into the computer when they voted. This suddenly made sense of the numbers we were constantly hearing as part of the songs for each candidate that continually blared from passing vehicles. The election was soon, and the campaigning was amping up, literally. It occurred to me that one could just follow this list and have no idea who one had just voted for. But then maybe that was no different from voting for a name in the United States just because one had heard of it.

I downed the last bit of my now-warm Coke and crossed the rest of the *praça* to enter Ki-Barato, an actual grocery store. Checking my market basket, I got a cart and zipped through the rest of my list: unrefrigerated cartons of milk; eighteen tiny, speckled *codorna* eggs; yogurt drink; frozen juice concentrate in square plastic packets (*graviola, acerola, pinga,* and more familiar ones: *açai,* pineapple, mango, passion fruit); and the Brazilian cook's mainstay, condensed milk. The young cashiers would smile as I pulled out my bundle of plastic bags for reuse (whether with admiration or benevolent tolerance of my eccentricity, I was never sure). The first time I did this, they nodded

knowingly: *"Ahh, melhor para o ambiente"*—Ahh, better for the environment. Judging from the plastic bags, pop bottles, and Styrofoam
washed up on the beaches, the litter in the streets, and the lack of
recycling, I was surprised they knew the concept.

"Mom, we don't know what to do. Our friends just drop their
wrappers on the street, or in the courtyard at school." Both Molly
and Skyler had wondered how to fit in when they couldn't quite bring
themselves to just drop paper on the ground.

As I waited to retrieve my market bag from the grocery checker, the
old beggar woman found me, as she always did. She'd tell me a story I
rarely understood. But I didn't need the story to give her money. It just
took her sunken breasts in the same loose shift over too-short pants,
her bare swollen feet, and her rheumy eyes to make me want to help
her. She wore a brown crocheted cap over her white hair that always
had interesting things stuck into it. That day, there were two plastic
spoons and some toothpicks. I wondered whether it was some sort of
amulet or just storage. Around her neck she'd tied a clump of beads,
a dried flower, and two tiny plastic babies on a string.

Ever since I'd lived in New York City in the eighties, where I'd felt
both beleaguered by beggars and guilty, my policy had been to give
to old men, women, and children, feeling somehow that they were the
most helpless. Although really, anyone reduced to asking for money
that way needs help. Abroad, I feel especially concerned about the
children. I've never forgotten my sense of guilty privilege as I sat, when
I was twelve, in the backseat of a taxi in Cairo, windows rolled down
in the heat. We were stopped at a traffic light when a barefoot girl
in a flower-print dress, worn thin with dirt, limply reached her arm
through the window, dangling pungently fragrant strands of jasmine
for sale. She looked to be my age. We paid her a few piastres, and as
she drifted onto the next car, the little boy following her, his potbelly
poking out from under his too-small shirt, held his cupped hand out
to me, his eyes encrusted with flies.

Rather than making a living this way, it would be far better for
children to be in school. However, I know school isn't always afford-
able. (Even the "free" schools in Mozambique required a uniform
and close-toed shoes, more than many could pay.) I've also heard too

many Oliver Twist stories, children being manipulated by adults into begging for them. Fearing what Fagan might do when the kids come back empty-handed, I mostly just give money all the time. If I have it with me, I also give food.

In Penedo, there weren't many beggars, just a few regulars: the old woman at the grocery; the blind man sitting cross-legged on the sidewalk, singing in his hoarse, tuneless voice; and the other man, shirtless, in a turban and ragged shorts, who sat in the doorway across the street from him. I never saw anyone else give them money.

Done with my shopping, I caught the bus. An alternative to the bus would have been to hire a man with a wheelbarrow to walk me home with my purchases. They hung out at the market and charged about six dollars to walk up the hill. For some reason, I was self-conscious about it; I guess it felt too much like a servant-master relationship. At the same time, I recognized my own hypocrisy: I *was* the upper class here and as such was expected to help out the lower classes by employing them.

"*Oi da casa!*" I shouted as I slung my bags through our front door. "Hello to the house!" Aniete came running.

"*É muito pesado!*" she cooed sympathetically, scooping up my straw bag. "It's so heavy!"

I was sweaty and tired but felt better for my daily ritual. The small talk with my market regulars had reinforced my connections to our chosen town.

19

Surfing Through the Presidential Election

LEARNING TO SURF had long been a goal of Peter's, one he set in Bali almost twenty years ago. At Jatiúca Beach, three-hours away from Penedo in Alagoas's capital city of Maceió, we found the ultimate surfing instructor, Disraelle. Once we learned how easy it was to use the van system, we'd begun going to the ocean a couple of weekends a month. We'd been sampling the smorgasbord of Brazilian beaches: the beach as highway and twenty-four-hour tailgating party at Peba; the itinerant-food and dental-floss-bikini flesh buffet at Praia do Francês; the classic Hallmark card of deserted beach and breeze-flushed palms at Pontal do Coruripe; and finally Jatiúca, a city beach along a busy drive, backed by ten- to twelve-story buildings.

Deeply tanned, tattooed, and ripped, Disraelle grinned with delight whenever his surfing pupils managed to catch a wave and stand. "*Ótimo, ótimo!*"—Awesome!

Disraelle immediately earned Skyler's respect when, riding a board in, he jumped lightly in a half turn to face the other direction and ended in a headstand, board still moving, just a toy in the waves. He drew diagrams in the sand, made Skyler and Molly lie facedown on the beach and jump to their feet in one smooth movement, ready to tame the board and the ocean. Out in the water, they learned how to flip the board over and slide under it to nose out through the crashing waves. Everyone stood, Skyler even pulling off a few 180-degree jumps as he coasted into the shallows.

While my family surfed, I hired a taxi and began my search for a nine-point FireWire camera cable. Ten electronics stores later, I decided it was not available in the state of Alagoas, a reminder that when traveling, advanced technology is often unusable. During the course of my two-hour search, however, I got a much better sense of the layout of the town.

A city of about eight hundred thousand, Maceió is built on a point jutting into the Atlantic. Beautiful beaches are lined with thatched-pavilion restaurants, palm trees, bike paths, and sailboats for rent. The cuisine ranges from the standard beach fare of grilled kebabs, corn on the cob, and *água de coco* to exquisitely prepared sashimi in a hermetic environment of white-cushioned sofas and bamboo mats. Along the beachfront is a parade of high-rise hotels and condominiums.

Behind the coastal strip rise hills, where a few four-lane roads snake in and out of the dips, passing through the *favelas* in the valleys. Apparently these ramshackle slums—clusters of smudged plaster boxes under red-tiled roofs at best, black plastic at worst—are slated to be torn down. They'll be replaced by high-rises into which the current residents are to move. Peter noted this had been done in the United States in the 1940s and '50s, when the trend was to replace American ghettos with "projects," high-rises that frequently became dens of crime. In the States, the plan has been abandoned. I wondered how it would turn out here, in a country notorious for political corruption where the money attached to grand plans often ends up in individuals' pockets.

My taxi ran the gauntlet between miles of banner wavers, each paid fifty *reais*, thirty-five dollars, to stand and wave a banner for eight hours that advertised a political candidate. It was about the chance to earn a little money, not about impassioned support. Given the history of post-colonial Brazilian politics, it's not hard to see why most voters seemed so apathetic. In the last two centuries, since independence from the Portuguese, Brazil has seen a monarchy, civilian presidents put in place and propped up by the military, an oppressive military dictatorship, and, only recently, twenty-five years of democracy, which is to say elected presidents largely coming from one of two parties, though there are others, and from the wealthy elite. Almost none of these governments would have given the ordinary man on the street the sense that he had any meaningful input. However, this particular election was especially interesting to me because there was a woman running for president who looked as though she might actually win. I was impressed that this macho country might elect a woman before the United States did.

The election was the next day. There, in Maceió, were miles of
turquoise banners for Teotonio Vilela Filho, the incumbent governor
(and son of a former senator); then miles of red, white, and blue
stripes for Ronaldo Lessa, his adversary. Zeca had said Lessa couldn't
serve even if he won. Apparently, after his last term as governor, he
was convicted of embezzling, and a law was passed prohibiting politicians who had committed crimes in office from ever serving again.
Evidently, Lessa was appealing this and blithely moving forward with
considerable support.

"If you can't look past the financial crimes of Brazilian politicians,"
Giovanni had observed at one of my lessons, "you will have no one
to vote for."

Having read an article in *The Economist* touting the accomplishments
of the president then in office, Luiz Inácio Lula da Silva, known
fondly as Lula, I was curious to hear what people here thought of
him, and of his hand-picked successor, Dilma Rousseff, whose future
would be decided the next day. If elected, she would be Brazil's first
female president. Lula stood out because he had come from both a
working-class family and from the northeast, from Pernambuco, the
next state over. His party was the labor party, and he was credited with
having made significant strides in defending the rights of workers and
increasing social programs for the poor. But even his government had
been weighed down with accusations of corruption. Not everyone
was a fan.

"Lula is just stealing money from hardworking people and giving
it to people too *preguiçoso*—lazy—to work!" My taxi driver was ges-
ticulating wildly, both hands off the wheel, he was so furious. He was
referring to Lula's *Bolsa Família*, a welfare program that provides up to
sixty-five dollars a month to poor families. Not enough, as my next
taxi driver pointed out, to support a family, but better than nothing.

So what of Dilma Rousseff? My first taxi driver hadn't liked her
either.

"*Ela era* [something I couldn't understand] *terrorista*," and he mimed
pulling a trigger. True enough. In the 1970s, she'd been part of a radi-
cal socialist group that promoted armed uprising against the military

dictatorship then in power. I'd thought that might be seen as heroic, but apparently not.

At the beach the next day, election day, we asked our surfing instructor, Disraelle, who he was voting for. He gave the response we'd heard most often: *"Estou indeciso . . ."*—I'm undecided. They're all robbers. With that, he sprinted back down to the water, arms swinging wide as if to embrace the ocean before narrowing above his head for a dive into the foaming water. Magically, he popped up two waves out, took a few powerful strokes, and caught a wave back in, twirling with a forestroke and backstroke, like an eggbeater being propelled into shore. He could vote later. Clearly this was his natural habitat and would continue to be, regardless of who won at the polls.

Those waves still break jade green and frothy white, as I imagine they have for millennia, watching the Dilmas come and go. Our lives are small in the scheme of time. The waves remind us of that.

Reluctant to leave, we finally dragged our collection of small bags to the empty lot where we'd caught our first van to Penedo three months before. No regular vans were available. They were needed to transport voters.

"But we can take you for two hundred *reais*," said a man relaxing by an unmarked one. "You can have the whole van to yourself. Two hours."

We tossed our bags onto the seats and chose places out of the fifteen empty possibilities.

It didn't take us long to clear town. We'd picked up a police officer who had been an election monitor and was allowed to ride for free. Apparently, his presence liberated the driver from any of the restrictions from speed limits that he might have felt otherwise.

The ride was that visceral, interactive experience that Brazilian public transport is. In the United States, I once saw words on the back of a T-shirt: "You know you're driving in Nicaragua if: the driver ignores the lane markings on the road; the driver passes near the crest of the hill; the driver speeds up for the curves; cars drive three abreast on a two-lane road." *Substitute Brazil,* I thought.

I was glad for the handle on the side of the seat in front of me. It grounded me when I found myself airborne, literally, from high-speed bumping through potholes. It also helped me brace for the curves that sent the rosary dangling from the rearview mirror out to a forty-five-degree angle. I swiveled in my seat to point out an enormous cross, constructed of wrecked cars, five high and three across. It marked a police checkpoint. I saw a roadside plaque in the shape of a black coffin with words in white saying, "*Quantas vidas são necessárias . . .*"—How many lives are necessary—but we were past before I could read the rest.

At that moment, I could have panicked and prayed our lives weren't about to join the list, but somehow, in these situations, I never do. I find it quite easy, almost a relief, to relinquish control. I'm not normally a person who likes being out of control. But I think, in situations like this, where I have little choice, I find it easier to give myself over to chance. Instead of gritting my teeth at every lurching turn, I rather enjoyed it, like a ride at the fair.

Two hours it was, right to our doorstep. Two hundred *reais* it wasn't. "*É trezentos!*"—Three hundred! the driver argued vehemently.

"Who heard him say two hundred?" Peter demanded.

"I did," I blurted. But then, did I? In another language, it was so hard to be sure.

We relented, feeling burned but too tired to really care. Hitching our bags through our narrow front door, we were happy to be home.

20

Hitting the Wall

MY CELL PHONE RANG. It was November 7—Zeca's birthday!

Peter had left before dawn to walk down to the *baixa* with his soccer pals and catch the bus to Pernambuco for a game. The rest of us had been quietly reading in the garden room.

"Yah, hello. So, if you want to come to the party . . . people are coming now . . . I can send a car. I can't come. You know it is my birthday, so . . . I haf to be here . . ."

"Zeca, that's okay, we can get there," I said hurriedly. I hung up and went to wrap our birthday present, some framed photos I'd taken of Zeca playing tennis. I asked Molly and Skyler to sign the back.

"Does that look bad? Oh, that's bad," Skyler said of his signature. In retrospect, that seems to have been the trigger. As Molly and I changed, Skyler lay on the sofa in his boxer shorts.

"I don't want to go."

"Why not?"

"I just don't want to."

"Well, I think Zeca has been really nice to you, and you owe it to him to at least show up at his birthday party. We're ready to leave." I was frustrated. "I'll give you five minutes." I could feel myself beginning to overreact. These sudden mood reversals were so hard to take, especially when my hopes had risen, when he had seemed more at peace with himself.

In the end, Skyler dragged out the door behind us, we crossed the *praça* and managed to catch a bus. A mile and a half down the road, we jumped out and began the short, hot trek to Robson's house. There, the freestanding houses were largely invisible behind walls rimmed with broken glass or electrified wires, and the streets, which in our neighborhood were normally full of people, were empty.

"I'm just a bad person," Skyler said.

"You're not a bad person. You're just a little moody these days. Adolescent hormones."

"Adolescent?"

"Yeah, teenage. I have the same thing. That's why you see premenopausal women crying all the time. You're moving into it; I'm moving out of it."

Skyler was slowing down. Stopping. "What is there to like about Brazil?"

"Okay, do you want me to answer you seriously? Can you listen seriously? This is what I think. I think the people here are exceptionally open and gracious, the place is beautiful, the history interesting, there's surfing, capoeira . . ." I went on and on, the floodgates open, four months of patience shoved aside as words tumbled out. By this time, we were stalled against a wall.

"I can't do this!" Now tears rolled down Skyler's cheeks.

"Okay, I'm going." Molly stalked off.

I felt bad for Skyler. For him to cry meant he was having a really hard time, and I knew he couldn't just figure out why and change it. At the same time, it was draining to boost him up.

"Skyman." I put my arm around him. "Robson's house is right around the corner. Go to the end of this street and turn right. We'll walk slowly. Come when you feel ready."

Around the corner, I rejoined Molly. We stopped and waited by an empty lot, full of weeds and trash, next to Robson's house. There seemed to be no zoning in Penedo. Large, beautiful houses were plunked down next to tire shops. The sidewalk was crumbling into sand.

Skyler appeared at the corner, bright in his red T-shirt, slumped in his spine. We waited until he caught up. Tears still trickled down his face.

"Now I look like I've been crying."

I smiled, put my hands on his shoulders, and looked into his face.

"No, you don't. You look fine. That's the beauty of youth. Those things disappear."

Eventually, we managed to enter Robson's yard.

"Oh, *this* place!" Skyler exclaimed. "I remember this place. It's really fun." Bang! We'd made it through another of his daily swings, whether because he was basically resilient and would pull himself together when something promising showed up, or because the daily testosterone flushes had hit another part of their cycle, I didn't know.

We wandered through an opening in a wall that connected two parts of the rambling house into the covered arcade behind. The women were seated there, resting from their kitchen labors, tending to toddlers, cooling off in the breeze. A row of songbirds in cages swung gently above their heads. Out back under an arbor of bougainvillea, we found Zeca in aviator sunglasses, cigarette in one hand, glass of beer in the other.

"Do I look like Johnny Knoxville from *Jackass?*" he asked, grinning.

"Yeah, kind of. Yeah, I can see it, the glasses." Molly, our in-house expert on American pop culture, saved me again.

Robson pulled me into a hug. "*Tudo bom?*" He was a handsome man, George Clooney's Brazilian twin, with cropped salt-and-pepper hair, lively eyes, and a quick smile.

All the usual suspects were there: Zeca's dad, the uncles (he had seven on his mother's side), and some friends. A man was playing a guitar while the others robustly sang along, led by Jacaré, a short, stocky guy, energetically rocking side to side in his folding chair. Skyler and Molly were spirited away by the young cousins. Hours later, Skyler reappeared, bare feet black with dirt. "How do you say Ghosts in the Graveyard?" he asked, wanting to teach this old camp game. We settled on "*Fantasmas de Cemitério.*" He ran off to explain the rules, and they scattered once again.

"This song gets me in the fetoo. How do you say it? Fetoo?" Zeca was indicating his low belly.

"Fetus?" I offered.

"Yeah." Zeca punched his fist high in the air. "This song gets me in the fetus," he shouted. It occurred to me as his voice reached full volume that he had probably meant "in the gut."

I helped myself to a plate of grilled meat, beans, *vinagrete* (chopped tomatoes and onions), and *farofa* (coarse manioc meal sautéed in butter). It was peaceful under the arbor, with all the boisterous singing, kids swinging in and out of sight, chickens and nursing dogs rummaging around in the dirt, and plates of food constantly appearing for informal grazing.

Zeca's mom waved me to a chair on one side of the arcade. "... *é mais ventilado.*" Molly was there, chatting with a young cousin, a slender fourteen-year-old with her hot pink blouse falling off one shoulder, a popular look.

I ended up passing the afternoon chatting with aunts and cousins, wandering down the road to buy freshly baked buns, eventually being invited to help chop hot dogs into leftover *vinagrete* for a six o'clock snack. In the evening, I wandered out into the dark backyard to check on Skyler, who had been happily climbing trees. He reported gleefully, "This is soooo funny. You know, Zeca's really drunk, so he's swearing a lot! You know, like, 'This is my fucking birthday.' So I wanted to say, '*Porra*'"—a common Brazilian swear word—"but I didn't want to do it in front of all his uncles, so I yelled, 'Sperm!'"—the literal translation that Zeca had given us—"and then Zeca yelled, 'Sperm!' and we were both yelling, 'Sperm!'"

It made me soar to see Skyler so happy and Molly so content.

I, too, felt content and wondered why, in the United States, I always felt so restless. I thought of the large family parties at Peter's mom's around the Fourth of July. There, similarly, lots of aunts and uncles and cousins would lounge on her lawn by a lake; lots of beer would go down. But I always felt there was something I should be doing. In Brazil, I didn't have a lot of demands on my time in general, so six hours wiled away didn't seem a waste, and I could fulfill my need for accomplishment simply by trying to speak Portuguese. But the ease also came simply from the aura of contentment that Brazilians exude, like a great quilt that makes you just want to curl up and sleep.

"It seems like every time I have a good day, the next day's a bad one," Skyler observed the following Sunday.

"Yeah, I've noticed that," I said, trying to sound matter-of-fact rather than accusatory. I stood by the white tile counter in the kitchen, blending milk and packets of Skyler's favorite *acerola* cherry juice in the *liquidificador*.

The previous day had been fabulous. Skyler had come back in the middle of the day bouncing with excitement about how he, Victor, Ricardo, and Paulinho had all done tons of back flips (we're talking seventy-five to a hundred) off some piles of construction sand.

"Mom, next time you have to come with the camera. We were all in the air at the same time."

They'd zipped through the house, devoured the passion-fruit popsicles, used and strewn all our glasses around the kitchen, and promptly left again—for another four hours of flipping, off walls, in grassy *praças*, anywhere they could find, all around town.

Molly had had a good day, too. School friends had invited her to go to Piaçabucu, a town thirty minutes away. "They said I should pack some clothes in case I stay overnight," she'd said with delight as she rushed out the door.

"Give us a call so we know what's happening," I'd called after her. We allowed her to do things we would never let her do at home, like sleep over in some other town, or go to parties and come home at five in the morning. We knew she was solid and trusted her to call if she was in trouble, and we usually met some of the players, so we could at least make sure they weren't *totally* scuzzy. But mostly we just crossed our fingers. We were so eager for her to connect that we canned most of the rules.

However, on that Sunday, Victor had knocked on the door just as Skyler woke, so he was feeling beleaguered. Peter and I had tried to convince Skyler that it was okay to just say you had other things to do, that you didn't always have to give a reason.

"I do say that. They just aren't like that here. They don't leave. There's not a day when there aren't tons of people knocking on the door!" His voice was shifting into fifth gear.

Even Molly, normally even keeled, was on edge that Sunday, stomping her foot in frustration, about what we could only guess. "I'm not upset. I'm just tired. Never mind!"

Peter, on a deadline to submit a new book proposal, had retreated into the greater isolation of our bedroom. He had his earphones on to block us out.

By dinnertime, Molly was telling me to "chill out." She'd taken to correcting our Portuguese, justifiably because she was quickly outstripping us, but in that way that stemmed from embarrassment at her parents' ineptness. I knew I was snappish but felt it was not my fault. I felt I was being robbed of my pleasure in this place. I was ready to find someone to blame.

I wondered if I were "hitting the wall." When Peter and I had taken our five-month honeymoon trip through China, we'd hit the wall at two months. In Mozambique, it had been a little later. The wall is the point when one can't put a good face on the adventure anymore. The exoticism is wearing off. The pride of "wow, look at this cool thing we're doing" has begun to wither. Life just seems hard, one long struggle. And maybe now, too, we were starting to need a break from each other.

It was probably good that I needed to make the two-hour trip to Praia do Francês to rent a beach house for the upcoming visit of our American friends. I'd begun to cry stirring sugar into the passion fruit juice.

The next morning, I threw a bathing suit and towel into my straw bag and slipped out the front door. In ten minutes, I'd made it down the ridge, passing the woodcarver, the bakery, and the market, and was in line at the bank before a set of four ATMs. I was lucky; there was money. Almost running now, I managed to wave down the van just as it was pulling out. I squeezed onto the end of a row of three seats. The man next to me was plugged into headphones, but I could still hear his music.

We barreled over cobblestones, picking up more passengers on our way out of town, until all fifteen seats were full and a man with a hooked nose sat on a plastic stool in the side aisle next to me, pinning my other leg. I took out my book, *The Handmaid's Tale*, a cheery little story about oppressed women in a hyperconservative religious society. No one read, at least not in public, at least not in this part of Brazil. All these silent people were either listening to my seatmate's music or just thinking or sleeping and dreaming. I imagined our van—a metal bubble full of thoughts and dreams, careening down the road. My thoughts were still angry—angry about the whining, the self-pity; angry that my family should criticize me about my snappish tone. *Me,*

Atlas, holding up our world, keeping everyone else's precarious mental states afloat!

I closed my book on my lap and looked out at the spindly trunks of coconut palms flitting by. The man in the headphones fiddled. The music shifted. Now it was in English. "I'll always be there for you . . ." the man's voice crooned. My eyes began to fill. Who, I wondered, was there for me? I could see the ocean now, brilliant turquoise with a ruffle of purest white where it hit the sand. Why was I having such a hard time?

At 10:00 AM, we swung into the Praia do Francês roundabout, and the van slowed to let me out. I paid and started the walk to the real estate office. Sweat began to trickle down the center of my back, like water being eased out of a dam and into the chute.

The business at the real estate office went surprisingly quickly. I counted out the deposit, the equivalent of $550 in cash, shook the agent's hand, and stopped to smear sunscreen on my bare arms in the shade of the office porch. There were vans passing almost every hour on their way to Penedo. I wondered when to go home. I turned and headed to the beach.

It wasn't as crowded as on weekends. The tide was out, making the sweep of hard sand look especially inviting. I stood in the shade of an almond tree and decided to rent a beach chair and umbrella from a guy wearing eyeliner and foundation. He'd risen up from behind the counter of an open-air restaurant, where he'd been sleeping on a makeshift mattress.

The water was delicious, warm on the surface and cool underneath. I swam in a calm lagoon created by a long reef and looked at the ripples of sun on my arms through the film of water.

Talk about multi-use. There were people in the water, not swimming so much, mostly sitting submerged up to their shoulders, in straw hats and baseball caps. Then there were the fishermen, like the white-mustachioed man standing on the beach watching his lines, which extended way out into the lagoon from rods planted in pipes sunk into the sand. Then there was the guy snorkeling with the harpoon gun, and finally there was the flying Zodiac that was taking off and landing every twelve minutes. As a mere swimmer, you could start to feel a little vulnerable.

Now, a flying Zodiac—that was something Skyler would really like. "It's everybody's dream to fly, Mom," he'd said a few days earlier. He'd recently become obsessed with YouTube videos of flying people in wing suits. "Do you think people will be able to fly in my lifetime?"

I swam back to my more deserted section of the beach, wary of hooks and harpoons. As I waded into shore, the tune from a CD-sales cart jumped out, Cyndi Lauper's "Girls Just Want to Have Fun." I felt the water getting warmer as I reached the shallows and thought, *What I really want is to watch my kids have fun.*

I walked over to buy a chilled coconut from a girl lounging in a beach chair. She picked one up, held it in one hand, and nonchalantly hacked off the top with a large machete. Puncturing the woody skin of the now-flat top, she inserted a straw. I retreated to my umbrella to savor its cold, sweet water. A bit later, I spied a teenage boy swinging a round charcoal brazier by its long looping handle. Raising a finger, I got an answering chin lift, and he ambled over and pulled what looked like a white popsicle out of his cooler. This porous white cheese was slightly sour, rubbery, and oily—perfect for grilling. After buying the cheese and a bag of roasted cashews and a plastic cup of mussel soup from other roving vendors, I was quite content.

Just as I put my book away and was sitting back to enjoy my last minutes on the beach, the coconut girl shuffled her way toward me through the powdery white sand, another coconut in hand. She jerked her head toward another set of chairs. Oh!

A mystery man was treating me to a coconut? Was this like buying a girl a drink? I had to laugh. I was so long out of this game, I had no idea what to do. I glanced furtively in the direction she'd come from, but not long enough to really see anyone. What if my look were taken as an invitation? I put the coconut on my beach table, not sure whether to drink. Was taking a sip like saying yes to something?

I suddenly felt exposed in my skimpy swimsuit. I hadn't worn anything so revealing since the red gingham two-piece I'd used when I was eight. I'd become a competitive swimmer and had been a steadfast one-piece wearer ever since. The suit I had on now was one piece, but barely. It was more like a bikini on end, running vertically rather than horizontally.

I sat a while longer, gingerly sipping my secret-admirer coconut and tapping my foot to the Brazilian pop song being played at the cart that had just pulled up in front of me. The song had the word *Americana* in it. Had he sent that over, too?

I decided to try to catch the van leaving the roundabout at 3:20. I picked up my things and left, carefully keeping my eyes on the sand, wondering if I were being watched. Squeezing into the small restaurant bathroom, I changed clothes, retrieved my purse, and began the hot trek back out to the highway.

I was glad I'd left early. The van arrived thirty minutes ahead of time. I flagged it down and climbed in, happy to head home, rearmed with gratitude for my intrepid family.

Pousada Colonial

Skyler "playing" Capoeira

Bentinho "playing" Capoeira

Giovanni

Karol

Aniete

Zeca

Lu, Peter, and Junior

The Coelho—
Skyler, Molly
and Valdir

At the beach
in Peba

View out the back window

Amy and Peter score a date in Salvador

21

Bands of Ants and Silent Horsemen

ONCE, WHILE LISTENING to a session of British Parliament on the radio in a rented car in England, I suddenly understood the cockeyed humor of Monty Python. Listening to that raucous parliamentary session, I realized context is everything, and when you don't have one, things can seem surreal. I began to understand where the magical realism that Latin American authors are famous for comes from. I had several experiences in Brazil that I'm sure actually happened but that in retrospect seem fantastic.

Like the time Molly got home at 11:00 PM from watching a *futsal* game with friends. I was half asleep but rousing myself to greet her.

"Mom, are there always this maweee ansheeez?"

"What? I didn't catch that."

She spit toothpaste into the little sink in the hallway outside the bathroom and jerked her chin up. "Look at the ants!"

Above us, on three walls, wrapping around two corners, were *thousands* of ants, big reddish-black ones. They were up near the ceiling, covering four rows of tiles—a solid band of squiggling black, one foot wide.

"Ohhh."

We'd been seeing more and more *formigas*, the almost-imperceptible little ants that I'd swipe up by the dozens with a wet rag, during the day. And I'd killed a few of these big ones at night, the only time I'd noticed them. My tolerance for insects is very low in tropical places, where mosquitoes carry dengue fever, flies have been who knows where, and I don't know whether the spiders bite and if they do what that might bring. I was taking no prisoners, practicing the brutality that comes with ignorance.

But this was beyond me. I tried to see where all the ants were coming from or going to but found nothing. They didn't appear to be moving down, where they could start invading all our food stores in open baskets below. It seemed there was nothing to do but go to bed. I suspected they'd be gone in the morning, and they were. Completely.

One day, I was following Skyler and Victor down an alley when Skyler urgently beckoned to me from across the street ahead, shouting, "Mom, hurry up!" I emerged out of the narrow side street and skittered across the intersection, just ahead of the first of a hundred or more horsemen. They were clicking noisily up the cobblestones, accompanied, of course, by the requisite speaker-mounted car, blaring music at high volume. The surreal part was that until I'd popped out of the side street, I'd heard nothing at all. It was as though they were part of a movie set and had just been given the go-ahead to start moving and turn on the speakers. I happened to be carrying my camera in preparation for photographing Skyler's upcoming game of street soccer, so I stopped to take pictures. Instead of the usual smiling, thumbs-up pose that I got when I pulled out a camera, the riders seemed oblivious, as though I were as invisible to them as they had been to me.

Then there were all the little piles in our house, fine little piles of black. From what? There was no visible trail of falling dust. Was it alive? Aniete swept them up daily, and then they reappeared. The pile by the dish drainer was a little different—a little more in the horror-movie vein. I wiped up a wet brown "accumulation" from behind the dish drainer. While I continued to wash dishes, I saw a drip in the same spot and the brown began to re-accumulate. I could see the drip land, but looking up, I could never see the drip leave. What was dripping?

Once I started to see things this way, there was no going back. The fantastical quality was increased by the fact that, as foreigners, we were so in the dark; we couldn't predict things coming, we didn't recognize what they were, we didn't understand what created them. They seemed to magically appear and then disappear, still a mystery.

22

A Viking Queen Floats Above a Chiffon Sea

FROM THE TIME they were in bassinets, both Molly and Skyler had been residents at the university, tucked into dance studio corners, immersed for years in music and diving, twirling bodies. It was not surprising then that by age three, Molly was looking for a tutu and Skyler was finding ways to spin and flip. While, as a modern dancer, tutus have never been a part of my life, by age sixteen, Molly had developed into an elegant and adept ballet dancer, and to our delight, we'd been able to find a wonderful teacher in Penedo, Fernando Ribeiro. He immediately invited Molly to perform in his Ballet das Alagoas recital. This meant finding new pointe shoes. The pair we'd ordered from the States three months before had never arrived. I'd begun to realize that global American business is global as long as you're in the United States.

Catching the van in Penedo, Molly and I made the three-hour trip to Maceió in a last-ditch effort to find the shoes. We took a cab from the van stop to Maceió's downtown shopping district, where streets were closed to traffic. Entering the flood of people on foot, streaming around sidewalk racks, squeezing into dark doorways, we found the fabric and notions store where we hoped to find shoes that would fit.

In Maceió, there was one brand of pointe shoe, and you chose a size. In the United States, there are many brands, as well as four toe widths, three shank lengths, and narrow heels versus wide. In the United States, when one is fitted, the sales person will pinch the heel, stick his or her finger inside the curve of the toe, and peel back the outer layer of shoe as you stand flat, then on demi-pointe, then on full pointe. It was a scientific operation with many variables. In Brazil, they asked, "Do you want to try it on?"

It seemed that in Brazil, shoes were something to cover your feet, not a high-performance device meant to help you better feel the floor, or touch the ball, or cushion your joints. Peter had bought Dalan a new pair of white soccer shoes.

"Did he just ask you to buy him a new pair of shoes?" I'd asked.

"No, not exactly. He told me that his shoes were broken."

"Did he choose the store?"

"Yeah. We went to Sportgol. I think he may have chosen the shoes because he liked the color. He didn't even try them on."

Nevertheless, we found pointe shoes for Molly that looked as though they would work.

Molly had been taking ballet twice a week with Fernando, who traveled every week from Maceió to teach dance in Penedo. With the lifted chest and rodlike back of a ballet dancer, he'd stride into the tiny studio at Imaculada, where the students were chatting in clusters, wearing board shorts, muscle shirt, and baseball cap, bare legs and feet in leg warmers and jazz shoes. "Molly, we going to dance," he'd say, forearms circling from the elbows as he talked, like a flower girl tossing petals.

He was warm and interested in us from the start and clearly enjoyed trying out his spattering of English. Neither Molly nor I told him that I, too, was a dance teacher, but he sniffed it out. Maybe it's in the way we stand, a little taller when we're around each other. One day he bent my ear about how pulling work out of these students here at Imaculada was like "squeezing blood out of a cockroach."

"*E as baratas não têm sangue*"—And cockroaches don't have blood, he whispered out of the corner of his mouth.

December 10. The Ballet das Alagoas performance was to start at 6:30 PM. Molly had already left to walk down the ridge to the theater, carrying her green tulle tutu hooked over her forearm like a wreath. Peter and Skyler had watched the dress rehearsal the night before because they'd had to leave that morning to meet friends from Missoula who were arriving that night in Salvador, eight hours away.

I decided to dress up for opening night. Sweating despite my cold shower, I ran down to the washroom, blouse and skirt in hand, to iron them. I never iron at home, but in Penedo, I felt compelled to, knowing I'd inevitably be on show.

I stepped out of the house in my new platform shoes—my concession, along with red toenail polish, to Brazilian womanhood—and struggled not to twist my ankles on the cobblestones.

At the theater, the doors were still closed. I stood outside in warm, heavy air, watching the sky slide from light blue to slate to black. I thought about buying a beer from a vendor with a Styrofoam cooler, despite the fact that I don't drink beer. A half hour later, Skyler's teacher Vanessa sauntered up with one of her daughters and her mother.

Vanessa was Skyler's English teacher at Imaculada, though she was so shy about speaking, you wouldn't have known. We'd recently hired her to tutor him privately as well. We had rapidly abandoned our homeschooling experiment, finding ourselves unable to engage Skyler in any constructive way. He was back at Imaculada full time, and we were now trying option three: the keep-up-with-homework-because-maybe-you'll-find-it-more-interesting-if-you-know-what's-going-on option.

That evening, Vanessa's habitually slow movement was overlaid by agitated conversation.

"*Os ladrões*—robbers—broke into my brother's house. They had a gun," she told me when I asked if she was all right. No one had been hurt. Like so many, while Vanessa was distressed, she seemed to shrug it off—nothing to be done.

Just as Molly's friend Karol and her mother, Maria, arrived, the theater opened, an hour late.

I was so proud of Molly, of the get-involved attitude that had brought her to this moment. She would be looking out at three tiers of curving balconies in dark, polished wood. This nineteenth-century theater reminded me of the nineteenth-century opera houses, so optimistically built, in small towns throughout the American West. In Penedo, the seats filled with ladies in long dresses, men in dress shirts, kids dangling their legs through the balusters. The nuns from Imaculada had come, all five, in their dove-gray habits, clustered in the first tier, near Giovanni and his girlfriend Sheila.

We'd also bought tickets for Aniete, who had come with her sister Gel, who was visiting from the country. They were dressed in their best jeans and delicate high heels, their black hair woven at the roots with glimmering beads. It was the first time they'd been in this theater, their first time seeing ballet. And I'd invited Zeca. It turned out several of his cousins, aunts, and uncles, including Robson, were there as well; they'd come to see Robson and Shirley's daughter, Julia, dance.

The theater was airless and hot, full of hands fanning white paper programs, like a flock of fluttering birds. Then the houselights went out, the chatter diminished, and the red velvet curtain opened, or one side of it did, revealing six bodies curled on the floor, Molly's blond head prominently in front. The other side of the curtain appeared to be stuck. The curled bodies waited patiently in their red light. After some tugging, the concert began.

As the dance went on, people in the audience began to chatter. Some sang along to the deafeningly loud *forró* music that accompanied this first, more modern piece.

At intermission, people fled the heat to stand outside in the cool night breeze. They drank beer and soda pop, ate popcorn coated in salt and condensed milk, smoked cigarettes.

There was no announcement of the beginning of the second half. I scurried back in just in time to see the curtain open to reveal a single, tiny dancer in a sparkling white leotard and splash of white netting rimming her bony hips. Opening her elbow-locked arms wide to embrace the audience, she earnestly plunked her foot out to the side. Cameras flashed. She blinked, hazarding a tentative smile but looked immensely relieved when she was joined by a troupe of others, twice her size.

They were followed by one group of earnestly gawky dancers after another—troops being put through their paces, in sparkling costumes of bright yellow, red, and sapphire blue. Gradually, the long Romantic tutus gave way to those that jut stiffly out from the hips, a delicate woman sprouting from a dinner plate, signaling a shift from the beginners to the more advanced. The steps got harder, and the dancers valiantly struggled through them, smiling bravely. But it wasn't until Molly and her partner Keyla appeared that one could see the ease and elegance that ballet is known for. Their feet fluttering, they floated through the quick shifts of direction, with the silk-stocking leg extensions that are ballet's trademark. The steady rumble of audience chatter and scraping of balcony chairs stopped.

Molly, so confident now, so calm and elegant, took command of the theater. She, too, had started at age six and had moved through the gawky troopings. The little girl I remembered from years of *Nutcracker* mice and party girls had grown into a queen. Like a Viking, tall, blond, and shining, eyes huge in winged blue eye shadow, she floated above a chiffon sea of tiny ballerinas.

At the end, the older girls led lines of younger ones out to bow. The audience whistled and hollered. To my surprise, Zeca, who seemed to start most sentences about the arts with, "I don' really like this . . ." was delighted by the whole thing. After Molly's duet, he said, "I like that one the *second* best. The first is that little girl." He pointed out the six-year-old in the blur of blue netting who had continually turned in the wrong direction and was consistently a count behind. "She is doing it all wrong, but she don't care at all. Thaz great."

After the performance, Zeca went outside to smoke. When Molly was ready, she and I joined Zeca and Robson and his family at an open-air restaurant down the street from our house. Robson looked debonair in a straw fedora, and his wife, Shirley, elegant in a tight black belted minidress showing off shapely hips. Her reddish-brown hair hung down, framing almond eyes. Smart, thoughtful eyes. *No one pushes this woman around*, I'd thought when I first met her. Once again, I felt totally content, sitting there in the breeze, picking at French fries and fried fish with a toothpick, drinking a Coke.

Live music floated in from somewhere in the back. "Wait, listen." Zeca had his finger in the air and craned his head.

"*Para Amilie e Mohlley,*" said the voice over the mic.

Zeca grinned. "It's for you."

The song seemed almost wistful, not what I associated with Zeca's love of acid rock.

He drove us home at 1:00 AM, down the middle of the unlined street. Now, in the silent deserted night, it all seemed a dream—unlikely that there'd be an elegant little theater, full of ballerinas in gauze, in a backwater town up a river in Brazil. But then, Penedo was full of surprises.

23

Compatible Travelers

WE WERE GEARING UP for the arrival of our American friends, the Kadas-Newells, whom Skyler and Peter had gone to pick up in Salvador, and Molly's friend, Brooke, who would come a week later. Maybe this would help Christmas feel a little more normal, a little more celebratory. While I loved the white-light-draped gazebo in the *praça* in front of our house and the flame tree branches wrapped in twinkling color, it still felt strange; the lights melted in the sun rather than sparkled in the snow.

But we were apprehensive about our friends' arrival, too. I wondered whether it would interfere with our efforts to adapt to life in Penedo. It would be exciting to share all that we'd learned, and perhaps their excitement would bring back our feeling of adventure. Peter and I missed my father in this way. He'd joined us almost everywhere in the world, and his affirmation, his pleasure in our traveling, had helped us get through the rough parts.

But were we going to have to adjust all over again after our friends left? Especially Skyler. Carson Kadas was one of his best pals. But it might be hard for Peter and me, too. It would be exhilarating to talk politics and compare cultures in full-length sentences, maybe even reeling off paragraphs. It would be a relief to have the ease that comes with shared backgrounds, to not have to explain the inside jokes.

Martha, Mike, Carson's older brother Bowen, and Carson arrived from the *Estados Unidos*, as we would repeatedly explain to everyone in Penedo. It had been a while—basically since we'd left the States— since I'd heard Skyler laugh with such unabashed hilarity as he did with Carson. I soaked in his laughter, like refilling a sponge that had been squeezed dry. Skyler and Carson made a good pair in their physical daring and their total willingness to sacrifice their bodies at the altar of soccer. Carson's bare feet were skinned and blistered by the second day, just as Skyler's had been five months before.

Wanting to treat our friends to something special, we'd waited for their arrival to explore the inland part of our state, the towns upriver along the Rio São Francisco. We caught a van to Arapiraca, the town with the trauma center, then clambered into the back of a pickup truck, the only conveyance available for transport to the smallest towns. Once in Piranhas, a picturesque town strung like beads up and down a couple of hillsides, Peter spontaneously contracted with eight *moto-taxi* drivers to take us to view the Xingó Dam. Martha, tan and blue-eyed, with her graying hair in a braid, laughed out loud. "This is why our families work so well together. I don't know how many moms would be so cool about seeing their kids go off on motorcycles, in Brazil!"

I've often thought an important requirement for good traveling companions is a matching tolerance for risk, discomfort, and unpredictability, which may be one reason Peter and I manage so well. Peter and I had thought through our worst nightmares before every trip abroad. But when it was just the two of us, our perception of the risks was different. Hiking across China for our honeymoon or crossing borders into small African countries on the brink of revolution didn't feel particularly risky. We had that youthful sense of invincibility. But then we had kids.

"Having kids opens you up to death in a whole new way," our birth-class instructor had said. When we were choosing where to go with newborn Skyler, we'd said no malaria; we chose Spain. When the kids were six and ten, we chose the capital city of Mozambique, close to Johannesburg and good medical care. Traveling with kids, Peter and I have both imagined our children stuck in the outback, bitten by a snake, too far from the anti-venom; or our children, without sufficient language skill or cultural understanding to stand up for themselves, being sexually abused by adults; we have both envisioned dengue fever, typhoid, cholera, malaria, hepatitis A, B, and C. And together we have redrawn our plans accordingly, but gone ahead.

Peter decided we should try to float home, from the town of Piranhas down to Penedo, one hundred miles. Few locals seemed to have done this. Asking around, he'd found Hugo, a fisherman.

Hugo was a football player of a man with a sensual mouth and soft brown eyes under thick black brows. He said we should leave at five thirty in the morning to get to Penedo well before dark. He showed up at six. The trip would take nine hours, or so he said.

Hugo clearly knew the river, "stone by stone," as we'd been told by one of his boating comrades that he would. We slid past dry, knuckled hills, river water boiling around us, Hugo's double-wide canoe with its canopy top surprisingly comfortable, even for nine. He steered the green-and-yellow craft, with its tiny propeller the size of my hand, close into steep-sided sand banks, out into the roiling middle, and around copper rocks—going wherever he needed to make maximum use of the current.

After an hour, we stopped at a settlement with an open-air restaurant and a log cabin. We wanted to hike up into the *mata branca*, the white forest, to visit the former hideout of the bandit Lampião and his gang. Following a red-dirt path over rocks, we climbed through the low scrub of small-leaved *caatinga* bushes and long-fingered cactus. We followed Valkyrie, a guide we'd picked up at the restaurant, to the site of the shooting of Lampião and ten of his gang, including his wife, Maria Bonita. I was struck by how Wild West the story was. Despite the abolition of slavery in 1888, wealthy landowners, popularly dubbed the "colonels," had continued to exploit laborers and amass fortunes in cattle and sugarcane. A white man, Lampião, had emerged as the strongest leader of the Robin Hood–like bands rebelling against them. Leaving their children in town to be raised by others, these *bandidos* and their women hid out in the hills, in places like this rocky draw, where they'd been surprised one early morning in 1938 and shot. Twenty-four had escaped, but the colonels' police carted away the severed heads of eleven others, to parade them around the region. We picked our way back down the rocky path.

Back at the restaurant, we went swimming in the cool teal of the river, waiting to be summoned for our lunch of fried fish. This spot, now inhabited by descendants of Pedro—the man who'd been sent to town to buy food for Lampião's band, who was captured, tortured, and threatened with the death of his pregnant wife into revealing the band's whereabouts—seemed idyllic. The restaurant perched high above the riverbank, surrounded by groves of mango, cashew, and papaya trees and a thriving vegetable garden, watered by a solar-powered pump that floated on the river like some strange metallic insect. Several women stitched with embroidery hoops; a couple of young men taking a break from an excavation project played dominoes under a tree. Zooming out to an aerial view of their small oasis, one would have seen miles and miles of empty hillsides, turning white in the summer as the *catingueira* lost their leaves.

I felt lulled, caught in some timeless twilight zone, though somewhere in the recesses of my mind, I knew we should probably get back on the river. When we left, we bought lumps of jellied cactus wrapped in foil to suck on as we continued our journey.

Skyler and Carson stretched out on cushions in the bow to sleep. Molly read. Bowen wove backpack pulls out of strands of plastic. I was grateful for the relaxed camaraderie of old friends. Having them there made me feel proud of the life we'd managed to fashion, of our fluency in Portuguese, of the Brazilian friends we could now share.

Floating along, we listened with a mixture of delight and distaste as Hugo imparted, and we translated, the local lore. Such as the bit about a black snake that crawled into houses at night and found the nipples of nursing women to suck out the milk.

"*É verdade.*" He nodded seriously. "It happened to my wife's mother. They killed the snake, and when they cut it open, it was full of milk." I shivered with distaste.

"Cliffs!" Skyler exclaimed a few hours later, scanning the riverbank. "Look at those cliffs. They're perfect for jumping. Can we stop? Can we?" He pointed eagerly at the sheaves of rock rising above us.

Shortly after, Hugo pulled into a *prainha*. This little beach was tucked behind a set of rocks, under a tree. I threw my legs over the canoe's side and unexpectedly dropped into water up to my ribs. It turned out the river reached depths of ninety meters in places. Skyler and Carson clambered out, shedding their shirts. Molly joined them, then Peter, then Mike, all flying off the fifteen-foot-high rocks in ecstatic shapes—tucked, splayed, arched—before splashing into the current and drifting down to a landing spot.

When we regathered at the canoe, Hugo was whacking at a brown coconut with a large machete. He drained the water, chipped off the shell, and broke the moist, white meat into pieces. He handed them to us with chunks of *rapadura*, dark brown raw cane sugar, miming one bite of coconut, one bite of sugar, and gave it the thumbs-up. "*A comida dos pescadores*"—The food of fishermen. It was fabulous— sweet, moist, and crunchy. This was hour five, theoretically more than halfway.

We'd left the rocks and swirling currents behind. The small wattle- and-daub farms in their desiccated draws were starting to be replaced by towns. Colorful houses lined the bank like a parade leading to the ubiquitous church with flanking towers. A clutch of boys tossed a volleyball over a line strung above the water.

By hour ten, we wondered if we would really make it home before dark. Remarkably, no one was restless, no one was getting irritable from claustrophobia or hunger. We'd all fallen into the soothing lull of the current. Peter and Mike examined a map, measuring distances and calculating time passed. It looked unlikely.

The rolling land was subsiding, and greening meadows swept away to the horizon, weeping green trees replaced scratchy scrub. Black cor- morants yielded to white egrets lazily grazing with cattle.

"Maybe we should pull over in Propriá, since there's a bridge there and a road, and take stock of where we are," I suggested an hour later. It was now five and would get dark at six, like the curtain closing on a play.

Propriá loomed larger, its city lights beginning to sparkle as the sky grew dark. It was by far the biggest town we'd come to and had the first bridge we'd seen in twelve hours. Hugo headed toward shore.

There was the *Maravilhosa* moored at the bank. I'd seen this rental boat, a double-decker like a Mississippi paddle wheeler, next to the ferry slip in Penedo. Before we knew it, Hugo was lifting our back- packs out of the canoe and handing them over to the crew of the larger boat. Told we'd be traveling the rest of the way with them, we obediently filed up the gangplank. There was no one on board but the crew and their kids. They'd tow Hugo's canoe behind. Inside, they put out rolls and cheese, a thermos of sweet, black coffee, and beer. "Just the ticket," as my father would have said. Our kids ran up to the top deck to watch as we passed under the bridge, then retired below decks to the hammock room to play Uno. The rest of us stayed above, surveying the oily dark river under a full moon.

"My son said, 'It's the woman and boy from capoeira!'" Anterior, the riverboat captain, told me in Portuguese. Our capoeira group had given a demonstration at this boy's school in Penedo, and, as usual, Skyler and I were hard to forget.

We slowly zigzagged our way downriver. "How do you know where to go?" I asked the captain.

"*Prática*," he said. Practice? They were steering this huge boat, around shifting sandbars in the dark, from memory?

Peter, Mike, Martha, and I stood at the top rail, faces to the wind, and peered lazily into the dark water and shadows of overhanging trees. I marveled at the fortuitous turn of events and how often this kind of thing happened to us. A month earlier, we'd taken a similar motorized covered canoe to the "*foz*," the mouth of the Rio São Francisco, where it emptied into the Atlantic. There, the canoe's motor had broken down out at the ocean, and it looked like we'd get home long after dark; we'd been saved that time by a high-tech catamaran and had been invited to join their gourmet buffet on deck. It felt like we'd jumped from backwoods Mississippi to the Riviera.

The trip to Penedo took not nine but thirteen hours. We gratefully lumbered down the gangplank and headed for an outdoor restaurant, hungry but pleased by our adventure.

There are lots of ways to travel. My mother prefers advance planning and lots of preparatory reading. My father preferred wandering on whim. There's something to be said for both. But either way, things inevitably go awry, especially when traveling off the beaten path. It helps to believe—believe things will turn out all right. I think that changes not only one's perception of the experience but maybe also what actually happens. One of our Penedo acquaintances had introduced us to a visiting friend, an Uruguayan professor teaching in the United States. He'd said he comes to Brazil to write because he finds there's more inspiration in the unpredictable. I understand that. There's something magical in not knowing. We've been surprised and delighted by what we've pulled out of the hat.

24

Holidays Unraveling

WE ROLLED INTO Christmas with a bang, starting the night of December 21. First, Brooke's mom called from the States to let us know that Brooke had missed the first of her string of four flights and would therefore arrive not thirty *minutes* away in Maceió, the original plan, but ten *hours* away in Salvador. (We had already moved into the rented beach house in Praia do Francês to be closer to Maceió, putting us now farther away from Salvador than we would have been if we'd stayed in Penedo.) Next, the power in our rental house went out (taking with it the air conditioning, in the middle of Brazil's steamy summer), and then the vomiting began—three kids, six times by morning.

By the next day, the power had returned and the kids' vomiting had mostly stopped. We never figured out what had caused it. They spent the day lounging in the living room, plowing through Christmas presents from my mother, DVDs transported by our friends—*Jurassic Park, Forrest Gump*. We decided to break them out early. Meanwhile, I tried to figure out how to meet Brooke at the airport in Salvador. She would be arriving the following night at midnight. I felt it would be too much to expect a high school student to arrive in a huge foreign city where she didn't speak the local language and then string together buses, vans, and ferries to make her way to a small town three states away on her own. After fruitless hours at the Internet café trying to book seats on the bus, I reluctantly dug my phone out of my straw bag and dialed the station. I dreaded making arrangements over the phone in another language, but this time I was spared. My phone server was down. Where was this world at our fingertips?

I trudged back to the rental house in the blazing sun, no further toward picking up Brooke.

Then one of those surprising things that happens in Brazil happened. Amid all the technological malfunctions, businesses closing early, and people being out, Peter managed, in about fifteen minutes, to hire a taxi. It was like finding a taxi in our small Montana town to drive us 1,200 miles to Seattle and back, nonstop, on Christmas Eve. At home, that would never happen.

Fifteen minutes after Molly and I climbed into the car, the driver and his pal announced they'd never been to Salvador, or in fact to the state of Bahia. We would eventually discover, as we wandered blindly through highway interchanges, that they had no map. I'd considered phoning Peter with their license plate number, in case we mysteriously disappeared into one of the "love" motels out in the middle of nowhere with names like Le Plaisir, Eros, and Korpus. But as time passed, I began to relax.

In fact, I must have dozed because I jerked awake as the car lurched to a halt and opened my eyes to see that we were backing up an exit ramp in the dark. We just made it back to the highway before another car shot down the ramp. Two U-turns later, it turned out that had been the right exit after all, and we found ourselves shunted onto a four-lane highway. As we cruised along in the left lane, ignoring the car behind us flashing its high beams, it occurred to me that maybe our driver had never driven on a four-lane road.

Nevertheless, we made it to the airport before Brooke appeared out of customs, hit the Subway in the food court, then found our driver in the airport parking garage, asleep. Remarkably, we arrived in Penedo at our front door at 8:00 AM on Christmas Eve. The trip cost about $800, which Brooke's parents gladly reimbursed.

Peter and I threw our feet out of bed. "Is someone throwing up?" he whispered. I opened the door to see Skyler precariously perched on Molly's shoulders in stifled hysterics at the end of the hall. "Go away. Go back to bed," they hissed.

"You can't come out!" they shouted an hour later when Peter tried to get up to go to the bathroom. It sounded now as though all five kids were awake.

"Okay, we're ready!"

We emerged from our refrigerated cell into the startling heat and bright whiteness of the hallway. Snowflakes dangled from the ceiling.

Hundreds of pieces of cut-up white paper were strewn around the floor. Molly cranked the tunes on her computer: "Rock around the Christmas Tree" and "Baby, It's Cold Outside." We sang along with Bing Crosby.

"Want to trim my tree?" I batted my lashes at Peter. Finally, it felt like Christmas.

Just as we began to open presents, we heard a shout through the front door. "*Petair!*" Dalan was leaning up against the side of the house. "*Minha mãe está morrendo*"—his mother was dying in Maceió. Could he borrow some money to go see her? As Peter gave him the hundred *reais*, he said, "Dalan, *você precisa trabalhar*"—work to make some money. Dalan explained shyly that he couldn't read. He'd dropped out of school after second grade.

"Oh, and by the way," he said as he left, "Junior is in jail. He knifed a man."

By midafternoon, we managed to straggle out into the heat and head down to the river for a family game of soccer. We aimed for the *campo*, the field of lumpy dirt and sad grass where the grown men played. As we passed their houses, Ricardo and Victor joined the group.

I loved these games of family soccer. They were the only time I played. Aniete and Gel came along. They hadn't been able to go home for Christmas because no buses ran to the country that day, and Aniete declined to take the longer vacation we'd offered. They found it amusing that we were all going to play, even Martha and I, being not only women but also old when it came to Brazilian sports.

Afterward, dusty and sweaty from a hard hour of running after the ball, we waded through a lagoon to get to the river, the sun disappearing fast behind the ridge across the São Francisco. Gel and Aniete stood, feet in the water, while the rest of us peeled down to swimsuits or underwear and drifted out into the current. Neither one of them knew how to swim.

The bottom was sandy, the water soft. This was the first time we'd swum in the river here, leery of the sewage dump upstream. Keeping my mouth above water, I slipped along in the cool dark, feeling like an otter, dark wet head skimming along the surface.

We pulled on our rumpled clothes and began the trek back up the ridge. Skyler and I fell behind.

"It just doesn't feel like Christmas," he said a little wistfully.

He'd had a hard day. I wondered if part of it was because since Brooke's arrival, his friend Carson had shifted to the older kids, Molly, Brooke, and Bowen, who liked to just lie around and talk. Lying around and talking was the last thing Skyler wanted to do when you could climb trees and jump off walls.

It reminded me of myself at the same age, living in Cairo and receiving handwritten letters from friends at home. Somewhere during that year and a half of middle school, the letters changed. Suddenly my friends wrote about kissing boys. I'd felt bewildered, left behind.

We walked along in silence. "I know," I ventured. "This does feel weird; all wrong."

Despite the businesses in the *baixa* festooned in white lights, and the cashiers at Ki-Barato in red Santa hats, it was hard for us Northerners, used to snow and cold and Santa arriving in a sleigh, to wrap our minds around this hot, sweaty, fans-whirring, people-asleep-in-hammocks day.

"Still," I reminded him, "it was pretty fun, all the same." I put my arm around him. "There will be lots of other Christmases. This one is just different."

25

New Year's Eve in Salvador

AFTER A FULL DAY of van and bus rides, the nine of us made it to Salvador, checked into the Barra Guest Hostel, and headed up to the Pelourinho, the historic neighborhood. We were in search of Afro-Brazilian music. The place was rocking. The sounds of drums and electric guitar ricocheted down narrow, stony streets. There were lots of talking hips and rapidly shuffling samba feet, hundreds of witty and flirtatious conversations, all spoken through the pelvis. We said the kids could wander around as long as they stuck together. I was happy just to sit and survey the scene. I had all of our credit cards, cash, and iPods and was leery of the tight crowd. From our vantage point at one end of the Terreiro de Jesus plaza, we heard several competing bands.

Skyler came running back with Carson. "Watch the guys in the back," he said excitedly, pointing to ten or twelve guys with big round drums threading through the crowd on the right. In the back, the biggest red, yellow, and green striped drum was flipped up into the air above the drummer's head each time before he hit it. I was entranced, but I could feel my mind being pulled away. Something was happening over on the left.

Molly and Brooke suddenly appeared out of the crowd. Molly was clearly flustered. The story poured out of her.

"I didn't think I would be that scared. But it was scary."

Big breath.

"But I'm okay. I'm okay."

She was stoically holding back tears.

"This boy, he wasn't very old, maybe like Skyler's age? He was hanging out with us—you know, 'Hey, *amigas*.'" She dropped into one hip in a casual, hanging-out way. "Then he just grabbed my necklace and ripped it off!"

For her sixteenth birthday, my mother had given her a gold chain with a teardrop pendant of small rubies.

"I grabbed his arm and was yelling, '*Cadê, cadê?*'"—Where is it?

Really, in Portuguese! I was impressed. I didn't think my mind would have jumped to a foreign language in an emergency.

"You were like a ninja," Brooke said excitedly.

"I was hanging onto him so hard, I think I really wanted to hurt him." Molly's mind was replaying the scene. "I've never felt like that before."

She seemed a little alarmed.

"Then this woman found it on the ground and gave it back to me. People were so nice and helpful. The boy was scared. Can you hold these?" she asked me as she pulled her crystal studs out of her ears. "I don't want to wear them."

It was clearly time to leave.

"I never thought it would be *that* scary," Molly mused as we searched for a taxi. "I always thought I'd just give over my cell phone or whatever."

We squeezed five into a car, Molly squished in between Skyler and me.

"I hope they didn't hurt the boy," she said, her voice fading. She sounded exhausted.

As I sank back into the cushioned seat, my own complicated net of emotions started to surface: pride in my ninja daughter, relief that nothing worse had happened, and the oddly analytical parenting thought that it was good to have a few scary things happen—as long as there was no lasting harm—to help your children brace for the less nurturing parts of the world.

Northeastern Brazilians are known for their practice of Candomblé, a religion brought by the slaves that blends pantheistic beliefs from Africa with Catholicism. When Peter and I had scored our date in Salvador by ourselves three months before, we'd hired a guide to take us to a Candomblé ceremony, some of which were now open to tourists.

Our guide, Luis, was a slender, balding man, wearing white pants and a pressed button-down shirt. He led us to a van full of other tourists, which would take us, after many stops to ask directions, to a house in a hilly, dirt-road neighborhood, about thirty minutes away. I couldn't tell if someone lived there or if it was used only for Candomblé.

That night, they would be invoking Logun Ede, one of many *orixás*, or ancestors with connections to the spirit world. People arrived, dressed in blue and yellow, the colors of this particular *orixá*. The men wore collarless African tunics and brimless caps, the women loose blouses, ankle-length ballooning hoop skirts, and wrapped headscarves—Aunt Jemima, of American-syrup fame, in brocade. Everyone shone, with sequins, satin, and borders of lace.

Inside a large room, people in everyday clothes sat in white plastic chairs set in rows at either end—women to the right, men to the left. Peter and I seated ourselves at opposite ends of the room. Leaves were strewn over the concrete floor. Fluorescent lights gave the room a bright, flat light that seemed a little surreal under the circumstance.

Three men entered and took their places behind the drums. The resounding, repetitive beat began. A stocky man sang out, and the people in the chairs responded. The others, dressed in their Candomblé clothes, began a circular dance that would go on for the next hour, step-touching in unison. They, too, sang. Each song seemed to have its special hand gestures, gestures Peter and I had seen many years before at a durbar, a gathering for chiefs, in Ghana, West Africa: a faint wave with the right hand, then with the left; stacked fists paddling right then left, all floating, dreamy.

Seamlessly, the trances began. Hands behind the back, knees buckling, a person would double over, emitting a groaning shout or several quick yips. Some shook. Those not in trance took care of them, placing a gentle hand on a shoulder, helping them to rise. All of a sudden, the whole group filed out through gold curtains into a long back hallway. The drummers took a break. Platters of savories and sweets and plastic cups of soda pop appeared, passed by some of the dancers who had just been in trance minutes before.

When the break was over, the drums started up, faster now, and out of the back hall came one man, then two, their shirts gone, their eyes closed. They danced with renewed energy, wildly spinning, step-cross-jump, chests pumping. The onlookers clapped, faster and faster, driving the dancers. The curtains parted, and Oxum, the mother of Logun Ede, appeared, several of her, in fact, in ballooning skirts and armbands of glittering gold. Sparkling tiaras sat atop their gold head wraps; veils of beads hid their faces.

That was when the chic white woman in patent-leather sandals and a strapless hot-pink top slipped out of the chair next to mine and collapsed at my feet. The young Brazilian woman on my other side looked dismayed, but she caught the white woman's Gucci purse as she fell. The regulars looked bemused. They shook the fallen woman's shoulders and cleared strands of hair from her face, but she didn't come to. She was rolled onto her stomach and covered from head to foot with a long white lace cloth. She began to vibrate and shake, pelvis bouncing off the ground. Then they lifted her up and carted her off to the back room. I thought she was a tourist like me, but I never saw her again.

Afterward, as Peter and I trudged back up the festooned driveway, I told him about the woman next to me going into a trance.

"Luis did, too," he told me. "He kind of fell back into my lap, then doubled over. They took him into the back room."

As we turned into the dirt street, Luis was there. Peter put a hand on his shoulder.

"How're you doing?"

"I'm fine. I'm fine," he said in his quick, efficient manner.

It was eleven thirty at night. People murmured quietly as the van picked its way over the ruts and through the potholes of the darkened neighborhood. I tried to sort out where we'd been—not so much geographically, but psychically. It was as though the rational bolts of my mind had been loosened, and now I wasn't quite sure how to piece it back together again.

On our return to Salvador in December, Adams, the reception-ist at the Barra Guest Hostel, found a guide for us to see another Candomblé ceremony. As a child of our rational, logical, scientific, everything-is-explicable Western world, I find I never tire of seeing trance ceremonies. Here in Brazil would be the fourth time, after

Ghana and Indonesia, that I'd sit mesmerized, initially trying to explain what happened to these transformed people—where they "went"—and finally giving up. This time, we had the Kadas-Newells, Brooke, Molly, and Skyler in tow, and, to our surprise, the guide turned out to be Luis.

"This will be a little different from what you saw last time," he told us confidentially. "It's a family ceremony. There will probably be more of us than them. They will be evoking Exu, the *orixá* of the street."

He was right. As before, the van took us to the outskirts of Salvador and wound through dark dirt streets before stopping outside a house. Not just any house: a burned-black life-size statue of a two-legged being holding a pitchfork stood outside. We filed through a door into a courtyard, where we were each turned in a circle by a man dangling an incense burner.

As before, leaves were strewn over the floor inside the ceremonial room. The ceremony was already in progress, and the thundering pulse of three drummers filled the space. That's where the similarities ended. This time, there was no separation of men and women, and only two participants went into trance. When one reappeared, he had been dressed in red brocade pantaloons, and his bare torso was wrapped in silver fabric tied in large bows in the back, like a Christmas package.

"Dressed like the Portuguese colonists," Luis told us.

On his head, he wore a black felt hat pierced with a feather and studded with teeth and cowry shells. Set at a rakish angle, it seemed in keeping with his strutting manner, the cigar he was smoking, and the cane he twirled like a Broadway dandy.

"Exu is open, like the street," Luis explained. "He leads the way to opportunities. He's free. He can smoke and drink."

Sweeping across the space with his eyes closed, he stopped quite miraculously two-inches from the stairs leading out of the room. He whipped up to a seated woman, pulled her out of her chair, kissed her on both cheeks, and proceeded right down the line until he'd kissed all of us, with his eyes closed. This was just the beginning.

Our dandy seemed to be methodically ticking through a list. He proceeded to go down the line of onlookers again, beckoning us to stand, sweeping a sheaf of leaves down our bodies top to bottom, then, taking hold of our pinky fingers, he gave a firm downward jerk. I wondered if the kids would want to laugh, but they didn't. Molly, with her dancer's elegance, stood tall and solemn while she was cleansed, front, side, and back. Sprinkling gunpowder in the center of the floor, the dandy lit it on fire, creating a burst of sparking flame. Circus antics for the tourists? He smudged baby powder crosses on our chests and the backs of our necks and poured cologne into the palms of our hands, all with his eyes closed. Plastic cups of Fanta, guarana, and beer were passed, and then finally a basket for donations. The ceremony was over.

Adams, who had come with us, was puzzled. A Candomblé practitioner himself, he said he'd never seen a family ceremony opened to the public.

"Well, maybe it serves everyone," Peter surmised. "We want to see what they do, and they get some money to support their ceremony."

"Yeah, but it seems as though it might be an intimate sort of act," I countered.

"I know. I wonder if it makes it harder to go into trance if you have all those people watching," Molly mused.

"I thought it was interesting watching the watchers," Mike said. "You could see some were buying into it more than others."

The conversation went on. What part of it was African, what part Christian? Had they really been in trance, or hadn't they? Had it been authentic or faked? I wondered why that mattered so much—why it was so important to at least some of us to feel we'd seen the real thing, not just something trumped up for tourists. I've realized that one reason I travel is to feel connected to people unlike myself, so I'm grateful when they let me in, in any way at all. Performances meant for tourists almost feel like a way to keep you out, to be sure you see only the external trappings, while the heart remains hidden.

The next day in the breakfast line, Adams, a white headband pulling back his voluminous afro, showed me the cowry armband hidden under the sleeve of his polo shirt.

"I don' tell my parents I do this. They are Catholic. People say Candomblé is not good. But then you go to a ceremony, and you see them there, those same people who just criticized it. It's racism, you know." Like capoeira, Candomblé was still associated with blacks, even though people of many other races were becoming practitioners.

I was told there were Candomblé ceremonies in our town, in Penedo. I was curious as to whether they were similar to the ones we'd seen, but I felt hesitant to ask to watch one. In Salvador, they'd been embraced as part of the Afro-Brazilian culture that, along with capoeira, was now being marketed to tourists. In Penedo, when I'd mentioned Candomblé, people seemed a little embarrassed. Their embarrassment made me feel like a voyeur.

We were about to head into the Amazon, where Peter was hoping to meet people from the Yanomami tribe. I imagined if we could, it would be with a guide. Would what we saw be "real" then? I supposed this was part of what drew me to live in places rather than just visit, to find out what they were really like. But even then, a year was not enough.

"We're not like other hostels, you know." Russell, the owner of the Barra Guest Hostel, was saying in his still-strong English accent. "We can't be. It's not enough to offer just a bed-and-breakfast these days. So we offer a bit more: a bit of fun, don't you know."

It was New Year's Eve, and our hostel was putting on a dinner. I'd been last in line for the shower, so by the time I made it downstairs, Molly and Brooke were ensconced with a couple of rangy Australians. I knew Molly had been self-conscious about being younger than all the other young people, so I wondered how old she was tonight.

"Mom, I said I was seventeen. It was just easier. Okay? I just want us all to be on the same page." At sixteen, she could easily pass for twenty, so I thought seventeen was quite conservative.

"Mom, Brooke and I just split a *caipirinha*. Is that okay?" She was heady with excitement.

By now, the tunes were cranked, a mixture of international pop and some American oldies, Men at Work, The Police. The Argentinean girls were trying to coax the Argentinean guys into dancing. Peter and I took a couple of turns. It struck me that this was one of the best New Year's Eves I'd had in a long time. But Skyler was sad. The Kadas-

Newells had left earlier in the day, starting the multi-flight journey home. Skyler had wanted to go, too.

At 10:00 PM, the music stopped and everyone prepared to head down to the beach, to the big sound stage. It was rumored Ivete Sangalo, Brazilian pop star and local darling, would be playing. Skyler didn't want to go, so he and I stayed behind. Peter and the girls left with the roving party, and the hostel dropped into quiet, as though someone had flipped a switch.

I sat on the bunk bed with Skyler. He didn't want to talk. I lay down and fell asleep, until I felt someone shaking me.

"Mom, Mom, were you sleeping? Can we play a game and then go to the beach?"

Skyler's anguish at losing his friend seemed to have passed. We played a couple of games of dominoes and then headed out at 11:00 PM. Everyone was walking toward the water. By the time we turned onto the shoreline drive, the street was thick with people, all in traditional New Year's Eve white. Being small and quick, Skyler was good at finding the cracks in the crowd. I hung on to the back of his shirt.

"*Cuidado,*" several women said to me as we passed. "Be careful."

Skyler managed to sneak us right up to the lip of the stage. The banks of speakers throbbed in our throats. Five feet above us, a man in tight jeans, long dreads, and a knit Rasta hat was shouting into a mic, his foot stomping, pelvis grinding, one hand pumping the air. TV cameras projected the scene onto large screens. Despite being at the center of the sound vortex, I couldn't make out a word, but the people around us were singing; as always, they knew every song. They began to jump, both arms in unison, slapping the air above their heads. Skyler was jumping, too. The camera zoomed down. Skyler was waving, giving the cameraman the thumb-and-pinky-finger sign, *hang loose.* Now everyone's arms were overhead, waving side to side to the beat.

Bidda, badda, badda, boom. Fireworks burst all around us. It was midnight. We'd never seen so many, so many kinds, all at once. Gold bursts of weeping willow dissolved into sparkling cauliflower florets; a silver ball split into dangling earrings. The woman next to me pulled me into a jubilant hug and kissed me on both cheeks.

Around 1:00 AM, Skyler and I began to wend our way back. We looked down at the beach as we passed. People were in the water in their clothes. A boney, nearly naked man was standing on a rock, awash in white waves. He punched triumphant fists at the dark sky. Made it through another year!

And we, I thought, *have made it almost halfway through ours.*

26

Home

AFTER SIX MONTHS I am still struggling with:

- watching Skyler struggle.
- how to, politely, ask the rafts of kids to leave our house so we can have a little alone time as a family.
- how to tactfully train them not to turn on every piece of electronic equipment in our house as they flow through.
- what I might do to be helpful in this town.

But I have learned:

- more of the small words, the *ehta*s and *neh*s, those expressive grunts that make you sound like a local.
- to get the phone numbers of particular van drivers to reserve seats for trips to the coast.
- to understand every fifth word when Bentinho is speaking.
- to drop to the floor to dodge kicks in the capoeira *roda*.
- that in the summer, it's best to get up at five, or stay at home until late afternoon to beat the heat.
- that there are more kinds of mangos than I'd ever imagined: *rosa, vermelho, commun, espada, tommy, maria . . .*
- that cynical Zeca has a soft heart.
- that Eeyore-like Giovanni can be playful and lively.
- that hesitant Aniete can be silly and coquettish.
- that I am beginning to call this place home.

PART III: *Widening the Circle*

JANUARY, FEBRUARY

27

The Dividing Line

THE DAY AFTER we got back to Penedo, Peter flung some groceries through the front door and panted, "I'm going back down to the *baixa*, to see if I can do something for Junior."

Peter's soccer buddy had been in jail for over a week. Dalan said Junior was waiting for the judge's decision, and the decision had been delayed because the judge was on vacation.

"What are you trying to do?" I asked when Peter clanged back through the front door a few hours later.

"Find out his last name."

Peter had found Dalan at Gordo's Lanchonete, and he knew the name but, being unable to read or write, couldn't tell Peter how to spell it. Peter walked a few blocks farther down and ran into some of the guys at the soccer field. The word was out.

"*Você vai pegar Junior*"—You're going to get Junior out of jail.

Peter explained he wanted to hire a lawyer, but he needed Junior's last name. They didn't know it. They offered to take him to Junior's mom.

Peter stood outside the small yellow box where she lived. Junior's sister came to the door, wrote out their last name, and invited Peter in. Built like a block and missing a few front teeth, Junior's mother ran a bar, inside her house.

Earlier in the day, Peter had read me an email from Zeca, whom he'd enlisted to check into Junior's case along with Zeca's dad, a retired criminal lawyer who knew the judge. "It doesn't look good," Zeca had written. "In the police file, it says it wasn't just a bar fight. It says he wanted to kill the man."

I remembered watching Junior deftly bend the soccer ball into the goal at one of Peter's games. After that, he'd graciously dropped out to let another player play and had gone to sit in the stands with his young wife and baby daughter, happily nosing his face into hers.

Peter had latched onto Junior after it became clear he was by far the most talented with his feet. Junior had taken Peter under his wing, always choosing him for his team, giving him tips, picking him to take the penalty shots, teaching him to dance the victory dance.

And now this. Would the real Junior please stand up? I guessed he was all these things: the tender father, the patient coach, the man curious enough to befriend a foreigner, and the drunken brawler.

I wondered what had really happened, what the future held for Junior, his wife, and six-month-old Bianca. Where was the dividing line that separated quick-footed, fun-loving Junior from quick-footed, fun-loving Marcelo, our friend who moved from the Penedo soccer team to Barcelona to coaching teams in Saudi Arabia and Dubai? I realized I didn't know much about Marcelo's background, what class he'd come from. My impression was that the professional Brazilian *futebol* leagues were not combing the poorer neighborhoods to fill their ranks. Too bad. There was a lot of talent there.

28

Balance and Joy

MY BIRTHDAY IS in January. I'll be turning fifty-three. I'd quit my full-time job as a university professor when I turned fifty, looking for more time at home with Molly and Skyler and time to promote my dance company, Headwaters. I'd been excited about this new chapter, though nervous, too, knowing it could throw our family into financial disarray. While I gained flexibility in my schedule, I didn't gain time. I was my own worst taskmaster, each week falling short of my oversized list of things to do.

Before the Kadas-Newells had left us in Salvador, Martha had initiated a New Year's activity for our families that involved spreading cards with words printed on them facedown on a table and asking each of us to pick two. We had the option to put the cards back if we didn't like them. My words could not have been more apropos.

Balance was the first. That was part of what I had been hoping to find in Brazil and what I couldn't seem to hang on to in the United States. *Joy* was the second—another thing I found easily disappeared into the maw of work at home but seemed to be exuded here by every boom-box-jiving, capoeira-flipping, surf-diving, market-chatting, *cachaça*-drinking, *futbol*-kicking Brazilian. Interestingly, the only word that got returned to the pile, and repeatedly, by several different people, old and young, was *responsibility*. That's one we took seriously in the States, one we'd been telling our kids more about lately. ("If you want to drive a car, it comes with responsibilities . . .") It was a word that, by our standards, Brazilians were a little more relaxed about. The van might fill, bumping your carefully made reservation; class might start an hour late; the repairman might never show up.

I was pleased with my picks. *Balance* and *joy* would be great gifts for turning fifty-three. I immediately had a chance to practice hanging on to them.

While in Salvador for New Years, I'd received an email from the U.S. government department that administers the grants that my dance company receives, called Grants.gov. It said I needed to go online and change my dance company's password before it expired, in the next seven days. I didn't have the list of numbers—the MPIN, TPIN, CAGE, NAIC, SIC, and DUNS numbers—that might be required to do this with me in Salvador. When I got home to Penedo, I'd have four days left. Judging from past experience, this would be cutting it close. When we got back to Penedo, I tried to log on. The error message told me my username didn't exist. When I clicked on *I forgot my username*, I got an email giving me the same nonexistent username. And so it went. I emailed support. No one answered.

"What happens if your password expires?" Peter asked, standing behind me in the garden room as I continued to hit the same keys over and over, trying to physically force the correct window on my computer to open.

"I don't know. I've never let it happen."

I tried again the next day. Nothing had changed. No one had responded to my questions, and then our Internet went down. Balance, joy. The day after this, we would be leaving for Pontal to stay at Ada's *pousada* and celebrate my birthday. There, the Internet would be sketchy at best. I bought extra cell phone time in case I had to call the United States, and then, amazingly for me, I decided to stop worrying.

On the morning of my birthday, I went down to the *baixa* to try my luck at the ATMs and reserve seats on a van for the kids and myself, a process that turned into the usual maze of misinformation and misunderstandings. I felt as though I were caught in an M.C. Escher painting, the one where the stairs lead up, down, and nowhere all at once, rather like my online username nightmare.

Five hours later, we managed to climb into a van. I should have found this trying, but in fact, it had been nice just to hang out and chat with the kids while we waited. Maybe I was learning to channel Brazilian patience. A patience one could call "resignation" or, with a better spin, an ability to enjoy oneself no matter what.

The van trip took longer than usual. We detoured through small villages. At Peba, we drove through town and right out onto the hard-sand beach, circling back to the highway through the high tide. When we got to Pontal, Ada was waiting. Cigarette in hand, she announced in her whiskey voice that our usual bungalow was ready. She'd left a small bouquet of hibiscus and bougainvillea on the table, for me.

While the kids changed into suits, grabbed the boogie board and flippers, and headed to the beach, I borrowed the modem from Ada and checked to see if "support" had contacted me. They hadn't. Okay, time to call. In Brazil, one had to buy minutes on cell phones, so it tended to run out. I'd bought the biggest increment I could, but as soon as the message came on—"your wait will be at least three minutes"—I knew it was going to be a gamble. I could envision the phone dying as the support-staff person was asking, "May I have your DUNS number?" Thirty-five dollars spent for nothing. I left a message, "I'm in Brazil . . ." and headed to the beach. Balance, joy.

While I was grappling with my phone situation, Skyler had shown up panting.

"Mom, the tide's high, but you know that empty lot, how there's a wall on the other side? You can kind of go along this little ledge, then climb the next wall and walk along the top, and you'll get to where there's still beach. Okay? Bye," and he'd ducked back out under the veranda roof and disappeared.

When I got to the first wall, I looked over and down the other side. There was the little ledge, a half inch wide. White-fingered waves hurled themselves hungrily against it. Was that where they'd gone? I looked down the beach. No one. The waves, the wall? I looked uneasily out to sea.

I remembered we'd seen a rickety gate in a sand dune farther down. I crossed back through the empty lot and circled around through town.

Pontal do Coruripe is a fishing village on a point that sticks out into the Atlantic Ocean, forming one end of a large bay. Its sweaty, slow pace makes Penedo feel like Manhattan. TV screens flicker behind sheets hung over open doors, revealing inhabitants asleep in their chairs. Birds hop lackadaisically in cages suspended over front verandas. Hole-in-the-wall shops sell biscuits, warm Coke, and *ouricuri*, the palm-frond handicrafts this village is famous for.

I ended up on a road where I'd never been, paralleling the beach. A large lagoon full of mangrove bushes ran along my left. The inhabitants of a fancy walled house on the right had dug holes in the concrete and planted spiky agave plants in the middle of the sidewalk. At home, one can't willfully block the sidewalk. At home, if you don't shovel the snow by ten in the morning to clear the passage, you can be fined. I shifted into the street.

I suspected the rickety gate was attached to Pousada Paradiso, so I asked permission to thread through its stucco bungalows. Standing at the flimsy gate wedged open in drifting sand, I looked out at the vastness of ocean then down the beach.

There they were, Skyler, Molly, and Brooke, three ecstatic figures jumping the waves, freeze-frames caught in silhouette against the shimmering water. I felt a flush of relief. Except for them, the great curve of beach was empty. Palm groves waved in the breeze. It was suddenly looking good: fifty-three, on a deserted Brazilian beach with happily cavorting kids, government password or no.

We ambled back hours later as the sun disappeared behind the trees. Peter, who'd stayed behind in Penedo to continue his research on a new book proposal, had arrived. Ada had set dinner under the arbor on the back patio, clay dishes of sweet sautéed vegetables, garlic beans, tomatoes with basil, and steamed dorado. Then came the mango cream and then the surprise, a chocolate cake with fresh strawberries. Peter must have called ahead. I was wearing my birthday presents from the kids, gold flip-flops and sparkly dangling earrings. I was feeling more Brazilian by the day.

Peter and Ada were talking about whether the villagers were going to succeed in thwarting the state's effort to put in a massive shipyard. Oil had been discovered seventy miles off the coast, and the government wanted a shipyard to service the offshore rigs. They'd offered each fishing family one hundred *reais* a month to go along with the plan, though they hadn't made it clear how long they'd continue to pay. At first, the fishermen had thought that sounded good, but then they'd begun to wonder how it might affect the fisheries and had started to organize against it.

As I listened quietly, my eyes began to close. Excusing myself, I ducked under the bamboo chimes and unlocked the door of our bungalow. I kicked off my new flip-flops. The stone floor felt cool under my sandy feet. I turned on the fan, crept under the diaphanous mosquito netting, and collapsed into bed. It had been a good day.

The next morning, the kids once again headed to the beach, and I logged on to Grants.gov. Two days to go. My "nonexistent" username worked! My pleas for help had been heard. I headed out to the beach. Balance and joy. I thought the fifties were going to be fine.

29

Walking Tall

SKYLER HAD HAD one rocky day after Carson and Bowen left, but he seemed notably better than he had been for the previous six months, as though he'd suddenly made a jump in the journey toward adulthood. He seemed to be handling things that would have sent him into a downward spiral two months before with philosophical equanimity.

After two days at Pontal, we moved on to Maceió, to spend a couple of days before putting Brooke on the plane back to the States. As soon as we arrived, she, Skyler, and Molly donned their suits and ran for Jatiúca Beach to go surfing. Disraelle, our favorite instructor, went out with Brooke, as it was her first time. Skyler ended up with Disraelle's wife, who forgot her flippers, swallowed a lot of water, and bailed before Skyler even made it out to where he could wait for waves. My heart sank as I watched this from my rented beach chair.

Skyler was also on the squirrely, smaller board, the one that was harder to control. He only got up once, but on the difficult board and on his own. The girls came in. He stayed out. *One more good ride, just one more*, I prayed to myself. I could see this was going to take a while. I dug my heels into the sand. My stamina for handling Skyler's downturns was definitely diminishing.

A group of Brazilian tourists from Amazonas asked about Skyler, as he flipped over time and again. *"Muita resistência"*—A lot of resilience, they said.

As I looked out at the incredible turquoise-green water and watched my boy miss wave after wave, I began to wonder about obsession— when it's helpful, when it's not. I supposed the Steve Jobses of the world had to have some degree of obsessiveness to bring their dreams to fruition. But when did it become self-destructive? How could we help Skyler navigate that line?

He finally came in. I said I'd seen him hanging upside down, under the water, feet hooked on top of the board, quite a few times, sometimes for a long time.

"I know," he said. "I was so pissed, I thought I should just hang upside down and chill out. But I like that board."

"You do?" I was surprised. "It's so difficult."

"I know, but did you see, I got up on it once, all by myself, and it's cool. I wasn't very steady, but it's really quick. You can move it all around."

This was definitely not the boy we'd known a few months before. The boy who was convinced, after he'd split his head, that he couldn't do anything. The next day, he asked if he could just rent a board, no lessons. The proprietor looked at him and advised him to go to the part of the beach with smaller waves.

"No, I want to go there," he replied.

"That's where the big waves are," I said uneasily.

"I know."

He hitched that same squirrely board under his arm and marched into the breaking waves. Paddling out, belly down, his already slight figure disappeared behind the swells. But then he reappeared, sitting upright on his board; out with the big guys, all rising and sinking on the building waves, face to the horizon, waiting. He got up several times in the next hour, not long rides, but solidly on his feet.

I felt tremendous pride. Not because Skyler was learning to surf, but because Skyler seemed to be walking out of the fire. Walking tall.

30

Surprising Finds

JANUARY. This was summer break for the students at Imaculada. I'd thought this would have been welcome news for Skyler, but despite this, the old misery was creeping back in: "Why can't we go back home?" he asked. "I just feel bad. I don't know why. Why am I like this? It's me. I just feel pissed off all the time." I wished I had an answer, but I was feeling as confused about his moodiness as he was.

When we'd made our hanging mobile of wishes for the year back home in the States, everyone had written, *Go up the Amazon.*

That would be the focus of our summer break and carrot enough, I hoped, to pull us through the next couple of months. I'd been developing the plan for some time. We would be making our now well-worn trek southwest to Salvador. There we'd catch a flight to Brasilia—the nation's capital—nine hundred miles away. From Brasilia, we'd take one more flight, the remaining two thousand miles, to Manaus—the capital of the state of Amazonas. This would be like scooping down from Boston to Nashville and back up to Seattle. After a few days in Manaus, we would take a boat for a full day upriver to the small town of Tefé, where we'd spend the night before catching a smaller boat to Mamirauá, the first sustainable development reserve in Amazonas. Our time at Mamirauá would be Part I, the viewing-flora-and-fauna part. Part II would involve catching a small plane in Tefé to São Gabriel da Cachoeira, still in the state of Amazonas, but near the Venezuelan border and a number of Yanomami villages, where we would see if we could meet any of this elusive tribe. This part was still up in the air.

We were on the second leg of our journey, our flight to Brasilia, when our baggage began to disintegrate. We'd each arrived in Brazil with one enormous duffel bag and a computer case—not good luggage for jungle trekking. Peter had combed the shops in Penedo and zeroed in on what seemed the most promising backpacks. We'd bought three. Two were now coming to pieces before our eyes. You can't really check baggage with the compartments gaping open and your underwear leaking out. We found a storage locker at the Brasilia airport and poured out the contents of our bags.

At one of Brasilia's slick multistory malls, we picked up two real camping packs. I wasn't surprised that these were such rare items, at least in Northeastern Brazil. I just couldn't picture Brazilians, at least the ones we knew, quietly hiking for miles into an isolated area to commune with nature. Where were the boomer cars, the firecrackers, the people, the vendors, the good times? At the mall, we also found a soccer ball (in orange, Skyler's favorite color) and English-language books. We immediately stocked up on more than we could comfortably carry.

I'd opted for the twelve-hour layover in Brazil's capital because I was curious about its architecture. A nineteenth-century Italian saint, Dom Bosco, had prophesied that a new civilization would grow up on this spot, between the fifteenth and twentieth parallels. In the 1950s, the Brazilians, who had been wishing to move the capital out of Rio de Janeiro to a more central location that would help them develop the interior, decided the priest's prediction was auspicious, that this was the appropriate spot from which to signal Brazil's rise to world prominence. They were going to do this with an ultra-modern, futuristic city. They enlisted Brazilian architects Lúcio Costa to create the layout and Oscar Niemeyer to design the government buildings. In three and a half years, a city of more than two million was created out of nothing. In 1960, when it was inaugurated, it must have looked like it was straight out of a futuristic *Jetsons* cartoon.

Costa said he was inspired by the shape of a cross, but in the end, the guidebooks describe the city as having the shape of an airplane. The description is apt. The fuselage is a wide-open grassy mall, reminiscent of the mall in Washington D.C., flanked by dominos of concrete and sea-green glass. The Plaza of the Three Powers—executive, judicial, and legislative—anchors one end. The executive and judicial buildings face each other, white and light, flat roofs suspend delicately above four paper-thin legs that sweep down past glass walls to perch on delicate points in the grass: modern versions of the Acropolis. On the third side, the legislative center, two tall slabs, white towers, rise out of a rectangular reflecting pool. A third slab lies, long and low, as though it had fallen over into the grass. On its roof are two giant bowls, one right side up, one upside down, put there, it seems, for the pure pleasure of design, a chance to luxuriate in the visual feast of contrasting shape.

There was almost no one there on a Tuesday morning, a strange feeling for Brazil. We wandered around the vast plaza looking at the stick-figure sculpture commemorating the *candangos*, the laborers out of whose toil this city rose. One wonders if it hadn't been rather like building the pyramids. Skyler kicked his newly acquired soccer ball as high as he could. It seemed to rise higher than the Eiffel Tower–like flagpole, a bunch of twenty-four upward-sweeping strands, each strand marking a state. Fifty years later, it was already out of date. Since, states had split and been renamed, making one realize how much this country was still in flux. Atop the pole, the green-and-yellow Brazilian flag thwapped in the wind like some massive sail in irons, looking for direction in guiding this ship of state.

People say that while Brasilia is impressive, it lacks soul. Certainly compared to the crammed, color-popping, music-blaring, rococo Northeast, this was feeling very empty and spare. I found it refreshing —a return to a sense of space more familiar to me, more like the vast empty of Montana.

After a cafeteria lunch in the basement of the judiciary (for which we'd had our backpacks x-rayed, our pictures taken, and badges issued) and a quick game of soccer on its lawn, we hailed a cab. Winding along Boulevard W-3, we headed to a restaurant on the shores of the man-made lake that wraps around the nose of the "plane."

The fuselage runs east to west, separating the plane's wings into north and south. The wings are divided into *quadras*, numbered rectangular blocks. So when you direct a cab driver, you ask, for example, for Quadra 407 North. The system was designed for a driving-oriented city (part of the reason the streets feel so empty). It seemed robotic, even by grid-oriented North American standards. It was so far from the organic growth of tiny, knotted streets in the Northeast that it hardly seemed Brazilian—at least not the Brazil we knew. It seemed the housing in the wings was largely in apartment buildings, mostly ten- to fifteen-stories high. As we crossed a bridge over the lake, we were greeted by a plaque. It translated as *Sector of Individual Habitations*.

"This is where the important people live," the driver said.

The houses were so huge that their rooflines were visible, despite the towering, dense hedges; no Northeastern walls bristling with broken glass here.

There were several restaurants in a beautifully landscaped garden, a garden run amok with brides. It must have been a hot photo spot because on this Tuesday evening, there were not one or two but five brides getting their pictures taken by this fountain or that cascading tropical plant. No grooms were in sight.

"They're probably getting drunk," murmured Skyler.

We ordered beef stroganoff, smoked salmon, and chicken with candied figs on beds of arugula. I got a glass of chilled white wine. At the arranged time, our taxi driver came back to pick us up. He juggled the soccer ball with Skyler on the lawn, while Peter, Molly, and I finished sipping sweet coffee and relished the last morsel of chocolate truffle, the perfect end to the perfect meal before we launched into the jungle.

On arrival back at the airport in plenty of time to repack our luggage and check in, we were summarily told that we'd arrived too late to board the plane for Manaus. After a bewildering conversation during which I repeatedly pointed to the clock to show that we were not past the half-hour deadline for boarding but had instead a full hour to go, Peter, who tends to leave the negotiating in Portuguese to me, finally stepped forward. Ah yes, well, they admitted under their breaths, they had in fact given away our seats. Were they coming out with this now simply because Peter had more clout, because he was a man?

The next afternoon, after one last plane flight and a luxurious night in a five-star hotel courtesy of the airline, we found ourselves in Manaus. Manaus did not fit my picture of the "Amazon." A city of 1.7 million, this hilly capital of the state of Amazonas rolled down to the Rio Negro, at this point already four miles wide. Oceangoing ships plied its waters. Eleven miles farther downstream, the Rio

Negro joined its brown with the white of the Rio Solimões, becoming the actual Amazon.

Like Brasilia, Manaus immediately felt different from the Northeast, quieter, more reserved. While Penedenses might be laid back about work, they were full of a feisty energy when it came to fun. In Penedo, sound bounced unmuted off stone-hard streets and stucco walls. Manaus was leafy. There sound was muffled by arcing shade trees, which lined streets of multistory office buildings, mildewing in the wet, and beautifully restored colonial mansions sandwiched between blocks of decay.

We checked into the Hostel Manaus and were pleased to get a second-story room all to ourselves. It looked out over an inner courtyard. Unlike the hostel in Salvador, which had exuded a cheerful exuberance, this hostel felt as though the energy had been sucked out of it. Its inhabitants lay immobile on dingy couches, recovering from their last hard trip into the bush. Thin from digestive ailments, they drifted about, catching up on weeks of accumulated laundry, emailing friends back home, comparing notes—the notes not of tourists but of travelers. While there's often a nice camaraderie among travelers, and invariably the people you meet are interesting, there can also be a kind of stagnancy in the draped bodies lounging on worn sofas, a malaise that sets in. We were like bouncy teens fresh out of a sock hop stumbling into an opium den. But it proved to be a good base of operations.

Just down the hill was a grassy park with soccer courts. Skyler was the first to venture into the pickup games. After months of honing his footwork on the streets of Penedo, he seemed to be champing at the bit to test himself in new venues. Peter asked the next day if he could join, not sure the young guys would want him, but they'd been open, finally even taking Molly, the only girl.

I got there just in time to watch Molly, Skyler, and Peter leave the sidelines and jump in.

"We're gonna get killed," Molly said, her blond ponytail swinging as she ran.

"We're gonna get killed," Peter agreed.

They spread out on the court, concrete covered with a thin layer of Astroturf.

"Oh my Gawd!" a fancy dancer of a player exclaimed in English as Molly took the ball away from him.

The Stark-Ragsdale team held up amazingly well, slamming more hard shots at the other team's goalie than the opposing team could get on theirs. Our family knew how to play position. They lost in the end, but the regulars were impressed.

It was Peter's birthday. That night, we walked through quiet streets to dinner at the Ristorante Fiorentina, fronting on a plaza with lush trees and a fountain. Looking through plate glass windows, we watched flirting couples and teen punks mill around a nineteenth-century beaux arts newsstand. Then it suddenly turned dark. Lightning and gusting rain flushed out the park's inhabitants.

The filet mignon in Madeira sauce with mashed potatoes and grilled peppers, then the crème caramel, sweet espresso, and port wine, were just the thing for a dark, rainy night in the Amazon. Who knew! We gave Peter his presents: a blow-dart gun, small vials of oil of pau rosa—for muscle and joint aches—and the fat of a snake with a name I didn't recognize—for flu and cold. His presents were more in line with the "Amazon" I'd expected, the National Geographic land of rare-plant-and-animal-filled jungle. The next day, we would be catching a boat to travel farther upriver. I wondered which Amazon we'd find there.

31

Guests in Their House

WE HAD TO BE at the floating terminal at 6:00 AM. This gave us time
to check our backpacks and buy a cup of sugary *cafezinho* and leathery
tapioca pancakes before our 7:00 AM. departure for Tefé. This town,
twelve hours upriver by "fast boat," would be the jumping-off point
for the Mamirauá Reserve.

The *Crystal I* left right on time. Sleek and white, it had *God is in
first place* emblazoned in Portuguese on its water-slicing bow. The boat
flexed its muscles and sped downstream away from Manaus, leaving
the shipyards and ferry landings behind. The four of us stood on a
small back deck, mesmerized by the frothing rooster tails shooting out
of its 1500 horsepower engines.

Ducking inside, we found a red interior with rows of seats, three on
a side, much like an airplane.

"There're our names!" Skyler exclaimed with wonder.

Molly, Skyler, Amy, and *Peter* had been written on four seat backs.
Rows of TV screens were suspended above them. They were perma-
nently on, and there was no choice of programming. As it turned out,
we would be treated to twelve straight hours of increasingly violent
American films, their actors' mismatched mouths earnestly spouting
Portuguese. But the first one looked fairly innocuous. It was set in a
Swiss ski resort. Snow in the Amazon.

The air conditioning was ferocious. I escaped into the open air
of the back deck, where there were also bathrooms and a kitchenette
with a two-burner stove. Two women cut vegetables into a boiling vat,
which would turn into succulent spare rib soup for dinner. (You don't
find that on an airplane!) Taking the fast boat wasn't cheap, $175 each,
but it was worth it.

Soon after our departure, we cut away from the Rio Negro, up
a narrow channel dredged through grass, a shortcut to the Rio

Solimões. The water turned from brown tea to café au lait, "black water" to "white water." Sediment from the Andes made the "white water" white, whereas the "black water" of the Rio Negro was fed by streams that were warmer and slower, so full of decomposing organic matter. The boat slowed to make the curves, honking to clear the few canoes in its path, like a cougar growling at mice.

We broke out into the Solimões, a river even vaster than the Rio Negro and certainly larger than any I'd seen in the United States. The Amazon is not the longest river in the world, but it is the largest in sheer volume of water. White water was mirrored in white sky, the land a thin pancake squeezed in between.

We sped past occasional tugboats pushing their cumbersome loads: barges laden with pink logs, cars, trucks, a two-story warehouse. There are so few roads in the state of Amazonas that in most places, goods must be transported by river.

Along much of our ride, the banks had been cleared for subsistence farming. The occasional small settlements had a few boxy houses on stilts, the first we'd seen in Brazil made out of wood. Their painted walls were fading; their window openings gaped black. The corrugated tin roofs looked dull. There were none of the bright colors and rambling verandas of the Northeast. An occasional cross on a steeple announced the presence of missionaries. A string of buzzards hunkered down on a fence next to a house. Dozens of them rimmed the village roofs. The buzzards were as common there as pigeons at home. Maybe such fertility also brings death.

Every settlement had a rope swing, suspended from towering trees, which dangled dizzyingly over the river. At one village, a boy ran along the bank with our boat, making us feel like an event.

I settled into a cushioned bench on the open back deck and watched the vast river stretch out behind us. Green banks curved together in the distance, narrowing to a point on the horizon where the river joined the sky. World traveler that he'd been, I didn't think my dad had ever made it to the Amazon. He would have loved the adventure of it, the boat, the river, the towns along the way. We were here, in Brazil, because of him—because of a little money he'd left me, because of his confidence that one could figure out how to make one's way in a strange place, because of his insatiable thirst for exploring the unknown, the different. That "different" that's threatening to many was fascinating to him. It was January 19, two years to the day since he'd died.

Thank you, Dad.

I went back inside in time for lunch. It was served on seat-back tray tables. We were on to the third movie, an action film with Tom Cruise and Cameron Diaz, when the boat began to slow. Looking out the window, I could see a large warehouse-sized building with the word *Açai* painted on the side. Just before we'd left the United States, this Amazonian berry was making its highly touted appearance in health-food stores. I stepped back out into the warmth of the back deck. We were pulling up to a covered floating dock. It was surreal, jumping from Tom and Cameron drinking champagne in a five-star hotel in Salzburg to the mud banks of a river town on stilts in the jungle. Sometimes I wonder if our human brains are made to switch gears this rapidly.

Pulling off the Solimões in a fast boat into the channel leading to Lake Tefé was like pulling off the interstate onto an exit ramp. The cougar lifted and settled its rear haunches into the water as it slowed to find a place to park—a formal slip or a slot of beach sand. Next to us, men were unloading a barge, by hand. Everything, in this region, was still unloaded by hand. That new van you ordered, or the fifteen-passenger motor boat, or that semitruck? Better find more than a few strong men.

The next morning, Molly, Skyler, Peter, an Irishman, a young woman from San Francisco, and I stood on a wooden dock, waiting to hand our backpacks to the driver of a small motorboat.

"Here, you can wear these," Eduardo said, handing Peter a brace of green, camouflage-patterned life jackets.

Eduardo and Bianca were from southern Brazil and spoke English. Young biology students, they would be our main guides for the next five days at the Mamirauá Reserve.

The six of us stepped carefully into the aluminum boat. The driver backed it away from the dock, cruised slowly past a floating gas station, then shifted into high gear.

We were headed farther up the Solimões River toward the Peruvian border and the floating bungalows of the Uakari Lodge. The trees along the banks were coated in vines, creating a fantastical, lumpy topiary of elephant trunks and wooly mammoths. A great egret stood, three feet tall, pure white, majestic against the curtain of green. This would be just one of hundreds. We would see trees festooned with them, like Christmas ornaments, delicate white question marks. We rounded a bend and flushed a flock of cormorants, though *flock* doesn't quite describe what we were seeing. A spray of black was scattering in front of us, and scattering, and scattering, and scattering. Thousands of black cormorants leaving stuttering lines of white, as their webbed feet ran across the surface of the water.

An hour and a half later, we docked. The Uakari Lodge floats gently at a bend in the Japurá River. Connected by a boardwalk were five thatched bungalows, a two-story central house, and some outbuildings, each on their own raft. In front of the central house, a square hole had been cut through the deck—a pool, in the river. A *netted* pool. We'd soon find out what we could have been swimming with had there not been that added protection.

After a lunch of catfish, we headed out for a hike in the *restinga*. This is a forest classification that seems mostly to refer to level—low, medium, high—because different flora survive at different heights, as rivers in this area can rise up to twelve meters, the height of a four-story building, in the rainy season. This is why the region is called the *várzea*, or the "flooded forest." For three or four months a year, people living along the banks are flooded out of their houses, even though they're built on stilts. They retreat into "floaters," cabins on rafts, just as the animals—the jaguars, monkeys, sloths—retreat into the trees. In those months, boats are the only way to get around.

Breaking through the matted vines, we emerged into an open forest. There are up to three hundred different kinds of trees in that forest, and I couldn't identify one of them. Looking up was like flipping through a leaf catalogue: huge and oblate, heart-shaped, frilly and fingered, pointed, rounded, ribbed, smooth, shiny, dull, some the size of a tire, and others so tiny it was like looking through green netting. Then there was the bark: the usual, plus trees sheathed in skins of peeling paper or suction-cup thorns or shaggy coats of long, needle-sharp prickers.

The kapok is one of many towering trees with smooth, elephant-skin bark and buttressed roots. I kept flashing back to a black-and-white photo by Richard Avedon of a tall, slim woman in a body-hugging evening gown that flares in flutes around her feet. I was in a forest of giant Avedon women. But beware their elegance. Some are lethal. Like the assacu, whose seed drops onto the trunk of another tree and over time strangles and engulfs it.

Francisco, our local guide, pointed out the trees used for medicine: sap to heal cut umbilical cords, or wood used to make tea to get rid of tapeworms. We heard how the jaguar ambushes the sloth. The jaguar knows the sloth poops only once a week and waits in a neighboring tree to pounce as soon as the sloth hits the ground. Other animals are happy to poop right out of the tree, like the red howler monkeys, who've wisely figured out the ground is a dangerous place. They like to sleep in certain trees so their scat is always under them, in the same place. We heard this a lot: the herons and egrets and cormorants settle in the tops of the same trees; the pirarucu fish lays its eggs in the same place. One began to understand the saying "creatures of habit."

It's strange to see a wok-shaped hole in dry ground and be told that's where a fish lays its eggs. But when you look almost forty feet up and see a clear line where the tree trunks turn from dark to light and are told that's the *water* line, it makes more sense. Here, the animals, plants, and people need to be able to adapt to living on both land and water.

One of the cooks at the lodge was missing a chunk out of his right cheek. He'd been fishing, in the high-water season, out of a canoe and had drifted under the branches of a tall tree, the wet-season home of a jaguar. The jaguar jumped him, hungry from weeks trapped in its branches. Both tumbled into the water. Luckily for the cook, the water was deep and the jaguar couldn't dive, so the man got away, minus only part of his face.

While we saw lots of signs of animals, it wasn't until we returned to the lodge that we started seeing the animals themselves. Peter and I sauntered out onto our bungalow porch and were stunned by the sight. On the way out for our post-lunch hike, we'd seen some cormorants heading downriver, but this was the Indy 500! Thousands of cormorants were now rounding the bend in a blur. One in the lead, no, now it's dropping back . . . number 504 swinging to the outside, beginning to pass . . . is he going to make it? Yes! But now passing on the inside, number 712 gaining speed, passing one, two, three . . . Wow, pulled right out in front, but there're more coming . . .five, six, twenty, a hundred, four hundred, a thousand. We stood transfixed.

"Whoa! Did you hear that?" Skyler exclaimed from inside.

"Yeah, sounds like a 250-pound man doing a cannonball," Peter guessed.

It was happening all around us, these great *ka-thunks*. Then we saw one; a huge, finned tail curled and lashed the surface of the water. The Loch Ness Monster: a pirarucu, the eight-foot-long fish, twice Skyler's height, that we'd seen in the fish market in Manaus, the one whose scales were sold for fingernail files. It was coming up to breathe. In addition to gills, pirarucu have swim bladders, allowing them to extract oxygen from the air. This unusual adaptation to oxygen-poor-water conditions in the Amazonian floodplains would seem to be an advantage, but instead it required what appeared to be a thrashingly desperate act of survival every few minutes. They rose and thrashed like self-flagellating penitents all through the night. I couldn't believe I'd made it to fifty-three without knowing that fish don't sleep.

But the *ka-thunks* weren't the only strange sound. There was that low groan, that icy wind howling through cavernous medieval halls— red howler monkeys marking their territory. Their otherworldly roar became a regular part of the soundscape.

We didn't see the caimans until the next day, when they surrounded our shallow-sided canoe. Two nostrils were followed a foot away by two glassy eyes and then a strip of scaly back. The semi-submersion was part of what gave them their stealthy quality, but really I thought it was their glide, that pulseless swimming, the skimming silence of it. We went out again in a motorboat that night. In the dark, Eduardo scanned the river with a powerful flashlight, looking for obstacles in the water. The eyes of the caimans, those trench-coated undercover agents, glowed red.

"I counted thirteen that time," whispered Skyler.

Despite this, the reserve is a tranquil place. A place where there is a lot of hunting going on—quiet, focused hunting. A lot of stalking, a lot of stillness. The anhinga paddles silently with webbed feet, then unexpectedly slides backward under the water, only to emerge somewhere else, golden neck first, actually only the neck, a pulsing, snake-like periscope. It is surprising to see how fast the caimans can cruise because more often they seem to be stopped, probably knowing it's the motion that gives them away. The egrets ride, white, on electric-green floating meadows, still lives on a conveyor belt of tall grass.

Between the hulking pirarucus, the diving anhingas, the plummeting kingfishers, the strafing large-billed terns, and the stealthily cruising caimans, being a small fish in the Amazon must be risky business. I wondered where we, as humans, fit into the hierarchy. Were we predators or prey? Clearly in this environment, we had the potential to be both. How much control did we really have?

I yearned to sit in one of the hammocks on our porch and immerse myself in the quiet, but we had a schedule: up at six, out by seven, back by twelve, lunch, out at three, back by seven, dinner, after-dinner activity.

When Bianca said the purpose of the night walk was to have a chance to "experience the night life," I thought, *Okay! Like party time in Salvador.* Well, I didn't really think that. There were no boomer cars or boom boxes; there wasn't even a radio here, only Eduardo's soothing guitar. Still, a walk in the soft jungle night sounded like fun until you heard the guide urgently hissing, *"Muito venenoso."* It didn't take any language skill to figure out what that meant when it was attached to *"Cobra!"* I was in the front, behind Francisco, the local guide, when he spotted the snake by the side of the path with his flashlight. I couldn't really tell you what it looked like, since I was backing up *rapidamente,* as I'd been instructed to. He had that excited, tight sound in his voice that you didn't question as he hissed its name, *"Surucucu, surucucu!"* Funny, that was the Brazilian name for the fer-de-lance, also known as the pit viper, also known as the most venomous snake in the Amazon, that we'd just been talking about, Molly and I.

As we'd paddled our canoe earlier that afternoon, Almir, our guide, said offhandedly that he'd been bitten by pit vipers, twice that year. Could they really swim? Jump into a canoe? Climb trees, do double backflips . . . ? Okay, maybe our minds were getting a little carried away. Maybe we just couldn't understand Almir's Portuguese. Later, talking to Bianca, we sorted it out. It was the anaconda, another friendly local, that could climb trees and hop into your canoe. The surucucu just kills you. Almir had gotten the antivenom in time but had been unable to walk the first time—for a month. The snake's venom had paralyzed his legs. When Francisco invited us to come forward for a look, I declined, unlike Molly, Skyler, and Peter.

That morning, we'd visited a village down the river. A woman there had told us how she'd seen an anaconda, at the edge of the water, already fully wrapped around a calf, starting to constrict it. She'd dashed into the river to free it. Now, would that be your first instinct? The anaconda had bitten her (she showed us the marks) and then had been unable to extract its curved teeth from her arm. Her husband, seeing that she was in trouble, dashed into the water, too, and, having no knife, bit the snake. I know, it's starting to sound like a tall tale. The calf lived.

They all had stories like that. You started to believe them when you walked back to your bungalow after lunch and found a caiman—just a *four-foot-long baby*—sunning itself on the flotation logs of your cabin.

Now, our night guide was shining his light into the base of a tree trunk. I'd dropped back safely into the middle of the pack. *"Carangue-jeira,"* was whispered along the line. *"Tem muitos nomes"*—It has lots of names. It turned out *tarantula* was the one I recognized. By the time I got up to the tree, she had slid back into her white pocket of a house, only a few of her long, furry black legs still stuck out, yellow on the tips. She'd done her nails.

Given that I was the child of a father who'd had a phobia for snakes and a mother with a phobia for spiders, this was not shaping up to be my kind of a stroll. I can't tell you much about the canopy at night, or the symphonic sounds of insects, as my eyes and ears were pretty solidly focused—okay, glued—to the ground.

We did, however, stop once to listen. And, in fact, the sounds were amazing. Like a percussion section, the cicadas played a steady blanket of sixteenth notes on high-pitched triangles; frogs, the washboard quarter notes; and toads, the low, belching whole note. An occasional rapid-fire rattle skimmed the surface. Here was a little of Salvador after all.

Soon afterward, we spotted the lights of the lodge through the trees. I was happy to return to our floating boardwalk. I'd take the *ka-thunk*s in the night anytime. But I was pleased, too, to have ventured into that other world, that Halloween night world of spiders and snakes, and to have had a small taste of what it might be like to live *with*, not just in fear of, those small creatures who are, after all, just defending themselves against those out to get them—the likes of us.

We were sorry to leave. I recognized specific places along the channel now, the entrance through the matted vines where our first walk had started, the corner where we'd gone fishing for piranhas, the path up the muddy bank to the lily pond.

We'd followed that path on our third hike when it had rained. Our guide had pulled us into a shelter of slender walls made by kapok roots and asked, "Who knows a joke?" in Portuguese, of course. Instantly, Skyler delivered several. Who knew that dumb-blond jokes would translate in a place where everyone's hair was black? It was then that I realized Skyler could really speak Portuguese!

How, without any concerted study of grammar, could *he* now conjugate verbs, when *I* still had to stop, think, translate, and envision the dictionary in order to tentatively venture forth with a possible verb ending, all the while wondering whether I'd really managed to select the *-er* and not the *-ar* or *-ir* verb, and the simple past, not the pluperfect? I guessed that was the difference between learning on the hoof—running with friends for hours every day—versus studying a textbook.

Now, as we sped through the green-walled channel, I could name most of the birdlife and recognized the knobbly bits of log that were actually caimans. I've always wondered why just the act of being able to label things is so pleasurable to me. It seems to help me see, as though I don't see things I can't name, or maybe just don't pay attention until I can.

The boat was now moving so fast that the air was pulling the spittle right out of my mouth. We passed a few small settlements, where the Ribeirinhos, river people sometimes generically referred to as the *caboclo*, live. They were descended from the mixing of indigenous Indians and northeastern Brazilians. The northeasterners had come here to find jobs a hundred years earlier, during the rubber boom.

Back in Tefé, the Irishman flew out, but the young woman from San Francisco was scheduled to spend a few more days in town like us. She was waiting for the "slow boat" to Manaus, while we gambled on getting onto a mail plane to São Gabriel da Cachoeira. Before she'd come to Brazil, she'd been camping in an abandoned cabin in the Columbian jungle, so she was clearly a toughened traveler. Even so, she was now rethinking her choice to take the slow boat. They were notorious for long lines outside bathrooms that made you gag, jammed sleeping quarters (hammocks packed elbow to elbow), and gut-twisting food. She was thinking she might switch to the fast.

Perhaps she was reaching that line that Peter and I had reached some years before, when you start to think, *Maybe I don't have to go totally native to be a "real traveler." Maybe I don't have to sleep on hard floors, sample all the local semi-edibles, tramp barefoot through microbe-laden mud, and pick up all the local bugs.* At some point, it loses its romance.

32

On Maintaining Respect

PETER HAD MAJORED in anthropology in college, and one of the classes that stuck with him, forty years later, was the one about the Yanomami. It stunned the world that there existed a people living totally detached from modern life as late as the 1950s, when these people, upriver in the Amazon, came into the public eye. Peter had read a book he still remembered, by a French anthropologist, titled *Yanomamo: The Fierce People*, which described the ritualized violence they used to settle disputes.

"In my youth, it was a benchmark tribe for exoticism," he'd told me. Perhaps this had been the beginning of Peter's lifelong motivation to go places and meet people before it was "too late," the birth of his fear that the worlds' cultures would become so homogenized that they would no longer be distinct.

When we decided to go to the Amazon for the kids' school break, there were two things we wanted to do—see animals and meet people, particularly the Yanomami. The first had been easy, with a guide to help us spot them. We knew the second would be hard. Perhaps surprisingly to some, the Yanomami, and many other Amazonian tribes, are not clamoring at the gate to get into this world of ours. Rather, they're slamming it shut to keep us, and our ways, out. We would need permission to visit, and that meant bureaucracy. Bureaucracy was not fast and not cheap. But we had wanted to try and had heard that São Gabriel da Cachoeira would be a good base of operations.

The Amazon River runs basically west to east, dropping out of the Andes Mountains and emptying into the Atlantic Ocean. Many tributaries feed into it, but ultimately, two main rivers emerge, the Rio Negro and the Solimões, like the two parallel arms of a tuning fork lying on its side. They join just east of Manaus to make what we call the Amazon. São Gabriel and Manaus are both on the north fork, the

Rio Negro. In Tefé, we were on the southern fork, but we were now about to fly even farther west and back north up to São Gabriel.

There were nine possible passenger seats on the mail plane. It flew on Tuesdays and Thursdays. Today was Tuesday. We'd been told our chances of getting on were good. Most of the mail was flying downriver to bigger population centers, not upriver to smaller ones, so they'd probably have room to leave some seats. We were getting to the end of the river road. A little farther, and we'd be in Venezuela.

I didn't realize what hermetic environments U.S. airports and planes were until we got on this little Cessna. There were as many flies as passengers. How do we have no flies on our planes? Hunched over, I squeezed through the boxes and slid sideways down the narrow aisle, past two swarthy, barrel-chested men; past a family of three, the young boy on the grandmother's lap; past Molly and Skyler. I was the last one on, so I was going to have to forgo my pledge to always sit in the back (something I'd done ever since I'd heard your chance of surviving a crash was better in the back). I imagined if this plane went down, there wouldn't be a lot of difference between the front and the back anyway. There was no one telling us to fasten our seat belts, no preflight demonstrations of oxygen masks and flotation cushions, no two-fingered pointing to the exits. They just piled the boxes of mail in the back, loose—no cargo netting to keep it from decapitating us when we landed. Then the two pilots climbed in front of Peter and me, and we bobbed down the runway. It felt rather jaunty.

The electronic map on the dash reoriented as we turned around and pointed ourselves west, farther up the Solimões River. I watched the dashboard instruments and realized everything was in English. There were explicit directions about weight load and something blinking red that said *Advisory*. The speedometer climbed to one hundred knots, and we lifted off. We were leaving Tefé, with its jumbled collection of wooden shacks on stilts rising up the high bank above Tefé Lake, like a wall of shingles in muted pastels.

We looked down at a mat of green, a vast flattened head of broccoli, cut by a milky brown ribbon. Cloud wisps spiraled out between the florets. Then we were engulfed in cloud altogether. I was enjoying that feeling of driving through the clouds, cutting between these two cumuli and banking right at that next one. Then I looked over and noticed the pilot. The older of the two was reading the paper. I craned around the other's seat back. Okay, good, his hands were on the wheel. The altimeter was at 6,500 feet. I went back to the clouds. When I looked again, the older pilot was asleep.

Two hours later, we were landing at a one-runway airport. The only hint of human life we'd seen while flying had been Fonte Boa, a square hacked out of the jungle with identical, tin-roofed houses plopped down in orderly rows, and then a tiny settlement of half a dozen cabins on a small, muddy lake. I expected *they* didn't just zip down to the grocery when they forgot a carton of milk. In fact, I expected they didn't zip anywhere. How did they even get there? I hadn't noticed a river; there had been only one runway, back at Fonte Boa, and no roads. Not one road, visible from the air, in all those trees. Back in Penedo, the kids' school director, Irma Francisca, had called the Amazon *"os pulmões do mundo"*—the lungs of the world. Over 50 percent of the world's rainforest was there, in that one area. It was like an ocean of breathing.

It was heartening to see the forest looking so healthy. The devastating deforestation we'd been hearing about in the States had not taken place there in the state of Amazonas, but in the neighboring state of Roraima, where in the 1980s they were cutting two and a half acres, the equivalent of two football fields, every five seconds—death sweeping through with an enormous scythe. Hard even to imagine the mechanics of it.

We sauntered over to the one taxi that sat beyond the airport building. As in Tefé, the evangelicals had been active here. On the side of our cab was written, *100% Jesus.*

São Gabriel da Cachoeira was immediately more appealing than motorcycle- and buzzard-ridden Tefé. Despite being smack on the equator, it felt cooler, perhaps because there was a little contour. Hills reclined blue in the distance. As in Manaus, we were once again on the Rio Negro. São Gabriel's waterfront bordered tea-colored rapids swirling around worn boulders and small islands. The view was stunning. Immediately I was struck by the leafy softness and the calm.

Driving up the hill away from the river, we checked into the Hotel

Deus Me Deu—Hotel God Gave Me. The hotel, on a second floor above the one-street business district, was a welcome change from the steamy hostels where we'd been staying. The white, convent-like corridors of Deus Me Deu, with their crisp lines of dark wood doors, offered a kind of antiseptic quiet and privacy I was ready for.

We were moving into more and more indigenous territory; the census listed São Gabriel as 90 percent Indian. It was proving to be far more cosmopolitan than we'd expected. We headed out in search of lunch and found a delicious "self-serve" with freshly prepared beef filet in a sauce of onions and carrots, chicken cordon bleu, and grilled fish. A slender woman, sitting kitty-corner from us, with perfect teeth, pinstriped pants, and red patent-leather pumps was clearly as curious about us as we were about her. She was married to someone in the army, she told us, in halting English, and was up from Rio de Janeiro for the week. This must explain who the clientele was for the amazing video store under our hotel. We'd passed the army base on the way in from the airport, the base that patrolled Brazil's borders with Venezuela and Columbia, a job fraught with drug trafficking and touchy tribes in tangled jungle. A good DVD might be just the break these soldiers needed.

The video store was unlike any we'd seen in our state of Alagoas, but here it was, over 1,500 miles up the Amazon River. It had a DVD selection as extensive as Hastings or Borders at home, in both Portuguese and English, and it had books, for rent. There weren't many, and nothing in English, but it was still a bookstore, more than we had in Penedo. It was an interesting collection: lots of Christian theology, but also the *Who Was* series—*Who was Darwin? Who was Einstein? Who was Leonardo da Vinci?* There were also a number of books that had been popular in the states: *The Da Vinci Code, Marley & Me*, the *Lightning Thief* series, plus *Eldest* and *Brisingr*. After lunch, Molly and Skyler combed the DVD aisles, settled on *Zoolander* and the TV series *Lost*, and put them away in their bedroom for an after-dinner treat.

It wasn't hard to imagine why the Yanomami didn't relish people coming to look at them, like curiosities in a zoo. I realized a big reason I travel, however, *is* to look at people, or rather at how they live.

"I think maybe it's about respect," Molly had said once. Respect can change the nature of a visit to an unfamiliar culture from being like going to see a circus freak into a healthy curiosity about difference. We had found, in Penedo, that this was a two-way street. We were looking at them. And they were definitely looking at us.

The next morning, we were sitting at the long, family-style table at Deus Me Deu when Sucy strode briskly into the breakfast room. Sucy was the man Peter had contacted at Instituto Socioambiental, a local nonprofit that advocates for the rights of indigenous peoples in the Upper Rio Negro.

"I have the man for you," he said in Portuguese. "He knows everything here. He knows everybody, and he speaks English!"

He nodded to the short leprechaunish man with flaring ears, twinkling eyes, and a lot of missing teeth who had followed him in.

"This is Valdir. He will be your guide."

At sixty-seven, Valdir was sprightly and liked to talk. He was full of stories, starting with his own. He was the son of a woman from the Macuxi tribe and a Portuguese worker who'd jumped ship and "gone native." A missionary family had come from California when Valdir was nine, and he'd befriended their kids. Two years later, when the family was leaving, he wanted to go along.

"I begged to go wit' them, wit' my friends, so my fadder say, okay," Valdir told us. But when he arrived in California, instead of living with the family, he was put in a school. It had a high fence and was surrounded by guards. "Santa Maria it called. I cry and I cry." He screwed the knobs of his fists into his eyes. He hadn't been allowed to go home. "I was nine years, tere."

Now he speaks English, German, Spanish, Portuguese, and Yanomami, and he doesn't have much good to say about missionaries.

The bureaucracy was starting to roll. But we needed to get permission to visit from the Fundação Nacional do Indio, or FUNAI, the Brazilian government's department of Indian affairs, as well as from the Yanomami themselves. Approximately thirty-two thousand Yanomami live on the border of Brazil and Venezuela. They're the largest still relatively isolated tribe in South America, residing in approximately 250 independent villages, scattered deep in the jungle.

"Berto, he can help us," Valdir said, full of confidence, his head cocked to one side, speaking of the son of a Yanomami headman. "I know him." Valdir had occasionally taken other westerners to Berto's village before, usually mountain climbers trekking to Pico da Neblina.

Berto showed up the morning of our third day in São Gabriel, in his Yanomami headman's son's garb: board shorts and a muscle shirt. It turned out he was living in São Gabriel studying to be a dentist. This was the first clue that we were about to enter a remarkably complicated, multilayered world.

"We can go today, if the final permission comes through," he told us in Portuguese. "But don't buy anything until we know for sure."

We'd been told we could have a lot to buy, about $2,000 worth. If we were given the permit, we'd begin the delicate matter of negotiating gifts for the tribe. Very specific gifts: fifty-three gallons of diesel for the electrical generators, eight gallons of oil, eighty gallons of gas for the motorized canoe to get us there, and four and a half pounds of bulk tobacco. (Everyone chewed, both men and women.) Plus there was payment for guides and transport. Our "ticket in" wasn't cheap, and it turned out we almost weren't able to buy it.

Valdir and Peter sat down to compile a list of the things we would need for ourselves: hammocks, ropes, blankets, mosquito nets, rain boots, rain jackets, food. At eleven, the permissions came through; stores would close for lunch at twelve. Berto said we should leave São Gabriel for the village at one. The journey would require two hours by truck and five by canoe. We jumped into action. I went for the dry goods, Peter and Valdir went for food, Molly and Skyler went for take-out lunch. By one, we were ready. At two, we were still there. At three, Valdir arrived to say he'd found the truck driver at work on his broken-down engine.

But he'd engaged another driver, whose nickname was Coelho, or "Rabbit," who rumbled up soon after in an old blue jalopy, coated in orange road dust.

"Not a *coelho*," Valdir joked.

The truck looked as though it might rattle apart. Peter and I climbed onto the cracked leather seats of the cab, and Berto, Valdir, and the kids pulled themselves over the wooden rails to stand in back, with a bed full of empty plastic barrels. Berto was accompanying us as far as the gas pumps. We filled the barrels. The station attendant, in her tight jeans and pink Dolce & Gabbana T-shirt, ran our card. It didn't clear. Nor did the next card, or the next, or the next. The truck stood pregnant with one hundred and thirty gallons of gas. We needed to come up with the money, $1,000, in cash.

I ran to tell the kids, still standing among the cans and barrels, that we were going to catch a taxi to the bank and try our luck with the ATMs there. Months before, we might have thought twice about leaving our kids with strangers, in a strange city, in a strange country. But we'd come to trust our intuition about people and places. There didn't seem to be anything threatening about this one.

Finally, one card gave us enough cash. Berto had never seemed worried. For the most part, people there didn't look worried. They were patient. They were used to waiting. They didn't curse and twitch and pace, the way we did in the States. Combined with the cash we already had, we pulled together enough, but it left us with almost nothing. This made us uneasy. You never knew when you might need to buy your way out of a fix.

We finally waved good-bye to Berto and left. It was four.

It took Coelho more than two hours to suck his way through the orange gumbo of the dirt road, that orange road that creeps through jungles all over the world. Peter and I had seen them in Ghana, Mozambique, Indonesia. Another truck was installing electric poles, and despite being a fancy Volkswagen, it wasn't equipped for the job. (We stopped to tug it out of the slurping goo.) We, on the other hand, in our rattletrap blue Toyota Bandeirante, motored steadily along like an animal perfectly adapted to the climate. Back on the truck bed, the kids weathered the wind and a burst of pounding rain. Their soaked clothes had nearly dried when the truck finally jolted to a stop, swung around, and backed down a muddy landing. It was almost dark.

We were in a clearing in the Amazon forest. A small creek seeped through a gloomy tunnel of tangled vines and branches. Molly and Skyler jumped down, and Peter and I spilled out of the cab. Down in the slough, two men lounged in a thirty-foot-long aluminum canoe, mounted with a forty-horsepower Yamaha motor. Although night was falling fast, nobody rushed.

"*Seu nome?*" Peter asked, as one of the men waded ashore and they shook hands. He had a lithe, athletic build and a soft smile.

"Anderson," he replied, pronouncing it *Ahn-deh-sohn.*

It was not a name I'd pick for a Yanomami—for a son of the headman of one of the Amazon's most traditional and famously fierce tribes. But I'd found in Brazil first names seemed to be as easily, and randomly, imported as T-shirts. He was Berto's brother.

While I was off using the bushes, Orlando, the other boatman; Coelho, the truck driver; and Anderson somehow managed to roll the barrels of oil and gas we'd brought—one thousand and forty pounds worth—out of the truck and into the canoe. It sat unnervingly low in the water. Valdir, the two boatmen, Peter, the kids, and I climbed in carefully. We said good-bye to Coelho. I didn't envy him the trip back through the gumbo in the dark.

Anderson pulled the starter. We slipped quietly into the channel. I felt like Nancy Drew in the Florida Everglades.

As we twisted down the narrow creek, Orlando sat facing forward, straddling the bow. He swung a flashlight beam from side to side. Was he looking for caiman eyes? Sunken logs? Both?

"*Em baixa! Em baixa!*" Anderson shouted. "Get down! Get down!"

We ducked under a thick, overhanging branch just as Anderson gunned the motor and rammed the boat over a fallen tree, deftly lifting the Yamaha to clear the propeller at the last minute. Anderson did this run a lot, anytime anyone in his village wanted to go grocery shopping.

No one spoke. At every bend of the creek, the boat rocked sideways nearly to its gunnels. Lightning flickered. It was going to be miserable if it rained. But for the present, I felt totally relaxed, almost elated.

We snaked our way into larger and larger channels. By the third one, Valdir, Molly, and Skyler had wrapped themselves in a tarp on the wooden floor of the boat to sleep. Peter and I sat in back with Anderson, our hair streaming in the wind, and stared into the blackness, into the backs of our minds. It occurred to me that when you travel, you often put yourself in the hands of people you barely know. We were in an overloaded boat—at night, on a small creek in the Amazonian jungle, going somewhere toward the Venezuelan border—with our children and two men we'd just met and one we'd known for a day. The only people who had any idea where we were, and then only in the most general terms, were Peter's and my mothers in the United States.

I've always loved that feeling of speeding in the wind in fast boats, and there, in the dark, I came the closest I ever had to flying. Peter had taught me that when white-water canoeing, I should look for the V in the water, the place where the bulk of the water squeezed through the rocks in a rapid. Here, Anderson was looking *up* for that narrow slot through towering trees, that V in the sky whose point kept bending right, then left, then right as the tangled banks twisted their distant nose, leading us farther in. In the slit of sky, furrows of cloud lighted by the moon separated, and there was Orion! Upside down. It was comforting somehow, to have one of our own up there, a constellation I recognized. Eventually, Peter and I, too, lay down, squeezed in between the gunnels and gas cans. My nose was inches from the stream of white water that split from the bow, giant catfish whiskers. It spattered like distant applause.

I think I slept, in small spurts, because the next six hours passed in surreal snapshots: a white beach, four men and a boy, peeing; a memory of cold, curling into Peter's warm side, thinking it had been a long time since it had been cold enough to want to do that; a flashlight shining up into an overhanging tree, a fleeting soft question in my mind of whether they were looking for snakes.

"*Estamos chegando,*" someone whispered. "We're arriving."

We clambered dopily into our new yellow rubber boots, hefted our packs, and started to climb a moonlit mountain meadow to the village of Ariabu. A man stood in the doorway of a wooden house. He pointed to the "hotel," as Valdir had called it. The hotel had no walls. It was too dark to see much else.

We rigged our hammocks and fell asleep. It was 3:00 AM. The trip on the river had taken us eight hours, not five; as long as it would take for us to drive from our hometown in western Montana across Idaho, across Washington, to Seattle. The entire time, we'd seen two lights, both fishing canoes.

33

Conflicting Worlds

PETER OPENED HIS EYES. There was an old man staring down at him.

"*Oi,*" Peter said. The man's face crinkled into a smile. Peter gazed into small, intent eyes, heavy brows, and a muzzle of a mouth with rotting teeth. This man had the textbook Yanomami haircut, short bangs cut straight across, black hair neatly sculpted around the ears. Far from fierce, he looked gentle, kindly, old.

We were not exactly being held prisoner, but it was clear that we were not free to leave our "hotel." The tribe was being careful. Their contacts with outsiders have not gone well. Many have died from imported diseases, first the measles and flu from Jesuit and Franciscan missionaries in the 1950s, then malaria from marauding gold miners starting in the 1980s.

Our hotel consisted of an octagonal concrete pad, a central pole, and eight posts around its circumference, supporting a thatch roof. We lounged in our hammocks, awaiting further notice, wondering about things like where to go to the bathroom. We were floating in an eddy, that currentless pool in a river where fish wait and watch for passing food. We were waiting for things, people, to drift by, and they did; they were coming to look at us, the animals in the zoo.

Later in the day, that same man returned, stooped and barefoot in loose shorts and an old red shirt, walking with a staff. His feet were wide and flat, his large toes separated a little from the others. He shook our hands, one after the other, holding our hands in both of his for a minute, as if resting with each of us.

He was saying something. "*Haiamahamohwahneefaoohchoh . . . ?*"

It wasn't Portuguese, definitely not English. He was smiling and nodding. We stood. He stood. We wondered what was next. We went back to reading and writing and swinging. He stood. Eventually he squatted down by a post. When I looked up again, he began plucking at his knees and tilting his head with his hand out. He was asking for something.

"*Remédio . . . meus pernas . . . ruim.*" That was Portuguese. "Medicine for bad legs."

I wondered what to do. I decided to give him water and an Aleve. Later, Valdir, who'd been off visiting in the village at the time, said, "Oh don't give tem anyting. You know, if tey die, ten ter grandchildren, tey say, tat tourist gave my grandpa someting and he die, and next time I come back here, tey shoot me."

The rest of the day passed in suspended animation. The old man, the chief of the neighboring village, a woman with a baby, and a woman selling baskets all drifted into our eddy. Eventually, we were summoned to lunch with Julio, the headman, and Adelaide, his wife (pronounced *adeh-lie-gee*), the parents of Berto and Anderson. Each Yanomami village is run by a headman, who governs by consensus, but each village is independent of all the others. There is no overarching tribal government.

Adelaide had grown up traveling with a German missionary—cooking his food, washing his clothes—and had prepared the meat we'd brought. We sat in their outdoor kitchen, on plastic stools at a long green-painted table. The floor was concrete, the roof corrugated tin. Adelaide washed dishes with funneled rainwater. Then there was the washing machine. I had another one of those double-take moments, as when I'd learned Berto was studying to be a dentist. Their grandkids tumbled underfoot with a gaggle of ducklings. Their daughter-in-law, a silent, almond-eyed beauty, flitted around the edges. It was homey. We sat. They sat. We were all feeling each other out. Why were we there?

When planning this trip, we'd had a family "meeting." A meeting to discuss what each of us was hoping to do in the Amazon, to get out of such a trip. Peter had been clear that he was interested in finding the Yanomami.

"Do you think they have blow guns?" Skyler had asked.

"I'd like to see animals, people, it's all good. But do you think we could really go to a village? Like, an aboriginal one?" Molly had asked.

I was eager for the kids to see a way of life that was really different from ours, even more different than that in Penedo, and it seemed the Yanomami would offer that. So basically, we were just there to watch them, but so far, they were mostly watching us.

It wasn't until four that afternoon that we were allowed to venture farther into the village. It turned out our eddy was at one end, next to Julio and Adelaide's house, which was also the only store. The village ran the length of a ridge. Through a fringe of *açai* and *pupunha* palms, one could see green, cloud-wreathed mountains in the distance, jutting out of thick jungle—just how I imagined Hawaii. The yellow dirt track running by our hammock pad widened into an expansive oval. It was ringed with a couple dozen thatched wattle-and-daub huts. Each was flanked by a small raised garden of what appeared to be solely green onions, and many had tetherball poles. The "ball" was a stuffed plastic bag.

"I wanna try it!" Skyler said (a phrase that popped out of his mouth about as often as its evil twin, "I hate Brazil, why are we here?").

At this hour, every tetherball court was occupied. Everyone was kicking back at the end of the day—everyone except males between thirteen and forty. They had all gone hunting. The village was preparing for their return after a two-week absence, looking forward to a feast of curassow (bush turkey), tapir, boar, monkey, and maybe even black jaguar. So now, under-thirteen boys played tetherball, flew kites, pulled toy trucks; young girls hefted toddlers; women nursed babies; and the old people prepared to dance. The dress code was casual: no shirts, no shoes, loose shorts, and bras or T-shirts for women.

Many young girls had swayed backs and protruding bellies. Malnutrition? Or had they all had children? We were told they started at thirteen.

"I'd like to meet some girls my age, but I think they all have kids," Molly said the next day.

I asked Valdir about malnutrition.

"Oh, it very good. Everybody have food, *mandioca, pupunha* . . ." he said with his usual good cheer. *Mandioca* is Portuguese for *cassava*, but I'd never seen a *pupunha* before. It looked rather like a persimmon.

But Julio, the village headman, said his people ran out of food.

They'd been nomadic when the missionaries arrived. The missionaries had encouraged them to settle, to become farmers. It seemed, sixty years later, farming was not in their blood.

No one seemed to take much notice of us. I guess our presence had been cleared. We saw Julio across the dirt oval. He was sitting on a long bench under a high shed roof hung with hundreds of bananas. With him were four other male elders. Their dress was surprising. They'd shed their shorts for skimpy Spandex swim trunks, and their bare bodies were painted in black, with dots, squiggling lines, and a thick black line extending from their mouths down their chests, a long tongue. White eagle down was stuck to their black hair, like fluttery 1950s bathing caps. Around their biceps were wrapped bands of black curassow skin pierced, like pincushions, with feathers, short green ones, long orange. The two-foot-long blowpipe Julio had shown us earlier lay in front of them, along with a small bottle of the special powder.

"I wanna try it!" Skyler had exclaimed when Julio had first come by our eddy and shown us the blowpipe.

We'd each snorted a pinch and instantly been sent into fits of chain sneezing. Julio grinned, delighted by the effect. Our sinuses were running, which explained why supposedly the powder was good for curing colds. However, if you put the special powder in a blowpipe and had someone else blow it up your nose, four pumps to each nostril, you'd hallucinate for an hour.

"*O mundo abri*"—The world opens. Julio smiled benignly and opened his arms wide, looking up with rheumy eyes. "You ask [the ancestors] for good things for the community, for health, for food . . . If you are stressed, *tudo é bom*"—everything is all right. He suggested one shouldn't do it more than once a day.

We joined the men on the bench. They were waiting for the women to dance.

"Can't I play tetherball?" Skyler was getting fidgety.

"I don't think so," I said, wishing he could. "We've been specially invited to this ceremony. We're their guests." To my relief, a few minutes later, Julio sensed Skyler's restlessness and gestured to him to join the tetherball game nearest us. Skyler peeled himself off the bench and ambled over. The young boys scattered. Skyler looked back at us, palms out. *Now what?* he seemed to be saying. Julio and the other elders laughed but called out to the boys, who slowly trickled back. Skyler was substantially taller than all of them, though we guessed they were about the same age. Finally, one got up the courage to face him and batted the plastic bag into the air. Skyler, hesitant to take advantage of his greater size, wasn't trying very hard, but eventually he wrapped the bag around the pole, which put an end to the encounter.

Meanwhile, at the far end of the yellow dirt oval, a woman appeared, then another and another. They were celebrating the harvest of bananas and *pupunha*. That morning at dawn, we'd heard a lone voice wailing, much like a muezzin's call to prayer. That had been the beginning.

Their chests were crisscrossed with beads, and their bodies and legs were painted like the men's. The string of women loped toward us in a slow-motion jog, each bearing a long arrow or machete. They seemed to come from a great distance. The men sitting on the bench shouted out to them as they passed, causing some of the women to break out of their trancelike state and crack up, laughing.

I wondered how all this squared with going to church on Sundays. We never saw the church but were told it was there, on the next ridge, the way the army base was there, just past the dip. (We'd had to be cleared by them, too.) How were the Yanomami straddling all these worlds? It was as though they had each hand and foot on one of four islands that were slowly floating apart. Julio snorted hallucinogens, painted his body, and communed with ancestors, but he had a son studying to be a dentist, and he had a washing machine, a telephone, and a TV on which Skyler thought he'd glimpsed the NBA. He had also flown to the country's capital, to Brasilia, to lobby for his tribe and ran several businesses: oranges, cattle, and gold.

At dinner that night, at the long green table in their outdoor kitchen, Julio waved to Adelaide to pull out the scales, to bring the small plastic bottle. He carefully poured its contents onto a piece of note-paper: a small, granular, richly yellow pile. Lifting the notepaper, he funneled the grains onto the scale: thirteen and a half grams, worth $945 on the world gold market. He knew the rates. Julio had bought it from some boys who'd panned for it in their rivers. Years before, in the 1980s, a Brazilian company from the south had wanted to bring their big equipment in, to dredge the Yanomami's rivers and mine for gold. Julio had gone to Brasilia to fight, to keep them out. He'd won—and been shot for his trouble. Twice. First by a man hired by the mining company, and a year later by another of his own tribe.

"*Ali*"—Right there. Adelaide pointed to where the second shooting had happened, in the corner of their kitchen.

It sounded familiar, shades of the trouble that follows wealth discovered anywhere: oil, diamonds, gold.

In 1992, the Brazilian government, under pressure from anthropologists and international NGOs, had delineated the boundaries of a Yanomami reserve, an area twice the size of Switzerland. This had been in response to the devastation wreaked by independent gold miners, numbering forty thousand, more than the Yanomami themselves, by the end of the 1980s. The Yanomami were dying from the malaria the miners had brought as well as from the mercury poisoning the fish in their rivers. The idea of the reserve was to keep the outsiders out, but little has been done to enforce this.

Julio didn't think much of the gold miners, but he thought things had been better since the missionaries had come. "*Muitas guerras antes*," he said. "Before, there had been many wars among the Yanomami."

But Valdir disagreed. "Tey don' come to convert. Tey come for da minerals. Da gold. An Indian village has gold, da missionaries are tere."

The next day, Julio showed up at our eddy pond with a teacher of indigenous arts from the neighboring village of Maturaca.

"Marcelino can teach your son to make an arrow," Julio said in Portuguese "and his daughter can teach your daughter to weave baskets."

We jumped up.

"When?"

"Later."

We sat down.

Eventually the time came. As we wound down a narrow path in our yellow rubber boots, a man and his two daughters caught up and followed us. We arrived at the river separating the two villages. There was no boat. In seconds, the daughters enthusiastically jumped in, swam across, and dragged back a large aluminum canoe. It had, however, no motor and no paddles. Valdir was shaking his head.

"How we goin' to cross?"

The man waved at us to get in. Climbing in last, he dangled his legs into the water where the motor would be and started to kick. Valdir's eyes sparkled.

"An Indian motor," he laughed—proudly, I thought.

Marcelino was lounging under a shed roof with his daughter and a clot of milling kids. He had a gentle, kindly smile. Hanging on his bare mahogany chest was a sky-blue beaded square in geometric designs.

"You want to make an arrow?" He asked Skyler in Portuguese.

"*Sim*," Skyler responded.

Marcelino proceeded to walk Skyler through the meticulous steps: choosing the right wood for each of the arrow's three parts—the tip, the shaft, the tail—inserting one into the other, wrapping the joint with string dredged in glue made of tree sap and beeswax. And so it went, both quietly concentrating—Marcelino putting an arm around Skyler's shoulders to show him how to hold a knife or wrap the hard tip of a curassow feather, Skyler intently hunched over the arrow, oblivious to the naked boy at his shoulder, clutching a tattered kitten to his bare belly.

Marcelino's daughter might have been in her thirties and had the same worn look I've seen on working mothers in the United States. She showed Molly how to build up the side of a basket, sewing together the coiled fibers. Marcelino's daughter spoke with that slow, cotton-headed sound of a person with a cold. A runny-nosed toddler clung to one of her knees. She looked less enthused to be "engaging" with the visitors. The number of curious kids leaning against the shed's poles and squatting in the dirt grew. Who were these blond kids? Why were they trying to make arrows and weave baskets?

It made me wonder what we pass down to our kids. The Yanomami seemed to be working hard to pass down both their values and their hands-on skills. In my circle at home, we don't pass down hands-on skill as much as we pass down ideas: ways of approaching the world, of handling problems, of dealing with people. Peter and I were trying to hand down experience, global experience, from our childhoods to theirs, hand down the idea that there are lots of ways to live and one is not inherently superior to another. We were trying to hand down our curiosity, our enthusiasm for trying different things. At the moment, it seemed to be working.

Gradually, the kids of the village, initially so shy and reticent, had begun to breach the barrier of our pad, and Molly and Skyler had started teaching Uno, using sign language, as the kids didn't seem to speak Portuguese. The kids took on the game with gusto, playing it their way—i.e., anyone can slap down a card at any time.

That night, when we got back from dinner with Julio and Adelaide, our eddy was full. A dozen villagers were watching *Rambo*, dubbed in Portuguese, on a TV mounted on one of the hammock posts. Our hotel was also the community center. The TV was running on a generator. The generator that was now burning the diesel we'd brought. In retrospect, except for the non sequitur of running into an American movie in a remote village up the Amazon, this particular movie made sense. Like Sylvester Stallone, the Yanomami were fighters who just wanted to be left alone.

After three nights in hammocks and an increasing number of people in our eddy, I was feeling ready for the hermetic corridors of the Hotel Deus Me Deu in São Gabriel. When we piled back into the long boat and waved good-bye to Julio and Adelaide, it felt like leaving family.

I'm always surprised at how quickly I bond to others when I'm in vulnerable situations, rather the way members of a mountain-climbing team might bond even though they've only just met. In the case of a mountain-climbing team, however, the members would be equally dependent on each other. In this case, I felt far more dependent on the villagers of Ariabu, especially on Julio and Adelaide, than I suspected they did on us. But in some ways, they may be growing dependent on people like us, as well, on the goods we bring and the positive "press" we take out into the world to support their traditional culture.

I was glad to retrace that midnight trip in the daylight. The walls of foliage on either side looked as impenetrable in the light as they'd looked in the dark. Occasional tatters of color broke the mass of green: the peacock's-neck blue of a giant butterfly and bits of orange, purple, yellow—bird-of-paradise and passion fruit flowers, trumpet vines. This was Hollywood-movie jungle. If you scrutinized the wall of green, you could find small openings leading into blackness, a way in. Into what? Now we knew, at least a bit.

We'd left our Uno cards back in Ariabu, with a child who lived in the hut next to our hammock pad. We'd left our blankets with Adelaide, and I'd given my rubber boots to Anderson. I realized it was impossible for us to visit such a place and leave no trace. Even if we'd left nothing, the mental picture of us in our yellow rubber boots and zip-off pants, reading paperbacks and toting high-tech backpacks, would still be there, along, perhaps, with a new germ of desire, and then maybe discontent. Or perhaps I flatter myself. Nevertheless, I felt guilty, greedy, for buying my way in to look at these people.

On the other hand, the gate had already been opened. The signs were everywhere: in the bras and T-shirts; in the new form of *mandioca*, introduced by missionaries; in the TVs and telephone, the generator that brought recorded music and movies, the washing machine and tetherballs. Some were probably improvements, others not. I was glad that the Yanomami were able to exert some control over who got in and at what price. I thought it was probably important, for both sides, that Molly and Skyler should continue on in the world knowing there are people like this living so differently; important that our kids should get a taste of what skill and knowledge these people have; important that they learn that these people don't always need help, at least not ours, and, if they do, to listen carefully and respect what they are asking for.

34

A Long Swim

BACK IN SÃO GABRIEL, we showered, rented a few more DVDs, found a cozy neighborhood dinner spot, and waged battle against the *moucouine*, tiny mites. I'd been the first to get them.

Dressing one day back at the Mamirauá Reserve, I'd looked down to see that anywhere my underpants and bra had been was covered in red bumps—a red-welt bikini. Apparently the mites were attracted to spots where it was warm, hence your underwear lines. I must have been a find—a premenopausal woman with hot flashes. I had to grit my teeth not to scratch.

By the time we left Ariabu, Peter, Molly, and Skyler were turning red as well. We spread the recommended antidote, the musty-smelling andiroba nut oil, on liberally, forming a layer of glue to which our clothes now stuck.

"Oh, Mom, I feel so yucky," Molly said. "I have about everything you could get. I have bites on my butt, pimples on my face, diarrhea, my period. I feel bloated, sweaty, and dirty." But she was laughing.

We enjoyed kicking back, waiting for the fast boat that would take us back to Manaus. It would be leaving in two days. Our time in the Amazon was coming to an end.

The taxi jounced through the ruts and came to a stop by the river-bank. At seven in the morning, a small line of passengers was forming. We suspected this fast boat was not going to be as luxurious as the one we'd taken at the beginning of our trip from Manaus to Tefé—and it was going to take twice as long, twenty-four hours. But we had high hopes anyway. Though smaller, this one still had the sleek, white promise of the first, and to our relief, the air conditioning was less ferocious. It had the same rows of airline seats, and I was glad to see the banks of TV screens, knowing that for Skyler, the nonstop string of action movies would make the time fly. The only things missing were the back deck and the writing emblazoned on the hull: *God is in first place.* This should have tipped us off.

Here on the Rio Negro, the bank was very different from that on the Rio Solimões. It was strikingly beautiful—with giant, rounded granite outcroppings and pure-white pocket beaches punctuating a lush tangle of forest. Maybe the rocks were the reason there seemed to be no farming and, as a result, almost no houses. It felt pristine, wilder. Initially there were those jutting peaks in the distance, but gradually the land flattened and spread, earth curving into sky bent around a fish-eye lens.

We were served a dinner of stewed beef, sautéed chicken, and rice, and then they turned out the lights. It was six thirty and dark. We fidgeted with our seat backs. They were anchored upright. We pulled the plexiglass windows shut against the rain. It was almost cozy, but not comfortable. The woman next to me finally decided to lie down in the center aisle. There we were again, racing through the night in a boat. I thought I might have preferred Anderson's open-air canoe, with its more visceral feeling of flying through deep space.

I was dreaming of dancers when my slumbering body lurched into the seat in front of me. There was a loud bang. People were screaming. "*Calma, calma!*" someone shouted. Awake in an instant, I wheeled around to find Molly, Skyler, and Peter in their seats behind me.

"What happened?"

"We crashed."

I glanced at my watch. It was 4:00 AM.

"If we need to bail, go out the window," Peter said quietly.

We all looked out the window. Blackness.

I thought about what I could swim with, which things we might need could survive the wet: credit cards, eyeglasses, passports.

Molly and Skyler said nothing.

I looked down. Our computer was gone. In fact, everything I'd stuffed under the seat in front of me was gone. People were out of their seats. None of the hundred-plus people seemed to want to sit down. There was water on the floor, but it seemed to be seeping, not gushing.

I flashed back to those tiny paragraphs I used to read at the bottom of some inside page in *The New York Times*. The ones that matter-of-factly described the sinking of yet another ferry in some faraway place, the tens of lives lost. Was this going to be it?

I got up and squeezed my way forward. Our computer and several bags had somehow ended up three rows in front of us. I continued to weave my way through the standing people up to the front. It was an astonishing sight. The bow had drilled into a sandbank all the way up to the windshield, which was now missing large slices of glass. Had the pilot really run into the shore at forty miles an hour? Had he fallen asleep? A man was outside standing on the sand, digging the boat out with a blunt two-by-four. I wondered whether this would be like pulling the knife out of someone who'd been stabbed. The person wouldn't die as long as the knife was plugging the hole. Were we not sinking because the sand was filling the gap?

I returned to Molly and Skyler, who were still quietly seated. Except for one passenger with a broken arm, no one was severely injured, and people were now surprisingly calm. The man in front of us said the same thing had happened last month.

It began to get light. We had not run into the bank; we were in the middle of the river! It would be a long swim. I began to think about what might be in the water. Unfortunately, I knew.

35

Dark-Skinned Nannies Wheel
White-Skinned Babies to the Park

I WAS LOOKING for a padlock.

"I don't know the word . . ." I said in Portuguese, miming a padlock with my hands, and the sales clerk responded, "Oh a lock. Over here." In English. That was when I knew I was in a different place.

A couple of weeks earlier, our fast boat, dug out of the sandbar in the middle of the Rio Negro, had been able to limp its way back to Manaus, late, but without further mishap. We'd checked back into our hostel and caught a plane the next day to Salvador, from whence we'd taken the bus to the van to the ferry back to Penedo. A week later, we'd reversed the transport chain back to Salvador to catch a flight to Rio de Janeiro, our last hurrah before the kids returned to school.

We felt we couldn't go to Brazil without going to Rio, one of the most visited cities in the Southern Hemisphere. It was immediately obvious why. This city of six and a half million has one of the most dramatic natural settings in the world. Rocky outcroppings rise above a looping coastline trimmed in white-sand beaches: Copacabana, Ipanema, names that have been immortalized in film and song. Rio's *carnaval* is second to none for spectacle. We've all seen the images of samba-dancing women on huge floats, all bare skin and feathers.

We were meeting Peter's mother, Judy, and sister Kate, and thanks to them were luxuriating in the hushed comfort of the Ipanema Plaza, a boutique hotel, where glittering cases of H. Stern jewels adorned the lobby and rooms were tastefully decorated in celadon green. Looking out from the fourteenth floor, we saw canyons of white dropping to rivers of green, through which wove schools of yellow taxis and lumbering white buses. Above the canyons, black sea birds soared and dropped, flapping on hinged wings, by the windows of white-upholstered apartments.

Down on the street, I was taken aback at how American the world outside felt. On the streets of Ipanema, we could have been on the Upper East Side of Manhattan. There were the same sidewalk cafés and plate glass window displays of elegant clothing and gleaming kitchen accessories, the same clusters of ficus trees for sale on the sidewalk. There were the same dark-skinned nannies wheeling white-skinned babies to the park. There was even a Citibank. We didn't have any of this in Penedo.

Molly and I salivated over Panama straw fedoras and gladiator sandals. I hankered after a cocktail dress I had no reason to buy. The off-the-shoulder sheath shimmered through filmy veils of organza, in peach and lime, sequins and beads, epitomizing my image of Rio, the Hollywood city of romance, with Roger Moore, Bing Crosby, and Jean-Paul Belmondo for guides.

Back in Missoula, on our hanging mobile of wishes for this year in Brazil, soccer had taken second place after "Go to the Amazon." In addition to wishing to play, Skyler had written, "Watch a live professional game."

Rio was home to many of Brazil's top *futebol* teams, and, amazingly, our four-day visit coincided with the semifinals of the Guanabara Cup, the tournament pitting Rio's teams against each other. We would have to forsake our loyalty to our chosen team, Corinthians, as they were based in São Paulo.

Choosing a team was no small matter. Team loyalties were handed down through generations, and once you had declared yours there was no going back. We'd sworn fealty to Corinthians out of loyalty to Zeca. But as we already knew, Zeca was a maverick. Most Penedenses were diehard Flamengo fans, and Flamengo would be playing in Rio.

"Flamengo is a team of criminals," Zeca had said dismissively when first recruiting us as Corinthians fans.

He didn't have to argue his case. On our arrival in Brazil, our morning cake and coffee at the Pousada Colonial had been accompanied by grisly TV reenactments of the murder of a model by Flamengo's beloved goalie, Bruno Fernandes de Souza, better known as Bruno. I intentionally sat with my back to the television so I wouldn't have to stomach, yet again, her bundled body parts being thrown into a pond as I ate my fried eggs.

"*Que pena* . . ."—How sad, what a waste of a life, the clerk in a Penedo furniture store had said, shaking her head, looking more stricken at the loss of the goalie she idolized than by what he'd purportedly done to the mother of his baby.

However, Flamengo, in an effort to regain lost ground, had recently taken on Ronaldo de Assis Moreira, known fondly as Ronaldinho, luring him back to Brazil from Milan. Skyler had been following Ronaldinho on YouTube in the States for years. It was clear which semifinal we'd be going to: Flamengo v. Botafogo.

Judy decided she could do without the sweaty, jostling crowd, but Kate, always up for a new experience, came along. Our hotel arranged for us to go in a group with a guide. Part of me wanted to go local, take public transport and find our own way to the stadium. But after seeing the streets swarming with shouting, fist-pumping Botafogo fans, clearly drunk and out for blood, I was relieved to be floating above the fray in the raised dais of our tour bus.

"We have to be sure we sit in the right section so we don't get gang beaten," Skyler had been saying. The appearance of military police walking skulking German shepherds in the no-man's land between the stands and the field confirmed my sense that things could get ugly.

Molly wanted to get Flamengo shirts, and fit in with the fans, so we bought a couple as we wound up the switchbacking ramp, almost running to keep up with our guide. We popped out into the stands. It was 104 degrees, and our side was in the sun. The fans from each team got a clearly delineated half of the stadium. Ours was awash in red and black and gargantuan, swooping banners with Ronaldinho's silhouetted face. An enormous red sheet, forty rows high and fifty people wide, was being passed overhead. You weren't allowed to bring any liquids into the stadium, and no alcohol was sold inside, but the ban hadn't stopped anyone from prepping before they got there. The stands were rocking.

"There's Ronaldinho." Skyler was pointing. "The one in the white cleats, with the long hair. See, he's shaking the refs' hands."

Like everyone else, we stood for most of the two-hour game. I looked at the tattoo in baroque cursive on the glistening, bare shoulder blade of the man next to me: *Flamengo.* The energy was intoxicating. We rode the heart-thumping din of shouted chants and hoarse songs. Suspecting that the words weren't totally flattering, I consulted Skyler, our in-house expert on insulting phrases. It turned out the fans were shouting, "Hey ref, go fuck yourself," repeatedly, in rhythm, at thundering volume—inconceivable in the States.

When the game ended, the teams were tied, one to one. Fantastic, a shoot out! We would get to see Ronaldinho bend the ball into the net. It was interesting how you could feel a player's personality, even when he was so far away that he appeared only an inch tall. Ronaldinho seemed calm and generous as he offered a hand to pull up a fallen player from the other team or passed off the ball for a teammate to take the shot. He didn't seem to be the usual chest-thumping, fist-pumping Brazilian footballer, which you'd think he might be when he could pull in a salary of $700,000 a month. But Ronaldinho was last in line to kick, and Flamengo sewed it up before they got to him. By that time, the Botafogo stands were almost empty. On our side, no one had moved. Ronaldinho was last to leave the field, raising his arms to his fans, who roared with approval, including sweat-matted Molly and Skyler, sated and happy.

That evening, we headed out for more sightseeing. After a taxi fiasco, in which our two taxis split and went in opposite directions, the kids and I stood waiting for Peter, Judy, and Kate at the base of the Sugarloaf cable car.

"Mom, we're going to miss the sunset. Couldn't Skyler and I go up by ourselves?"

I succumbed. I coughed up my last bits of change and watched as my children disappeared in a dangling box headed to the top of Sugarloaf, a rocky precipice in the middle of Rio.

"If we don't show up in an hour and a half, come back down," I shouted after them.

Eventually, the others limped up in their yellow cab, tired and frustrated. We'd missed the sunset but in the end got something equally magical. Balanced atop the Sugarloaf, we soared in the soft, cool air. We watched as the city's night-lights sparked on. The bustle of this six-million-person city settled into a soothing sea of shimmering fairy dust spilling around dark volcanoes. The lights of streaming cars piped a scalloped shoreline. The slums of Rio, the *favelas*, trickled like silver lava down volcanic gullies. At night, everything looked equally jewel-like, the condominiums of the rich and the shacks of the poor. I remembered what Giovanni had said back in Penedo: "Everything looks good from a distance."

I guessed it could also be said, "Everything looks good in the dark."

36

Put to the Test

I WAS HAPPY to go home to Penedo. We'd been gone for most of five weeks. Molly was eager to start up at Imaculada, where her class would now be the *segundo ano*, the second-to-oldest class in the school. At the recommendation of Iracema, one of the *coordenadors*, we'd decided that Skyler would go back and complete the first semester of his seventh-grade year (when we'd arrived, he'd entered into the second). This meant he'd be switching to a younger class. He wasn't thrilled, but he seemed to accept it as yet another part of his bad-school-year package. Despite the return of his perpetual postural slump, things actually seemed to be improving.

"Well, this is a reversal of fortune," Peter whispered one day wandering into the garden room. "Check out Skyler." I got up from my desk and looked down the hall.

"Do you think we can trust it?" I whispered back.

We'd come to the end of the first week of classes, and Skyler had miraculously settled onto the red couch to do his homework with no resistance. Sitting down beside him, I paged through his multi-subject notebook and was quite astonished. Last semester, it seemed he'd never gotten a grip on which classes he had what days, who the teachers were, or whether he had any homework. We'd engaged Vanessa, Skyler's English teacher, largely to find out what his homework was.

"Skyler, I'm so impressed. Your *caderno* is so much more organized than it was."

He leafed through the notebook to show me his history notes.

"And I actually understand it, too." He recounted how the barbarians had attacked European cities and how the inhabitants had gone to feudal lords for protection.

"And here in math, I've already done all of this. My teacher, Valmir, he told how good I am to everyone in math. He told them in math how good I am . . . How do you say it?"

He'd been repeating phrases in English recently, with wonderment and some pride, I thought, that he was getting so much better at Portuguese that it was interfering with his English.

"He told them I wasn't held back because I couldn't do it, that I'm one of the best in math, but because I need to complete the other half of the year for my school in the States and because of the language." Skyler seemed relieved.

I was grateful for Valmir's tact. Along with Mario, the kids' PE teacher, he'd been exceptionally kind and empathetic, much as the *capoeiristas* had been.

At the capoeira salon that Monday, I mentioned to Bentinho that Skyler's birthday, his thirteenth, was coming up.

"*Podemos celebrar . . . ?*"—Could we celebrate on Wednesday, with cake?

"*Certo.*" Bentinho seemed pleased.

When Wednesday came, I was on alert. I'd been anticipating this evening for four months, since we'd witnessed the other boy's thirteenth birthday, and I'd begun to hope that Skyler might be put to a similar challenge, have the fortune to be part of a male rite of passage, so rare now in the United States, and pass the test. I knew I was hoping that somehow this rite would ease his fraught journey through adolescence, instilling him with the deep confidence that I hoped would eventually ground him as a man. I knew it was a lot to ask, more than this one event could really deliver, but still . . . Now I was nervous.

I'd been vigilantly guarding the remains of the last of three cakes from a surprise birthday party that Skyler's friends had thrown him the night before. Victor and Ricardo had been eager to mount a surprise party at our house, not easy to do when punctuality is about as foreign to Brazilians as patience is to Americans. But they'd pulled it off, enlisting neighborhood friends to blow up balloons and string crepe paper above our dining table in a delicious frenzy of secret plotting.

Considering the number of times we'd trudged up and down the ridge carrying cakes and platters of *brigadeiro*, cloyingly rich balls of condensed milk and cocoa powder, made by Karol and other friends, everyone in the neighborhood must have known by then that it was Skyler's birthday. This time, on my way down to the capoeira salon, I was carrying a heavy platter of watermelon, so I was walking fast.

"*Cadê Eskyloh?*" The standard greeting rang out every few meters.

"*Lá.*" I jerked my head back to where Skyler was slowly making his way down the hill, surrounded by his friends.

"*Salve,*" I shouted as I entered the salon and shook off my flip-flops.

"*Salve,*" they shouted back.

I put the watermelon and pop on one of the tables that had been pushed to the side, and I headed into the back courtyard to change. I'd recently managed to overcome my self-consciousness enough to start wearing the capoeira white. By the time I reentered the salon, Skyler and his entourage were coming through the door.

Bentinho smiled and nodded his head as if to say, *Ah, here he is, the sacrificial lamb.*

More and more people kept arriving throughout the warm-up, which was unusually strenuous. Recently, Bentinho had lectured the advanced students, telling them they couldn't just show up to "play"; they also had to continue to train. I hoped Skyler had caught that life message.

By the time we broke for the *roda*, there were nineteen people besides Skyler. Nineteen people he'd have to spar against, nineteen people who were going to try to trip him up. Peter had arrived with the camera.

Skyler didn't look the least bit uneasy. Maybe he didn't realize what was coming. Or maybe he did and was eager to see if he could meet the challenge. I'd begun to notice in him an almost-reckless desire to prove himself, as though testosterone had taken the helm.

The drumming was starting, and the circle was beginning to form. When everyone had gathered, they all fell silent. Bentinho was smiling. "It's Skyler's birthday," he began in Portuguese. "He's twenty-three." Everyone laughed. Skyler nodded, going along with the joke. "No, he's thirteen," Bentinho continued. "We're going to play with him. Right?" An image of panthers batting around a mouse flashed into my head. "Okay. Let's go."

The *berimbau* player began to sing. *"Parabéns para você . . ."*

I laughed. It was "Happy Birthday," but stretched out and synco-pated to fit the capoeira rhythm. Then, suddenly, they shifted into our birthday song in English fit into the capoeira call-and-response mode. Everyone joined in, *"'Appy birtday, 'appy birtday . . ."* grinning at their own attempts at the language.

I think then it began to dawn on Skyler what was going on. Bentinho invited Skyler into the circle. As usual, the tempo was slow, at first. They circled each other, crouching and rocking, almost in slow-motion, both pairs of eyes fixed on the other—the tall, powerful black man, the small, slight blond boy. Then Bentinho's foot swept out, almost hooking Skyler's, but Skyler dodged and spun. Bentinho regrouped. Skyler tilted and kicked toward Bentinho's head. Bentin-ho's arm darted into the space under his leg, but he didn't grab the leg and flip Skyler to the ground, not this time. Instead he flipped over onto his head and waited, legs bent, ready to shoot forward should Skyler advance. Skyler lunged sideways, switched his legs, killed time. Then Bentinho was up, sweeping one leg behind Skyler's knees, the other leg in front, and Skyler was down, his legs locked in a scissor grip. Skyler laughed, surprised, and squiggled out of Bentinho's hold, rising and darting away. Bentinho smiled.

Ningo cut in. He and Skyler touched hands, and the bout started anew, over and over, eighteen more times. Fabio was the last. By this time, the tempo had picked up and the "game" had moved into the realm of fast-spinning high kicks, and Skyler was doing well, holding his own, but Fabio could see he was exhausted. After a few slicing fan kicks, Fabio held out his palms and put an arm around Skyler's shoulders to lead him out of the ring. Skyler bent over, hands on his knees, and filled his lungs with air. There were quiet nods as the play-ers looked his way. He'd done it.

Bentinho started speaking, and, as usual, I could only catch a few words: *"rapaz de treze"*—boy of thirteen; *"agradecido para seu participação em capoeira"*—grateful for his participation in capoeira. He looked my way. "Do you want to speak?"

I nodded and started haltingly, *"Estou orgulhosa dele"*—I'm proud of him—*"porque eu sei . . . "*—because I know it's not easy to come to another country where you don't speak the language, where you know no one. It takes courage. But he has this courage. We are—*"agradavel?"*

"Agradecido."

"Agradecido,"—grateful—I continued, "for all of you because you help us a lot." I was starting to tear up.

They clapped. Bentinho nodded to Skyler. *"Fala?"*—Speak?

Skyler looked uncertain then came out with a simple *"Obrigado"*— Thank you.

Yes, thank you, I thought, *for taking my small, uncertain, stumbling boy and helping him to find his strength in this time of insecurity. Thank you for your generosity, your willingness to take in this boy who is richer and more privileged than any of you and offer him something that is more valuable than anything he could buy—the knowledge that he can walk into the unknown and come out the other side, stronger for it.*

They all smiled and burst into applause.

37

Gratitude

IN NINE MONTHS, I have found:

- friends I would never have in the United States.
- patience with myself and others.
- a new language that I can now converse in with people of my own age.
- a feeling of belonging in a culture very different from my own.
- immense gratitude for the generosity of the people in this town.

PART IV: *Crossing the River*

MARCH, APRIL, MAY

38

A Five-Day Orgy

WE COULD SEE IT coming. First the multicolored plastic fringe, zig-zagging pole to pole down the street, thick and shaggy, rustling like dry palms; then the banners on every light post; then the sparkling, harlequin-painted faces like giant eggs grinning down from gazebo pillars; and finally the wiring of the extra-bright white lights. It had been going on for days. Here, finally, was the excited buildup we had for Christmas in the United States, a holiday that had passed in Brazil with a dull thud.

Tired from traveling and ready to settle back into our quiet routine, we didn't find the prospect of five nonstop, sleepless days of jostling crowds drinking and shouting and drinking and singing and drinking too appealing. But finally, even I was finding it hard to resist the insistent gaiety. It was hard not to smile at the burly man in the tutu and clown wig waving from his motorcycle, or the sleek black car spotted with rainbow confetti stickers, or the little band of jiving drummers wandering around town, a flip-flop-footed dancing bull leading the way.

"*Vai a Neópolis?*" my tennis coach had asked me at the end of my lesson one day, as we'd picked up balls strewn around the court and tossed them into an old shopping cart. Everyone said *carnaval* in Neópolis, the town across and downriver in Sergipe, was better. There they brought in name-brand bands at night and hosted the *Mela-Mela*, a major food fight, during the day.

"Do we need to take our own eggs and flour?" I'd asked.

"Yeah, and condensed milk and sugar water to throw." He'd grinned.

Zeca had warned us to watch out for people putting things in our mouths. Or was it to keep our mouths closed because there would be a lot flying through the air?

On the day we decided to go over for the *Mela-Mela*, Peter and I and the "gang" (Skyler, Victor, and Ricardo) were strung along one wall waiting for the *lancha* to cast off. We were headed to Neópolis, and we were armed. We'd hidden four supermarket bags full of flour in several backpacks. No one else, however, seemed to have anything. I started to feel very American. Had we supersized it again?

Molly had been largely on her own for the past two days, coming home at 6:00 AM after staying out all night. (Schools wisely canceled classes for this five-day stretch.) Surprisingly, I felt fine about it. She was good at checking in; had, in her friends, a phalanx of bodyguards; and seemed to know how to handle herself. When I'd asked if men were ever a problem, she'd said matter-of-factly, "Sometimes you just have to pry them off your face." *Okay, she's immersed,* I thought.

The *lancha's* motor started up, rumbling like a long fart. The little tube of a boat had filled and was listing to one side. I glanced at Ricardo. At age ten, he was crossing the river for the first time, and I knew his aunt was anxious about it given his rudimentary swimming skills. But he was looking cool, relaxed back into the bench, legs wide like all those men who ride the New York subway as if they're the only ones on it. This was day three of *carnaval* in Brazil, day three of sweaty crowds, pumping music, crazy chaos, pre-Lent excess.

Twenty minutes later, we coasted into the concrete landing on the other side. We squeezed our way out of the little boat and followed the crowd trudging up a narrow, twisting street. Neópolis has a pretty central *praça* full of benches and trees. We'd assumed the *Mela-Mela* would be there. But instead, like the sedated castle from *Sleeping Beauty,* it was full of sleeping people, tucked under bushes, on top of market tables. The crowd from the *lancha* was turning, disappearing down a side street. We hurried to catch up.

A block later, we were in it, carried along by the crowd through a canyon of sound. A guy who reminded me of the Michelin Man, with his skin painted silver the better to showcase his bulging biceps, stood on a stoop. He held his arms high to show off his tiny, Speedo-clad hips, slowly gyyyyyyyyrating to the upbeat brass of the *frevo* music (a northeastern Brazilian folk music that's especially popular around *carnaval* time). On a rooftop, a man in a black jumpsuit painted with a Day-Glo Halloween skeleton stepped side to side to the chest-throbbing beat, then gave a powerful pelvic thrust to the front, a thrust to the back, and a slow, juicy grind. A line of four men in swimsuits step-touched in unison, like backup dancers, then spread their legs wide and dropped their hips in a come-and-get-it, side-to-side swing. Much as I think I am, as a dancer, unusually comfortable in my body for an American, in that crowd, I felt like a buttoned-up, Bible-toting Calvinist.

We sidestepped deadpan grandmothers, holding flaccid water hoses out living-room windows. A few hours later, we'd be grateful for the service. As we moved deeper in, we began to see people with faces patched with white, hair matted with flour. We scooped flour out of our bags, eager to join the fray—but how? A slimy hand swept over my face; its wet fingers seemed to be trying to crawl into my mouth. I squirmed away and instinctively flung my fistful. The man behind me laughed. In minutes, Peter's face was dripping with green and red. Skyler had clods of something pink stuck to his eyebrows. A tall man in an oversized diaper rubbed a goopy hand in Ricardo's hair. Ricardo didn't look amused. I wondered if, in Ricardo's mind, this would come to represent what was "across the river." People stuck their hands in our flour bags as we squeezed through the increasingly dense pack of pulsing, flour-and-slime-coated flesh. Earnest vendors sold beer from Styrofoam coolers, looking as though they were wondering if the great sales were worth the sprays of shaving cream and beer. Two tank trucks were parked at a street corner, manned by bands of bare-chested studs pelting the crowd with a fire hose. The *Mela-Mela* continued as far as we could see.

Several hours later, we wound our way back past the expressionless grandmothers, the sleeping square, and down to the river.

"That was fun!" Skyler exclaimed. Ricardo was eager to wash off. I wandered into the water in my clothes and dunked. It would take me a week to pick the hardened scabs of flour out of my hair and a month to clean up Skyler.

At home, we found Molly, who'd gone to the *Mela-Mela* with her friends.

"I . . . have . . . never had," Molly was saying emphatically, "so many disgusting things put in my mouth. I have had flour, eggs, butter—oh my God, I was so glad I was wearing my sunglasses. This huge hand just smeared my whole face in butter. I was dripping."

"Was it fun?" I asked her.

"Yeah, it was really fun. They would tell you to say a word, like *chuva*—I said that one twice—and then, WHAM, in the mouth."

I flopped down on the couch, mentally preparing for the last two days of the festival. Our house was located at *carnaval* central. We just had to open our front windows to watch hours and hours of *blocos* —the slow-moving masses of bouncing people in their matching fluorescent T-shirts, following a little brass *frevo* band or a blast-you-out-of-your-seat *equip som* car. But Day Four turned out to be a rest day.

On the last night, we stood on our wicker couch in the garden room, propping our elbows on the windowsill. Each *bloco* seemed to have a designated route. Many were accompanied by towering *bonecas*, swirling, swaying puppets with gaping teeth and wild hair on oversized heads. The blue satin skirts of an eight-foot-tall woman with enormous white teeth leering out of glossy red lips split open to reveal Victor's dark head.

"*Oi, Eskyloh!*" he shouted up to us from under his precariously balanced ward.

Bentinho passed by, twirling his teenage daughter from the end of a raised finger. The lovely white-haired woman who lived down the block bounced by in a gold tutu and angel wings. "*Vem!*" she called, waving her wand at us. "Come!"

Our perpetually drunken neighbor tilted by, careening from one side of the street to the other. A woman in a platinum wig, cow-print skirt, and cowboy boots passed out condoms. Or was her low, hoarse voice a man's? A clutch of Peter's soccer buddies, their cheeks rouged and eyelids painted blue, had squeezed their muscled bodies into slinky polyester dresses. They raised their beers to our window as they went by.

The kaleidoscopic color, the pop-your-ear-drums volume of the music—the energy—had been maintained for almost five days. During *carnaval*, as on other occasions, it seemed that Brazilians had an insatiable appetite for fun.

Molly showed up with her school friends Leila, Larissa, and Keyla, her carefully pre-torn *bloco* shirt falling off one shoulder. Breathless, she ducked into her bedroom, slipped on her blue flower-print dress, and slid out the door, geared up for one more all-night trip to Neópolis, one more night of rapid shuffling feet talking to the music, dancing hip to hip under a dark Brazilian sky. Peter, Skyler, and I propped our eyes open for another hour, then battened down the hatches and hoped for sleep.

39

The Doldrums of March

ONCE CARNAVAL ENDED, March quickly degenerated into a scene by Tennessee Williams—stagnant, sweaty, and seething. Even the water hyacinths floating in the river had come to a standstill. Tensions were running high. Molly slapped Skyler, then burst into tears; Skyler was in our faces, then retreated, refusing to talk; Peter and I hid in the "cooler," our windowless, air-conditioned cubicle of a bedroom. My patience declined as the heat rose. We all just wanted to go home. Peter was the only one who seemed to be handling it all with equanimity.

The sugarcane fires burned. Though illegal, the practice continued. It made the cane easier to cut, and most companies were still hiring laborers to harvest by hand—laborers, like Fabio from capoeira, whom the company would perennially underpay, "somehow" never delivering what they'd promised. The factory bus lumbered by with a limp dummy of a man tied to the front grill. I was surprised the company would allow such a protest. In the afternoon, great spirals of smoke appeared upriver. At night, we'd see the fields alight, distant flames orange against black. By morning, the far hills had faded into brown haze. This had been going on for six months, though common wisdom said it should have ended by now.

Skyler, like any kid running barefoot, had three cuts, swollen red and oozing pus around his ankles. Peter ended up in the emergency room, having punctured his foot with a kebab skewer that was lying in wait on a soccer field that had supposedly recently been cleaned. Peter had paid for the cleaning.

The ants were multiplying. The smaller ones had established regular highways—by the dish drainer, under the bathroom door—while the big ones were descending from their ceiling perches and now appeared disconcertingly out of the trash, on the food shelves, underfoot—like one-night stands, still there rummaging around in the morning, over-staying their welcome.

Our house was turning into a clubhouse-cum-sports-equipment-outlet-cum-soup-kitchen-cum-Internet café.

Gangs of boys, Skyler's friends, swept through every afternoon, sometimes settling in for hours, taking careening rides in the hammock, walking on their hands down the hall, juggling soccer balls. Some days I'd walk in and find all four of our computers in use by magnetized boys, bodies frozen, eyes flitting, fingers jerking spasmodically. They devoured *biscoitos* and peanuts and drained our water jugs.

People we didn't know—skateboarders, little girls, parade partici-pants (Brazilians love using parades to advertise, to celebrate)—were knocking on our door asking for water, throats parched by the relent-less heat.

People we did know—Skyler's friends, Peter's soccer buddies, the neighbor boys—asked to borrow soccer balls, swimming masks, pad-dle ball sets. We began to insist they bring them back the same day, as we found ourselves more and more frequently cleaned out and clueless about where things had gone.

Then people started knocking on the door for food. First Ryan, which they pronounced *Heon*, a bony, taut boy from capoeira, who made that fluttering gesture in front of his mouth—palm down, fin-gers digging toward his lips—as he waited for Skyler to change into his capoeira clothes. He crouched in a corner of the kitchen on the floor, turning down my offer of the couch, and inhaled a plate of rice and meat.

Two days later, a pregnant woman appeared, dangling a small boy by his wrist, asking for water and *comida*. She sat on the front step, leav-ing the door open—half in, half out. Eyes drooping with exhaustion, she was gentle with the boy, cajoling him into drinking water while she picked through cold stew. She left the empty dish on the floor and thanked me quietly before hefting the boy onto her hip and heading back out into the beating sunshine.

A few months earlier, around Christmas, Aniete had gotten a job working in a clothing store down in the *baixa*. Sorry as we were to lose her, we'd let her go, knowing it was a good opportunity. But by March, Aniete had started using our house as her *lanchonete*, as we were within walking distance of her work. I'd find her on the bench by the back window just when I was ready to take a break and gaze out the window myself, and then hunkered over rice and beans at our dining table, chattering with Shirley, Aniete's cousin and our new *empregada*, just as I was ready to sit down for lunch.

Things were falling apart at home in the States as well. Our cat got shot with a BB and stopped eating. Our dog tore her leg on a fence and needed stitches. My mother had to put her dog to sleep.

"This is the longest month." Skyler groaned.

March was rough.

Peter banged through the front door into the garden room.

"I've just been informed I've been telling nurses all over town that I've been playing soccer without my shorts."

He was returning from his Portuguese lesson with Giovanni.

"At all those clinics, I've been saying *calções*, shorts, when I should have been saying *calçados*, shoes."

Molly and I laughed uproariously.

I felt as if my Portuguese were falling apart. I'd probably hit my peak in about November; after that, all our English-speaking friends had begun to arrive.

"That's a beautiful expensive!" I called out to Elizia as I crossed the *praça* on my way back from the stationery store. She was sitting in front of the school in her sleek new silver Fiat.

Oh, jeez, I thought as I waved cheerfully and realized I'd said "expensive" instead of "car," the two words separated by one *r* in Portuguese. God, they're tolerant.

April passed much like March, rather the way months did at home, mostly indistinguishable one from the other except for the markers of holidays—Halloween, Thanksgiving, Christmas—and, where we lived in the north, the change of seasons, though even those were mostly indistinguishable from year to year, one winter being much like another. Looking back at my childhood, it was the years we lived abroad that I really remembered. The others were the filler in between.

It made me think that it was probably time to go home, that Penedo was losing part of its great value, the power of the new and different to open one's eyes.

One night, Skyler wrangled open the front door, slammed some things around in the kitchen, then dropped into his chair at the table. The rest of us had just finished dinner.

"How was the *roda*?" I asked. Too tired, I'd stayed home from capoeira.

"Fine."

"So what's bothering you?"

"Nothing."

Then, a few minutes later, "It's what happened after the *roda*. Can I be excused?"

An hour later, he flopped down on our bed.

"I don't think I'm going to be Ricardo's friend anymore," he announced.

"Why not?" I asked.

"He gets in so many fights." Then it all spilled out. Ricardo had run after Pedro and kicked him, hard. Pedro had started crying and throwing rocks at Ricardo, and then Pedro's mom had come out and dragged him away.

"We could hear him screaming inside and her, you know, hitting him." Skyler paused then continued. "And Ricardo didn't even care. He just forgot about it." The flow of words subsided. "I tried to stop them," he added.

"I think maybe the same thing happens to Ricardo with his mom. That's why he lives with his aunt," I said now to Skyler, lying on the bed. "So maybe for him it doesn't seem . . . You know, it's just life," I ended lamely.

"Oh, and you know why Bazooka hasn't been at capoeira?" Skyler continued, on a roll. Skyler and I especially admired Bazooka. We'd nicknamed him "the cat" because he moved with a big cat's quiet ease but startling strength. "He got shot in the face. He's in the hospital. He still has one bullet in his face and two in his chest. Fabio told me. I guess he'd been drinking *cachaça* and got in a fight, and the other guy went home and came back with a .22."

I recalled that Giovanni had said that five people had been shot in Penedo during *carnaval.* Maybe Bazooka had been one of them.

After a while, Skyler lightened up. "Maybe this could be *my* job. You know how you've started teaching Fabio English and Molly's started teaching dance at the girls' orphanage and Dad's trying to get Junior out of jail? Maybe I could help Ricardo stop fighting."

"Yeah," Molly said, appearing through the door, her physics textbook in hand. "Otherwise, when he starts drinking, he's going to end up like all these others."

The next morning, I picked up the *Gazeta de Alagoas* from where it had been pushed under our front door. "*Capitão P M é assassinado*" was the headline. "The Captain of the Military Police Has Been Assassinated." "Assassinations," as they called murders, were our daily bread.

That day at lunch, Aniete limped through the door, looking drained from her climb up the hill. She sank into a chair at the dining table with a plate of rice and beans. "*Ontem, as cinco horas . . .*"—Yesterday at five o'clock, some young guys in a car shot a guy sitting in a plaza, right by O Laçador. "You know O Laçador?" she asked, referring to the Brazilian grill near her house. "There were lots of people. Everybody ran. The guy they shot, he shot another guy last week." She shoveled in another mouthful, rolled her eyes, and shook her head. "*Muita violência, muita violência.*"

Alagoans seemed to wear their first-place ribbon for highest incidence of violence in the country as a badge of distinction, as though if you couldn't do anything about it, you might as well claim it. Another nod to fate.

"*Eskyloh!*" The afternoon shout came through the front window.

"Skyler, it's Ricardo," I shouted from the front room.

Skyler ambled to the front door and jangled it open.

"*Oi.*"

"*Quer jogar* parkour?"

Skyler loves parkour, the sport of jumping railings, scaling walls, leaping stairs. A few days earlier, after joining a roving band of "park-ouristas," he'd said, "Mom, I think I've found my sport."

But today, after a short conversation, he closed the door and ambled back into the house.

"Don't you want to go out?" I asked.

"No." He sounded dejected. "I told him I couldn't play with him anymore if he keeps fighting so much."

"You did? Wow, that's hard to do, Skyler. What did he say?"

"I don't think he understood at first. But after about three times, he said, '*Tchau*.'"

As I opened the door to go out for my tennis lesson, a shout came out of the tree in the *praça*. "*Eskyloh!*"

Skyler looked torn.

When I came back from tennis, I could see Skyler's blue-and-orange tennis shoes dangling from a branch. He dropped to the ground, grinning.

"Ricardo said he would stop fighting," he told me, clearly proud.

I wondered what kind of impact Skyler could really have. Whether we were doing the "American thing" that I often objected to: step-ping in and telling others how they should behave with the barest understanding of their culture. On the other hand, where was Ricardo headed, with his toothless, drunken mother and stern aunt? Down Bazooka's path? It wasn't hard to picture, with Ricardo's hothead-edness and the inevitability that he'd start to drink. So maybe it was better to try something rather than give into nothing, even knowing intervening might be ineffectual in the end.

Iracema, the kids' school guidance counselor, invited us over for Sun-day brunch. We asked about the recent spate of violence.

"It's the police, too," Iracema said. "Sometimes it's easier to just shoot a repeat offender than keep throwing them in jail."

We thought about Junior. We knew this wasn't his first offense.

"Don't get involved," her husband Alexandre, a fisheries engineer, said, when we told him about Junior's case. "You don't know our cul-ture, how things are done. You say he's a *boa pessoa*, but you don't know. They aren't all good people."

We felt like children, being told to stay out of trouble.

Junior was still in prison in the neighboring town of Igreja Nova. It had been three months. Peter and Zeca had been to visit him.

"If you can say you were employing him, that could be good. It will look better if he has a job," Zeca had told Peter on the way to take a deposition.

"I felt so sad saying good-bye," Peter told me on his return, "seeing him there, behind bars. We went down to the store to get him some other things to eat. They just get rice and beans and salami. He's gaining weight because he's not playing soccer." Peter put his backpack down on the wicker couch and pulled something out.

"He gave me this." On the palm of his hand sat a delicate swan, fit together from origami-like pieces of folded newspaper. "Another guy in there taught him how to make them."

40

The Sensitive Cross-Cultural Approach

I CALLED SKYLER to the window. The *sanguin*, the little monkeys, were climbing the tallest coconut palm in our neighbor's yard. There were five of them, including a mom with her tiny baby burrowed into the fur on her back. The palm must have been fifty feet high, but they walked up it as though they were going upstairs to bed.

"How do they hang on like that?" Skyler exclaimed with admiration.

As the last one reached the fronds, a light rain began to fall. It looked cozy up there under the palm thatch.

A couple of days later, Peter walked into the garden room.

"A guy's in back climbing the big coconut," he announced offhandedly.

Skyler and I hurried to the back window. A man was squatting in its top, hacking off the lower fronds. They'd turned orangey-brown in the last few weeks—the palm's way of shedding as it put out new fronds above to continue its upward climb. The man hopped himself down the long skinny trunk, placing his left hand, fingers pointing down, between his squatting feet, to hold his weight as he jumped his feet down—like a monkey. He repeated this—hand, feet, hand, feet—until he landed lightly in the weeds at the bottom.

Skyler was an intrepid tree climber, but coconut palms were in a category all their own. There wasn't much to hang on to except that snake-like trunk.

"Could you teach our son to climb the tree?" I shouted in Portuguese to the man below.

He looked up at our window, surprised, but nodded tentatively.

"Do you want him to show you how he climbs?" I asked Skyler.

"Sure. I guess so," he replied.

He left to put on a T-shirt, then sauntered down our back stairs, through the laundry room, and out into our overgrown backyard.

The man demonstrated walking up the tree. He looked as casual as the monkeys had. Hands looped around the trunk like a tree climber's belt, he just walked up it, hips jutting out into the air, taking big steps so his feet were always in front of him, not below, where they could slide down. Skyler tried. He made it about ten feet, once, twice, three times, then would get too tired and back his way down. Skyler thanked him and reemerged up the stairs.

It turned out the man was doing more than trimming our neighbor's palm trees. A couple of hours later, he'd uprooted the entire yard's entanglement of green, revealing an astonishing amount of trash—plastic pop bottles, cans, white Styrofoam takeout boxes. Our neighbor, a bachelor who'd had a hard time pulling his eyes out of Molly's cleavage, must have been chucking his dinner "dishes" out the window. Peter, Aniete, and I peered out the back, surveying the destruction.

Aniete explained that our neighbor had killed a big, venomous spider in his house and thought it had come from outside. So this: Aniete waved at the denuded plot.

Peter shouted down to the tree climber in Portuguese, "Are you going to clear the trash as well?"

"*Sim, sim.*"—Yes.

We looked out the window that evening; the plant "trash" had been assiduously cleared, leaving nothing but bare ground and the human trash that had been left behind.

For days after that, I went over in my mind how I might ask our neighbor to clean up his backyard. It was an eyesore for us, never mind a rat haven. Using my Portuguese dictionary, I carefully planned out the sentences.

"Did you know men from the city come every day to pick up our trash, right here in front?" Maybe too indirect.

How about, "*O lixo*"—The trash behind your house—"*não é muito bonita*"—is not so pretty. We'd be happy to pay someone to pick it up." But maybe then we'd become the perpetual pick-up crew.

How about the sensitive cross-cultural approach, "*Nos Estados Unidos . . .*"—In the United States, we collect our trash to be taken away by the trash collectors. I know the custom is different here, but . . ." I decided I'd try this.

But then when I ran into him the next day washing his motorcycle in the *praça* and the day after that sitting on a plastic chair blocking the sidewalk, I just couldn't quite do it. Was it because I was questioning whether it was my place, as the foreigner, to ask the locals to change their ways? Partly, and partly I just didn't want to embarrass my neighbor; but then who's to say he'd have been embarrassed?

41

The Long Arm of American Ambition

THE LONG ARM of American ambition had finally snaked its way up the Rio São Francisco. Molly, a high school junior, was in crisis over the upcoming SAT, which she was registered to take in Salvador in early May.

Molly had come to Brazil armed with the Princeton guide to practice tests, which she'd begun to plow through a few weeks before.

"Everybody quiet. Molly's taking a test. She's being timed," I'd hiss at the parade of people slamming through our front door.

"Mom, all my friends back home are getting tutors or taking prep courses," she said, sounding increasingly dejected as she ticked off another practice. I had to admit, her scores were surprisingly low, but not wanting to discourage her, I said nothing.

"Mom, I feel so overwhelmed. I don't even want to think about going back to the United States." Molly groaned. "I can't fit everything I need to graduate into my schedule next year. It's ridiculous that I can't get language credit for Portuguese, when I'm practically fluent . . . And there's so much I want to do outside of school—*The Nutcracker*, a play, soccer, the newspaper. At home there's always so much to do!" she continued. "It's so much easier here."

She was experiencing what my father, giving it the good spin, would have called "an embarrassment of riches." In the United States, if one has the means, there are many activities to choose from. In Penedo, Skyler's street friends do the same thing every day after school: look around for something to do. They house surf, hoping to juggle some lemons here, scare up a ball there. In the States, one can try out for myriad sports, join extracurricular clubs to fit any interest, and suffocate under the load. In the States, the current norm of "I want to do it all"—or is it "I *should* do it all," or maybe "everyone else is doing it all, so . . ."—has turned excitement into dread, at least for Molly. In my own life, I've often felt relief—relief that I'm done. I check things off the list, and, in the process, I check off my life.

Molly had been Skyping with friends back home, which you'd think might have established a reassuring and calming camaraderie, but instead they seemed to relish whipping themselves into a stressed-out frenzy, as though the height of the stress were the measure of the import of the situation. And God knows the situation was important. They were suddenly standing at the gateway to the rest of their lives: that gateway to college, the name of which was going to determine everything that came afterward. At least that's how they seemed to feel.

Finally I was beginning to worry myself. Watching Molly struggle to pick up her speed on the practice tests reminded me how much Americans value "fast"—fast food, fast answers, fast results. (This is probably why we also value "young." We don't have time for the not-so-fast old.) We want things *now*. This leads to 24/7, to sound bites. If you can't give me that information, that service, those goods *now*, I'll find somebody else who can. So of course, to get into college, our kids need to prove that they are not just smart, reflective, and knowledgeable, but fast.

Brazil is the opposite. It is the country of "slow," the country of waiting, the country of patience. The country where you assume you can't get it *now*; in fact, you might never get it. So the question becomes: *When?* And the answer is: "*Quem sabe?*"—Who knows?

We found Brazilians *living* their lives, slowly and languorously, feeling the weight of the lemons in their hands, savoring a morsel of roasted meat at lunch, enjoying the sexual electricity of hips moving in tandem to samba music, lounging in the blissful cool shade of an almond tree. This seemed to be true regardless of class, at least in the Northeast. It was not just street kids who, at loose ends without lessons and school sports, had this kind of time. We saw it with Zeca's family, too, among the successful lawyers and businessmen. They made the time to be in the present.

I knew I was romanticizing. But maybe in Brazil, expectations weren't so high; consequently, the production was lower, and maybe that was okay. Maybe the added misery of "I should be doing better than this, more than this" was not so profound.

Molly's idea of ending her high school career with a bang was to do everything, and as a result, she wasn't sure she wanted to go at all. Fun and excitement had turned into a slog and a chore. Molly is a smart, perceptive person who often surprises me with her thoughtful reflections. But being thoughtful takes time, and the SAT test is not about taking time. It's about speed. Who cares about thoughtful?

"Molly, how are you scoring your tests?" I finally asked, beginning to think that maybe there was something wrong. Could she really be getting three hundreds out of a possible eight hundred?

She showed me how she'd been calculating the score.

"Sweetie, you need to add these first then divide that," I said, reading the directions for scoring for the first time. Her scores more than doubled.

"Oh my God, I'm so relieved." A gush of air seemed to whoosh out of her.

Why was it that Penedo seemed to have only new cars—until you needed one to take you long distance? The driver of the shared taxi jiggled and yanked the passenger door open. It emitted a rusty yawn like an irascible heron. I usually happily ceded the front seat to Peter, preferring not to see how abrupt the shoulders were and how close the oncoming trucks, but as Peter wasn't there, I seemed to be the next in line and landed shotgun. Once the four of us were seated— two other women, Molly, and I—the driver crossed himself, and the car rolled uneasily forward. Some metallic thumping rhythmically pumped up into my right foot.

Despite my trepidation, I found I enjoyed speeding past the orderly rows of eucalyptus plantations on the other side of the river and was beginning to feel nostalgic, realizing that this would be our last trip to Salvador. The clanking had disappeared, and we were skimming along the two-lane road at one hundred kilometers an hour. We passed the sod farm, with the same arcing rods of irrigation pipe that we had at home, like linked dinosaur skeletons. The grass looked as smooth, and out of place, as a golf course.

As we sped along past the more-prosperous fields in the state of Sergipe, I immediately felt more at ease. It made me realize how emotionally stressful it could be to be surrounded by hardscrabble lives, even when you weren't living one. It reminded me of how guilty, but relieved, I had felt when I had left New York City and its sad panhandlers behind to move to Montana, where there were so many fewer. I knew then I was avoiding taking my share of the responsibility—out of sight, out of mind—but I was relieved nevertheless.

We got to the bus station in Aracaju with an hour to spare.

Molly and I talked for the entire, luxurious, six-hour bus trip to Salvador—of family and friends, our choice to live in Penedo, and then through ten SAT essay questions. Questions like: "What is your view of the idea that every obstacle can be turned into an opportunity?" "Does having courage mean that we have no fear, or that we act despite being afraid?" I knew she needed to bolster her answers with examples from art, science, and politics. Too bad she couldn't just write from personal experience. She would have had a lot to say about overcoming obstacles and the nature of courage just writing about her year in Brazil.

The bus slowed as we hit Salvador's evening traffic. Rolling into the station an hour late, we found a taxi to the beach suburb where the international school hosting the SAT was located.

The next morning, we walked to the school, passing the jumping ring of an equestrian center, which reminded me of the afternoons I'd spent on a horse circling a tree, learning to post, English style, when I was twelve years old in Cairo.

The school guard took down our passport numbers and admitted us. The place was so different from Imaculada, so light and airy with its sprawling white buildings connected by aerial ramps and bright blue awnings against expanses of green grass. A book fair was spread out on tables inside the entrance. Bright collages, students' artwork, were displayed along the walkway; so like Sussex, the kids' school at home. Two boys, about Skyler's age, ran past—speaking English. My chest tightened, and my eyes began to tear.

"Oh no, Mom. Not here," Molly whispered.

"Don't worry, I won't," I said, doubting my own words. I walked over to look at a framed certificate in the reception area, trying to get a grip on my welling emotions, then walked up to the receptionist and asked what time Molly should arrive the next day. She answered politely in good English. I thanked her, then turned to Molly. "Sweetie, I need to leave."

Once outside the gate and across a weedy median, I let myself cry. The year would have been so different, Skyler would have been so much happier, if we'd done what we'd done in Mozambique, if we'd chosen an international school in a big city. All the pain of his year flooded through me.

"Mom, it's not your fault."

"Sweetie, it's okay. I know why we made the choices we did. I just need to cry for a bit, and then I'll be fine."

We hailed a passing cab. I took a breath and asked for the biggest mall in Salvador. I had promised Molly she could buy a pair of sandals.

I cried for much of the twenty-minute ride, but by the time we pulled up in front of the enormous glass-and-marble complex, I'd stopped. I'd convinced myself that the experience of language immersion and the hardship of coping with the confusion and feelings of inadequacy would still be worth it in the long run. But I knew the jury was still out. I barely glanced at the driver as I paid, wondering how many sobbing women he carted around in a normal day.

Salvador Shopping was like a scene from a futuristic cartoon. Workers wearing roller skates skimmed by mopping the floors; security guards, tall, bereted figures in black, passed silently on two-wheeled Segways; frosted-glass stairways, shining escalators, and black glass elevators connected floors of swank shops—Calvin Klein, Tommy Hilfiger, Billabong, Jorge Bischoff, Sony, and Apple.

"Coffee shops, Molly, they have coffee shops." We immediately settled in for a café mocha and "chease chake."

Brazilians have raised the flip-flop to the level of haute couture. You've got your sequins, your gemstones, your encrusted sea shells, your gold and silver and glow-in-the-dark; and then there are the leather options: glossy and suede, woven, braided, ruffled, studded with gemstones and bows, wrapped in straps and buckles. We scoped out every shoe store in the place.

We spent nearly ten hours in that mall, more time than I—a hard-core anti-mall mom—had spent in such a place in years. We squealed with delight on our discovery of a Brazilian clothing brand called Skyler and bought him several shirts.

"Do you think he'll wear this one?" I asked Molly. "The name is so big; he's always worrying about looking as though he's bragging."

We ended the day in the Bom Preço, a gourmet grocery.

We stocked up on Gorgonzola, Parmesan, and Gruyere, Toblerone chocolate, raspberry jam, and Argentinean wine. I was eager to take our treasures back to Peter, the true gourmand in our house.

Finally, after dark, we headed back to the hotel, made a picnic in our room of good, seedy, whole wheat bread, strawberries, and cheese, and tucked into bed, listening to *Inkheart*, a children's tale of medieval characters who come alive out of books. I hoped this would take Molly's mind off her impending test and drown out the TV we could hear through the thin walls from the room next door.

Looking at her drifting into sleep, I thought that one of the great results of this year was that Molly and I had shifted into another phase. We'd become friends. I found her interesting and funny and was often in awe of how well she handled herself.

I knew she was worried about how she'd do on the SAT. But I wasn't. She'd do however she'd do; in the long run, it wasn't going to matter. She was going to forge ahead with the same ease and confidence, the same gracious openness, the same curiosity and energy with which she'd approached the year in Brazil. And the year we'd spent in Brazil would only enhance what she already had.

42

Floating Anger

I WALKED INTO the garden room to my desk, to be greeted by a giant *FUCK* shining out of my computer screen. I had to laugh. It captured so perfectly how I felt.

It was one of the random photographs on my screen saver. Skyler, the artist who'd meticulously dug the word an inch deep into beach sand during a trip to the coast the previous October, was the reason I'd been ranting that morning to Peter. I was feeling exhausted and out of strategies.

After the lovely, mostly stress-free weekend in Salvador with Molly, I'd wakened that morning to hear Skyler storming out of the bathroom.

"I need to work out more!"

Oh. My. God. "Skyler, you don't need to work out more."

"I do. I'm so out of shape!" He was looking really distressed.

"How can you be out of shape when, yesterday, you surfed, played a soccer game, then ran nine miles on a soft sand beach?!" He and Peter had gone to the ocean while Molly and I had made our trip to Salvador. "Out-of-shape people can't do that," I protested.

"Why am I getting side aches then?!"

"I don't know!" I was at a loss. "Let's research it," I said finally. After Molly left for school, Skyler and I Googled. With three weeks left of our time in Brazil, we'd given up on pushing Skyler out the door on time.

"The cause of side aches is unclear . . ."

"Let's look at another entry," I said starting to feel desperate.

"No, I need to get changed."

"For what?"

"I'm going to school."

Ten minutes later, Skyler walked out the door, in time for his second class. I collapsed into my desk chair, exhausted and angry.

What do you do with anger that really has no place to land? I wasn't angry *at* Skyler. It was hard to feel angry at someone who was struggling so much that his mind was sprouting strange fruit. I think I was angry *because* of Skyler, and because I couldn't, for this hour at least, hold anything more up. I couldn't think of any more convincing arguments. I couldn't find any more engaging distractions. And I couldn't stand the thought of another three weeks of this.

The thing that kept me forging on that entire year was the conviction that things would surely get better. Had to get better. That as Skyler spoke more Portuguese, he would feel more at ease. As he felt more at ease, he would like school better. As he liked school better, he would have more things to do, more people to hang out with. As he had more people to hang out with, he would feel more connected to Penedo, maybe even come to like it.

But none of this had happened.

Well, he had come to speak more Portuguese. He could rattle away without thinking, sounding like a native Alagoano, even conjugating verbs! Incredible. He was bilingual. But then the rest didn't follow. Why not, God dammit!

In my calm, collected, rational moments, I can see—now—that this year was not a good setup for a twelve-turning-thirteen-year-old boy, especially not one with perfectionist inclinations. This was not a good time in his life for language immersion in a strange, macho culture.

So what does one do with floating anger?

In my case: cry. Sit by the back window and cry and watch the sheets of rain blowing sideways across the valley. We were coming full circle. The torrential rains that had sent me diving for cover when we'd first arrived eleven months earlier were returning.

From our perch on the ridge, the picture was one-quarter land and three-quarters sky. I'd never been so aware of clouds. I felt I was looking down at the whole planet and out into the universe. It was good for perspective. I remembered once thinking—as I strode at high speed across the University of Montana campus, head down, planning my next class—that I needed to remember to look up, both literally and metaphorically. Now was a good time to look up.

When some people look up, they're looking for God. I'd wondered a number of times about ducking into Nossa Senhora dos Pretos, the church down the street. As a person raised without a religion and little experience of going to church (my foreign catholic school experiences hadn't been encouraging), I didn't know quite what I'd do once in there. Just sit, probably. Its giant open doors spreading into that arching white space seemed inviting and peaceful. Perhaps that arching space would make room for thoughts and feelings that might not be able to squeeze their way in otherwise; perhaps they'd be able to spread out and sort themselves.

But I never did. I felt too watched in this town, and religion is such a loaded subject, like a freighter lying low in the water, waiting out in the harbor for permission to come in. I'd always been afraid to let it in, afraid to let go of my rational grounding in the world, afraid to make those leaps of "faith." Funny, as there were lots of leaps of faith I was willing to take, like moving to a foreign country, with my kids, to live in a town where we knew no one and couldn't understand what anyone was saying. But then, those leaps of faith were familiar to me from my childhood.

So instead, I went to the back window and looked up, out into the sky—the infinite, ever-changing, expanding sky—and it calmed me down. By the time Skyler clunked back through the door at eleven thirty, I was able to be half civil.

"How was school?"

"It was okay." He cocked his head, assessing the morning. "It was actually pretty good. Hey, you want to see my drawing? It started out abstract. Guess what it is."

I looked at the paper he held out. On it in pencil was an intricate mandala of tiny puzzle pieces.

"Well, it looks like a city."

"It's the planet. You know, how it seems really full, but really varied. That could be New York or Paris," he said, pointing to a skinny rectangle with a spiked top. "This is a forest, these are the Himalayas or the Andes . . ."

I felt so much relief hearing him prattling away and so much love for this boy who kept getting knocked down, by the place, and by his own brain, but kept getting back up, over and over again.

Maybe this was all going to end up all right after all. Maybe he'd end up loving this planet, his planet, with its confusion, its challenges, its infinite variety.

43

More Important Things

I WOKE UP EARLY on Good Friday. Peter had his back to me, his bare shoulder poking out from under the soft white pile of our blanket. It was only 5:45, but it was light. I padded barefoot down the white-tile hallway to the back window, slipped the key into the padlock, and opened the windows wide. It was like letting your breath out, a huge sigh of relief spreading down the hill, across the meadow, up through Bairro Vermelho, and out to the river and hills beyond.

There was the usual morning rooster orchestra. It didn't change in pitch so much as shift in density and location, a sudden clatch to the right, a pair below, pulling to a chorus in the distance, spraying left. A furry clump of *sanguin* picked through each other's fur on a palm frond at the bottom of our yard. Half-clothed people appeared in open doorways, tiny across the valley, wandered aimlessly into the dirt streets to stand for a minute before disappearing back into the dark maws of their houses. Nothing moved quickly.

A church bell began to clang. It had a hollow, toneless sound that said, *This is a practical bell*—announcing the time, calling people to prayer—not some highfalutin musical thing. It reminded me of the procession Molly and I had run into the night before with monks and nuns in robes of brown or white stepping slowly in time down the cobblestone street. Their somber chant, *"Nossa senhora . . ."*—Our mother full of grace—filled the darkness.

I poured cold coffee, milk, and a lot of sugar into a glass and folded myself onto the bench by the window. It was overcast, but not that taut, Saran Wrap sky—rather pillows of jostling cloud. One burst, and the rain came in a gushing drop. Within minutes, it was pinging on the PVC ceiling in the dining room. There must have been another hole in the roof tiles. I felt so grateful that the rains had come, to beat back the heat.

The isolated thunderstorms brought a little relief after the sodden lethargy of March and April—a lethargy that I'd begun to feel might never go away. I think this tendency to wonder whether this is it, whether *this*, whatever it is, is now for the rest of my life, started at about age forty, when it suddenly felt like my body was falling apart and like Humpty Dumpty wasn't fitting back together again, at least not "good as new."

Finishing my coffee, I headed out to the market, squeezing onto the bus just before the rain hit again. By the time I got off, the streets were flooded, ankle-deep by the curbs. I carefully hopped from bit to bit of visible sidewalk. Somewhere along the way, I'd learned not to flip my flops when it was wet. Just as somewhere along the way, I'd stopped saying everything in my head in English and had jumped directly to Portuguese.

This was a day for circling crowds in the *praça* near the ferry slip. Some things are timeless, like snake-oil salesmen with a good patter. A group pressed in to see the burly bare-chested man, who was putting screwdrivers and kitchen knives up his nose. For the finale, he dove through a lethal-looking bicycle rim spiked with inward-pointing machetes. All the while, he sold small tins of salve, guaranteed to cure everything: headaches, sore throat, back pain, and even your crotch (whatever ailed it).

I smiled. Just another day in Penedo.

Moving on, I stopped in at the "workers'" pharmacy, where the pharmacist asked if I knew the price of the medicine I sought. When I shook my head, he smiled with delight and quoted a price outrageously high. We both laughed at his joke. He then instructed the cashier not to put the little box in a plastic bag.

"*A senhora é salvando o ambiente*"—The lady is saving the environment.

By the time I'd moved through the market, I'd had several more good conversations: with Nené, the butcher; Celia, the fruit seller; and Nilda, a relative of Aniete's, who was manning her vegetable stand. I was feeling elated by my fluency.

A week later, Peter and I stepped out of the taxi, returning home from Oratorio, the restaurant where we'd been going weekly for our date night, which was also Molly and Skyler's "date night." They would go out to dinner on their own and do whatever they wanted; usually that meant watching a movie on the computer. That is, if they could disentangle themselves from all their hangers-on.

I pushed open the door and was met by Molly on the brink of tears. "We haven't even gone out yet. I am so frustrated. I feel so pissed off!"

Past her, I could see Karol and then two of Karol's friends using our computers in the front room.

"I will be *so* happy when we go home," Molly sighed emphatically. "At home we think our house is a refuge, but here . . ." She drifted off.

People in the United States value privacy and a chance for peace and quiet. Of course, people in the United States need the break from a "grueling day at work," their "dog-eat-dog" lives. A Brazilian home is not a refuge, at least not if our home was an example.

"Disturbing the peace" was not a concept in Northeastern Brazil, maybe because there was no peace to disturb. Or maybe the disturbance was the good part—the part with friends and music, the fun part.

The concept of "this is mine," so prevalent in our culture—my space, my time, my things, my quiet—was not so strong there. At dinner, Peter routinely swatted Molly's and Skyler's marauding hands as they tried to siphon food off his plate. "Dad, here everybody shares their food," Molly would retort.

Shares their food, shares their time, shares their space, shares their taste in music.

It strikes me that this is common to cultures where people have less. They have less space, so they sleep eight to a room (as Sarah, our Mozambican cook, did with her kids and grandkids); they have less food, so they share the hunt (as the Yanomami did); they have no running water, so they share the well (as the people in Aniete's village did). One would think it could go the other way, but it seems to be the opposite. The lack seems to build a kind of understanding about the need to work together, a kind of empathy that those of us who have more can lose.

This sharing of space wasn't an easy adaptation for us to make. In fact, I wouldn't say we adapted; we more sucked in our breath and tolerated it.

But I'm trying to hang onto the Brazilians' generosity with time. For me, time has always been an especially precious and contested commodity. As a child, I was already convinced that I was not going to have enough time in my whole life to do all the things I would want to do. I began to hoard time. So now I'm trying to learn to share time—with friends, family, community. This will be part of my newfound balance. Balance and joy.

The next day, I wandered into Sportgol, the best soccer shop in town, looking for a Vasco da Gama cap for Giovanni as a going-away present. Vasco was the soccer team to which he'd sworn his lifelong allegiance. I was pleased to have a chance to say good-bye to Sportgol's owner, a man whose name I'd never learned but who always greeted me, "*Oi, amiga*"—Hello, friend—and smiled gently from behind the glasses that slid down his nose.

Usually I'd initiated the conversations, trying to find out where a girl could play soccer, why official team shirts were so much more expensive than the replicas. But on that day, he was full of questions for me.

"My friend who lived over there," he said, meaning the United States, "for twelve years, he was married to an American." It was all spilling out in Portuguese. "When I told my friend about you and your family, he said he didn't understand how an American could come live here. He said you wouldn't like it. There's no organization here. The streets are bad. There, if your child doesn't go to school, they come to your house and knock on the door, to see if he's really sick. Here, nothing. It's all corrupt."

I said that our family had traveled a lot, so maybe we were more accustomed to a little disorganization, that maybe some Americans would find it difficult here.

"But you should tell your friend," I continued, "that there are things that are more important than organization—there are people. And here in Brazil, the people are open and kind; they know how to relax, how to have fun, how to take time with their friends, their family. This is what *you* have. This is why Americans should come to Brazil."

As the word got out that we were leaving, all the "wavers"—the people stationed along our daily paths who always smiled and waved—suddenly wanted to talk, to find out where we were from before it was too late.

"*Vai embora?*"—You're going away?—they asked, suddenly finding their tongues.

One was the elderly woman who lived down the ridge in the cream house with the sage-green shutters. She waved me over a few days before we left.

"*Onde vão?*" she asked in a whisper of a voice. "Where are you all going?"

"What is your name?" I finally asked.

"Mafalda," she replied, her eyes twinkling.

Of course! The kindly, diminutive witch who saved Harry Potter from the soul-sucking dementors, then faded back into her little English cottage to watch protectively through the cracks in her shutters. I knew she'd always been there for me.

44

The Long Stutter of Good-Byes

LEAVING WAS EXPENSIVE. First there were the parties, then the thank-you presents, then finally the eight hundred *reais* for each of us at the airport for overstaying our visas.

Peter, Molly, Skyler, and I sat around the dinner table one night and debated whether to throw a going-away party.

"Well, Lu's already talking about having a soccer-team party at Jane-la's. He's already figured out how much beer and *cachaça* I should buy," Peter laughed. "But another idea would be to have a cocktail party," he suggested. "We could say this is how we do it, in our country."

"No music, no dancing," I said, thinking of what we do at home.

"And it ends," Molly added.

"Yes, it ends. Talk for a few hours, just talk, then it's over," Peter said soberly.

"A little to eat, but not much, and a little to drink, but not so much that you can't talk or stand," I chimed in.

"Could be good," Peter concluded.

"They'll hate it," the kids said. We laughed in agreement.

After mulling it over, we decided to go ahead, to invite 175 of our best friends to a final bash at the tennis club.

Some might think Northeastern Brazilians are slackers when it comes to work, but when it comes to organizing a party, they are on it. Half the fun, I realized, was the planning. I visited Shirley and Robson at their beverage store down in the *baixa* almost every day for a week. Shirley helped me calculate quantity, told me whom to contact for coolers and ice, arranged for all the drinks to be delivered two days ahead of time.

When I started handing around invitations at capoeira, Bentinho offered to hold a *roda* at the party. Peter consulted with Eduardo, the president of the tennis club, to see if we could use the pool and the *futsal* court. Everyone was excited.

A friend of Skyler's, Francisco, asked if he could be our DJ. I was dubious. A thirteen-year-old DJ? But we said we'd try him out.

I handed Skyler's classmate Mateus an invitation and realized, as his face lit up, that instead of saying, "You need to present this invitation to enter," I'd just said, "There will be presents at the entrance." Oh well.

By the time we'd rented the club; hired five servers, a sound system with disco lights, and Francisco as DJ; ordered a thousand savories and five hundred sweets; bought ten cases of beer and seventeen cases of soda pop; and printed out invitations and photos of our friends for a display, we'd spent $2,000, more than we'd ever spent for a party.

But what a party.

It started at four on a Sunday afternoon with small-court soccer on a cracked cement court. The gals watched, chattering excitedly. The guys subbed in and out, even Robson and Zeca.

"When I got my nose broken playing soccer, I quit," Zeca had told us when we first met. But not surprisingly, he hadn't forgotten how to play.

The *capoeiristas* were in there, deftly weaving with the ball, and Victor and his older brother Italo and his friends and of course Peter and Skyler. Then the party moved on to a treasure hunt we'd set up ranging all over the top of the ridge, then an exhibition *roda*, *forró* dancing for young and old, and finally lots of eating and drinking until it was dark outside and people stumbled out the door seven hours later.

As the last people left, Skyler and I stood with Zeca in the vestibule.

"No, but you know, I jus remember," Zeca was saying, his speech a little slurry and his eyes beginning to droop, "I was thinking, it was you and Peter. You remember the time we were at the *pousada* and you were telling me I should do now what I want, that I can do it if I want it enough? I needed someone to tell me that. So now I am going to open this English school, and I am so happy. I have no money in the bank; I can't buy underwear, but it's okay."

"Yeah, who needs underwear?" I said. "You can set a new trend."

"Yah, in ten years, no one will be wearing it anyway." He smiled, turning to Skyler. "Do you wear underwear?"

The next day, Francisco, our DJ, appeared in our garden room, come to collect his payment. He'd done a great job choosing music and keeping it moving. His eyes widened at the sight of the bills. He confided quietly that this was the first time he'd ever been paid. We'd launched a career, and sure enough, I now follow it weekly on Facebook.

Saying good-bye felt like one long stutter.

Only when we began to pull the duffel bags out from under our beds did our imminent departure begin to seem real.

"This is our last Tuesday in Brazil," Skyler said with wonder.

How strange. You create a whole life, and then it evaporates, as though you'd just conjured up a town, full of people and houses, a river and a ridge, ferry boats and horse carts, school kids in uniform, *capoeiristas* and *futebol* players, coconut palms and mango trees, buzzards and egrets, *cachaça* and beer, holidays with parades and bouncing crowds behind *frevo* bands and *equip som* cars, people getting drunk, young men getting shot and friends going to prison.

Before leaving, Molly wrote a note to each of her friends. To Karol she wrote, *I know this is not the end of our life together. You will visit me, and I will return to Brazil. We will be friends always. You were like a sister to me this year, Karol. I don't know how we did it, but we always talked even when I couldn't speak Portuguese . . .*

Skyler exclaimed, "I don't know if I want to leave now. We might never come back. Are we going to come back?"

"Maybe we could come back in three years for the World Cup," Peter threw out. We all seemed to breathe a sigh of relief at the suggestion, relief at not having to confront a leave-taking that was suddenly feeling so final.

"Our struggles make me proud," Molly said as we walked back up the ridge one night. "Like, through our struggles, we've really dug ourselves a place here, each of us."

45

Crossing the River

THE FLEET OF LADIES was lined up on the shore—*Renata, Valeria, Liziane, Elizabeth, Vitoria*. I stood on the grass bank, sucking a stream of cold sweet juice out of a green coconut, and surveyed these brightly striped *lanchas*. It was still unclear to me how anyone knew which ones were going where and when, just as I could never figure out where to catch the bus when there were no clues, like signs or benches.

"*Qual está para Carrapichu?*" I asked the man lazily stirring ropes in the water.

He pointed to *Vitoria*, a slim white boat with splashy stripes of red, yellow, and green. It would be the next to head to Carrapichu, the mound of town across the river that I'd chosen for my weekly getaway.

I bounced up the gangplank and boarded. I liked being on the water and had decided I was going to take advantage of these floating ladies being so convenient in my last few months in Penedo. I was also running an experiment: Could I break out of my everything-must-have-a-purpose, must-lead-to-an-achievement pattern and give myself time just to think random, free-floating, non-pragmatic thoughts? This was not something I'd given myself time to do in my adult, working-mom life. Besides, I had a decision to make. I designated Thursday mornings.

I loved that twenty-minute trip—the initial cross to the island, jockeying for position with the car ferry, then hugging the island's far shore to sneak upriver through the currentless eddies, and the final cross to the other side with the blast of welcome breeze through the *lancha's* open windows. Slowing as we neared the shore, the captain killed the engine, and the little boat nuzzled up onto the sand.

Carrapichu was a busy place. Fully clothed women in floppy sun hats sat semisubmerged in the water, beating laundry on flat rocks; others cleaned fish. Clutches of glistening boys dove off rounded boulders, shooting sprays of shining water. Men backed their motorcycles into the shallows for a wash or stood on carts like Roman charioteers, urging their horses into the river. After their bath, the unhooked horse and rider went for a friendly swim. Then the dripping horse cantered out of the water, jubilant, electrified, exuding virility, its rider glued to its bare back. I envied the ease and companionship these horses and their riders seemed to feel.

My routine was to cross the road to the Pousada Terrazo and retreat into its quiet courtyard. There I sat under the potted palms, next to the pile of construction scrap and a murky goldfish pond, and helped myself to a thermos of dark, sweet *cafezinho*. I opened my newly purchased notebook, the one with the word *Happy*, in English, printed on the front. Now for the decision: to move forward with my dance company, i.e., stick to my old life, or chuck it and jump. It had taken me eight months to be able to even confront the question.

I'd spent twenty years of my life the American way, making my job my life—early mornings, nights, weekends. At least, that seemed to be the way for ambitious, career-oriented Americans on the track to "success." I had loved teaching dance and running the dance program at the University of Montana: the openness of new students, the stimulation of old ones who'd become friends, the camaraderie of shared passions with colleagues, the exhilaration of putting on dance performances. But it was hard, too, especially when Peter and I became parents.

When Molly was born, we split the days. I stayed home with her in the morning, working of course, and Peter stayed with her in the afternoons. We thought we'd figured it out. But it only took watching the top of her little blond head bobbing along inside the picket fence, wailing, "Mommy, Mommy!" as I drove away, to make me dissolve. Ten minutes later, I'd stand in front of my class, trying to hold myself together.

Then Skyler was born. At first, it was great. I had a sabbatical. We carted our five-week-old little boy and Molly, now three and a half, off for the five-month stint in Spain. I rented the dance studio and made a bed for Skyler on the floor, as I had for Molly in studios at home. My muses. But when the sabbatical ended and we returned home, our earlier system didn't work so well. Molly, a highly social being, was enrolled in preschool in the mornings, while I was home with Skyler. By the time I got home at night, she was often asleep. I'd barely seen her.

I started the long process of divesting. That was hard, too. The dance program felt like my other baby. But by the time I could apply for a second sabbatical, I'd managed to hand over the helm and was lobbying for a teaching schedule that would free me up in the afternoons—free me up to work, but at home. That sabbatical felt like a reprieve from a situation I knew in my heart wasn't working.

We headed to Mozambique. This time, when we returned to the States, I was determined to learn how to say no: no to 7:00 AM faculty meetings, no to more university committees, no to students wanting me to figure out their schedules and proofread their papers. My student evaluations went down. *Ms. Ragsdale seems distant,* they said; they didn't understand that my veins had run dry.

A friend had suggested I look at the world in terms of "breathers" and "suckers," that I look at situations and people and assess whether they are breathing life into me or sucking it out. After twenty years and the addition of two children and a dance company, my job at the university was falling hard into the sucker category. It was, however, our family's primary means of support.

I asked Peter for a meeting on "the rock," the rock by the creek across from our house—neutral ground, a calm setting. I wanted to quit.

"Okay," he said.

Just like that? Okay? But *how,* I wanted to know. How were we going to make it work—financially? He'd been freelancing for the last twenty years. So for him, *somehow* was a sufficient answer. For me, it was unnerving. We had a piece of land we could sell. The neighboring plot had sold for a lot. Maybe we could sell ours and buy a rental for some regular monthly income.

Okay, I'll make the jump. I quit.

Three years later, sitting between the construction scrap and mouthing goldfish, sweating over a *cafezinho*, I decided it was time to assess. How was I doing?

I watched the water hyacinths float down this slow, winding Brazilian river, the horses and their young men, the laughing women, and a brightly striped *lancha* swinging out into the current. I thought about Molly and Skyler, sitting at desks in a Portuguese-speaking classroom, now able to understand almost everything. I saw Molly's brilliant smile as she posed for photographs with her Brazilian friends and heard Skyler's rapid-fire voice debating in Portuguese with his. I remembered Molly performing with the Ballet Alagoas, tall, blond, and elegant, and Skyler, barefoot, deftly zigzagging with a soccer ball through his black-haired friends down a cobblestone street. I thought about how the capoeira men hadn't blinked when this fifty-two-year-old foreign woman and her slight blond boy wanted to join them, how they'd gently guided me into the *roda*. I heard the phone ring as Lu called Peter for another daily consultation about how to get Junior out of jail and sensed Peter's pleasure at being asked to travel with the team. I remembered Mario's smiling, crinkled eyes, a soccer ball cradled between hip and elbow, as he gazed with pleasure at Molly and Skyler running hard, sneakers squeaking, on the *futsal* court. I saw Aniete and Katia shaking their heads, saying, "*Que pena,*" sad and disbelieving that we were actually going home.

I pictured Robson flapping his saloon-door fingers, understanding nothing as we chatted in English but wanting to understand, wanting to engage.

I heard Giovanni, head thrown back, mouth wide in a huge laugh, responding to another of my "But why can't Brazilians . . . ?" in our ongoing debate about the powerlessness of the little man.

And Zeca.

Zeca picking us up, innumerable times, in the little black Fiat. Zeca knocking on the door for Skyler, to take him out for a guys-eating-meat lunch. Zeca putting bait on our hooks at his family fishpond. Zeca telling us he had never wanted to be a lawyer, but he needed to take care of his new nephew. Zeca, fortified by our encouragement, announcing he was going to open an English-language school.

I thought of all these people and this place that were now part of my life and Molly's and Skyler's and Peter's.

So what about the dance company? I'd come to Carrapichu to decide. The fact was, I loved to dance, but there were lots of other things I loved, too. Mostly it wasn't in my personality to make drastic changes. I was more of a "tweaker." So I decided to tweak, to downsize. I'd give it two years and then see—keep my eye on the "breathers" and "suckers" gauge.

But, too, I was going to remember to lie in a hammock, to sit at the "back window," to invite friends over on a Sunday for *feijoada*. I was going to find a physical community to replace my capoeira community. And mostly, I was going to remember with pride how my children staunchly hung on—through hours of incoherent Portuguese, the lines of girls and young men wanting to make out, and the onslaught of knockers at the door—and how my husband stood by my desire to raise "global children," despite his doubts about the size of the town and the emotional challenges.

And lastly, I was going to remember "balance" and "joy," and I was going to laugh.

46

A Quick White Smile in a Dark Face

WHAT I MISS from Brazil:

- the dry rustle of palm fronds
- cream church towers against a robin's-egg-blue sky and whipped cream clouds
- sorbet-colored houses
- monkeys in the morning
- men who can dance
- the crazy quilt of music
- *lanchas* crossing the river
- fast, cheap, home-cooked stews at a self-serve
- speckled *codorna* eggs dipped in spiced pepper
- chilled coconut water
- warm churros
- five kinds of mangos at ten cents apiece
- the Brazilian thumbs-up
- the twangy sound of the *berimbau*
- Bentinho, Fabio, Azul, Elton, Tijolo, Pirulito, Sombra, Ningo, Lampião, Taciana—the Grupo Pura Ginga do Capoeira
- Zeca, Aniete, Giovanni, Katia, Elizia, Robson and Shirley, Irma Joanna, Iracema, Mario, Pedro, Dalan, Fernando, Victor, Ricardo, Breno, Karol, Italo, Junior, Maria, and Celia
- Brazilian patience, Brazilian pace
- a quick white smile in a dark face

Epilogue

WE PACKED OUR BAGS and sold our furniture at half price, mostly to Aniete, who had decided to leave Aunt Laura's and move out on her own, something Brazilian women her age never did. Then we moved back into the Pousada Colonial, the B and B where we'd started, coming full circle.

The next day, we would throw our two bags each into the back of a hired pick-up and make the three-hour trip up the coast once more to Maceió, where we'd catch the first of five flights back home.

Molly's friends and Skyler's gang were all there, little Pedro hugging Skyler, his eyes beginning to tear. The staff of the *pousada* was lined up at the balconies to watch us leave. They hugged us and whispered a now-familiar litany of good wishes.

"*Vai com deus . . .*"—Go with God.

The one I really loved came from Maria, Victor and Karol's mom. "God will lift you up and bring you back here once again."

We stopped in at Robson's, on our way out of town, to wish him a happy birthday and say good-bye to Zeca and all his family. The women were seated under the songbird cages in the arcade, and the men were lounging out back under the bougainvillea arbor, just as they had been seven months earlier, on Zeca's birthday.

I slipped Zeca an envelope and told him, "This is to pay for Fabio, so he can take English lessons at your new school. Call him when you open."

"And if my school doesn't work," he said, taking it, "maybe I'm going to be a criminal lawyer. It feels so good to help people like that." He was referring to Junior, who'd finally been acquitted and released from jail.

Zeca walked us back out to the pick-up, closing the door as we climbed in and the car pulled away. We passed the Centro Cultural next door, where I'd taught dance to the daughters of sugarcane factory workers; circled through the roundabout; sped down the stretch past Natalia's house, where Skyler had gone to his first birthday party; and circled the next roundabout around *Christ in a Boat*, our nickname for the towering bronze statue of Jesus standing in a canoe, which had been one of our early markers as we'd sought to learn our way around town. Then we were speeding out of town, toward the ocean, toward the beaches.

We shuffled off the plane in Miami at six thirty in the morning, our stream of passengers merging with others all flowing toward baggage claim and customs. We entered a wider portion of the hall, the river splitting around large armed men scattered through the crowd, scanning for people to pull aside and question.

"Wow, not too warm; not even a smile," Molly noted.

"Pick up the ball! Pick up the BALL! PICK. UP. THE. BALL!" It took Skyler a minute to realize the uniformed man with the rearing German shepherd was talking to him. Chagrinned, he snatched up the soccer ball he'd been dribbling with his feet.

"Don't worry, Skyler. The dog just wanted your ball."

We managed to find all our bags, make it through customs, recheck the bags, and enter security. There we stood, one by one, in the beam-me-up-Scotty "imaging station," our hands raised over our heads, while our bodies were stripped to their bones.

I wondered what Bentinho and the other *capoeiristas* would make of all this if I managed to bring them to the United States to visit as I hoped to do—this and the self-flushing toilets and automatic paper towel dispensers.

As we were repacking and dressing (the TSA agents had even scrutinized our flip-flops), we were put through not one but two episodes of shouted, "Halt! Everybody, don't move . . . Okay, you can go, just a drill."

We were definitely *not* in Brazil.

"Whew, this is intense," Skyler said. "Let's get out of here, before they do another one."

Things had gone smoothly until we hit the first world. Then things began to go awry. When we finally made it to Chicago, two hours late, after a delayed flight from Miami, we discovered our bags had some- how been put on three different flights, arriving several hours apart. Luckily, we had a long layover.

As we were waiting at the baggage carousel for the third flight, an overweight woman with dyed blond hair walked up to the man next to us.

"Honey?" She sounded tentative.

"I can't hear you," her husband snapped.

"They've lost our bag," she almost whispered.

"What!" His voice rose. "Fucking hell!" He kicked their red carry- on. "Where the hell is it!" he shouted as he stomped off to the help desk.

Okay, we were definitely not in Brazil.

Back in Missoula, Tom—the Verizon man—convinced Peter that he didn't really want an iPhone because, after all, it was going to take ten days to hook up the Internet at our house and God forbid we should be without Internet for ten days. But never fear, the Droid was here, and we could "tether" it to our computer to go online. So Peter bought it.

It used to be that you tethered horses, but now you tether yourself —to the communications network. And the communications net- work is like a cancer that keeps dividing, requiring more and more vigilance to keep up, not just via email but via Facebook, LinkedIn, Twitter . . . you know the list. And the time it takes to stay "checked in" threatens, like that cancer, to take over one's life. At least, that's the way it feels to me.

Peter and I ran into a friend walking his dog in the park across from our house.

"Can you come on Sunday?" he asked. "Oh, Facebook," he said, seeing our confusion. "My housewarming? The invitation was on Facebook."

It used to be you had one landline for the family and called it good. Now Peter was negotiating for a landline and four cell phones. It used to cost thirty dollars a month; now it cost $240, but it was a bargain.

Tom made it all sound so simple. So simple that ten days later, my new cell phone, using my old office number, still told callers it had been disconnected. Likewise, our landline, a simple reconnection of our old number, refused to be reconnected. We had to hurl ourselves down the stairs, skid around the corner, accelerate through the living room, and clip the kitchen door in the hope that we could pick up the phone in the first three rings, before it told the caller we didn't exist.

People were finally able to get through on my new cell phone after I spent an hour and a half on the line with two Qwest and four Verizon agents, several simultaneously as I refused to let them hang up, knowing that if they did, I'd be back to scratch. We knew things took time in the developing world, but this was the first world, the place where we expected efficiency, friendly instant service, convenience—where things were supposed to work. How could we reset the expectations so they would produce contentment rather than total frustration?

So, being home was weird. What could we say to all the people asking, "How was it?" "I bet it was great." What was the sound bite that would somehow encapsulate our hearts cradling the people of Penedo, the quilt of sherbet colors, the ragged collage of sound—palm fronds clacking in the breeze, horse hooves on cobblestones?

It had been a full year. Full literally of blood, tears, and sweat, exhilaration and discouragement, fearful hearts and bursting hearts—and while we had been eager to return home, we'd also been sad. Sad to leave people who had been incredibly generous, who'd given us their time, shared their families, come by with avocados and mangos, taught us to dart and dodge with a soccer ball, to kick and duck in the capoeira ring—people who'd invited us to the beach, to their birthday parties and weddings, who'd waved and called out to us every day as we passed.

So when questioned, I settled on, "Well, it was really rich and, well, really hard, so I feel relieved to be back but . . . sad, too." It was lame, but it was the best I could do. Then I'd flip the conversation. "I hear you produced your Christmas play again this year."

There was still too much to say. It would take months to boil it down. So it seemed simpler to say nothing, turn the conversation away. Besides, no one really wanted more than that ten-second sound bite anyway.

Home was so familiar. Had we ever left? I resented it a little. I wasn't ready for Brazil to be reduced to a dream. As I rode around on my bike and drove around in my car, I realized we couldn't have chosen a town more the opposite of home. Penedo's hard surfaces and chute-like streets were met with Missoula's sprawling-wide, leafy-soft avenues; Penedo's bright oranges and pinks contrasted with Missoula's muted greens; Penedo's constant scraps of ricocheting sound juxtaposed the quiet, steady susurration of Missoula's water. In both places, the beginning of winter there and of summer here, the rivers were rising. But there, up on our ridge, we watched it at a distance, measuring the spread of green—the influx of water hyacinths. Here, we watched at eye level, as the stream across the street from our house, swollen with snowmelt, started to invade the paths of the park it runs through.

I kept finding myself thinking here—there, here—there.

I wondered if I were going to be able to maintain my effort to get off "the track," be able to hang on to the slower pace, hang on to the recognition that nothing is so important that it should stop you from spending time with people you love, hang on to the realization that there's real value in doing some things just for fun, even if they don't make you more productive or help you climb a ladder. I knew that to do this, I'd have to wade upstream, against a current that seems only to be building in strength (despite the increase in grumbling)— that work-comes-first, follow-the-prescribed-path-to-success current that continues to sweep us out to sea, that has caused us to lose our moorings.

For her senior project in her last year of high school, Molly organized a fundraiser for the capoeira salon back in Penedo, raising $3,000 for their program to help the street kids in Bairro Vermelho. She slugged her way through an overloaded senior year, and by the time she decided to go to Macalester, a college known for its focus on global citizenship, she was burned out on school.

She decided she wanted to travel abroad, on her own this time. Taking a gap year, she left for Europe: starting with family friends in

Sweden, moving on to work on a fig orchard in southern Portugal, and finally teaching English in a village of one hundred in Nepal. I thought how much more relaxed I would have felt if she'd just gone to college, into a safe, familiar structure, but then I knew, too, that she would know how to find her family wherever she was. That family would take her in and watch out for her.

I wish every American teenager were fortunate enough to go abroad, preferably to a developing country. It would change our relationship to the world, as individuals and as a nation, completely. Those kids would come back with a visceral understanding of why they're so lucky to have been born in the United States, recognizing how precious is their ability to speak out without risking their lives, seeing how well the law works, mostly.

But they'd see, too, that we're not so different, nor are we so far ahead, that our breakneck speed may be breaking us down, that our touted 24/7 access to work may be sapping our energy and stealing time, time we could be spending with others, face-to-face, the way Zeca's family did every Sunday in Brazil. Those kids would learn that maybe we need to look a little farther afield before we claim the bragging rights we seem to cherish as Americans. They would be shocked, as I was, that we have congressional leaders who have never left our shores, who have never been issued a passport but who make our foreign policy.

Some of those kids would decide they never want to leave the United States again, that they're in the place they love. Others might decide, as I did, that the world is their home, and it's both inexhaustibly big and very small—that it's full of people just like them, trying to find their place, their role, their identities, trying to take care of people they love.

I hope that my children will be able to see how they can fit into a larger world—one bigger than nations, broader than race—and feel comfortable enough in it to know they can jump and then look, because they'll know they can cope when they land.

I think they will, and when they do, I hope they take me with them.

Postscript

WHEN WE RETURNED to Brazil three years later, nothing had changed, and everything had changed.

Penedo appeared much the same. Some houses were newly painted, others faded; the market was still covered in black plastic; brightly striped *lanchas* still plied the river; music blaring from mobile speakers still bounced off plaster walls. But the rusting shells of the old buses had been replaced by Mercedes-Benzes; the motley collection of taxis at the ferry slip were now a uniform, shiny white. The peeling face of the capoeira salon continued to peel, but on either side were now a black-glass-chandeliered pastry shop and a designer clothing store.

"*É nossa, é nossa,*" Skyler laughed as he danced across the tiny *praça*, rolling the soccer ball forward, back, kicking it into the steps to ricochet into the goal delineated by two flip-flops against the retaining wall. "*Gol!*" he and Italo shouted, their fists raised triumphantly in the air.

His old friend Victor gave him a friendly shove on the back, a good-to-see-you, but how-did-you-get-another-goal shove. Victor had grown a foot and was filling out into a man. But he was still as patient and quick as ever.

We were back in the site where they first met, the very first night we arrived in Penedo four years earlier—the Praça do Convento, the tiny, bricked-in area sandwiched between the steps of the tiered plaza and a stone cross. Same people, same place, doing just what they'd done then, but now deftly using the stairs, the statue, the retaining walls to ricochet the ball around their opponents to their partners.

Though we'd arrived in town late at night, the first thing Skyler wanted to do was to run up the cobbled street to Victor's house, the blue house with the worn steps and dark, cool interior. Despite all the trials of his year in Brazil, now, at sixteen, Skyler was thrilled to be back.

Peter, Molly, and I, tired after a day of bus and van travel from Salvador, had retreated to Oratorio, the airy restaurant cantilevered out over the river that had been Peter's and my date-night spot. We'd installed ourselves in the hard wooden seats, ordered beans and rice, fried fish, beer, and *caipirinhas*. The waiters smiled in recognition and welcome. I felt a wash of contentment as I relaxed into the warm, moist night air.

Appendixes

Where Are They Now?

Ana Licia, **Keyla**, **Leila**, and **Sara** (Molly's friends) have enrolled in universities in Maceió to become nurses, physical therapists, and chemical engineers. When we visited, they returned to Penedo in force to pull Molly out to *passear* around town and dance till dawn.

Aniete has married Roberto, a man she'd just met when we lived there, and has a baby daughter.

Bazooka killed a man—a vengeance killing for the death of his brother—and is in prison.

Bentinho is teaching capoeira at the Centro Cultural, where I'd gotten him a job before we'd left, and is now employed by the city, teaching capoeira in all the public schools.

Elizia is still there behind the teller bars of her bookkeeper's office at Imaculada, her seriousness bursting into smiles and engulfing hugs.

Fabio left the sugarcane factory to enroll in the small local university to study tourism.

Giovanni is finishing law school and is hot to become a labor lawyer, defending the worker.

Junior had been arrested again, but when we visited, he was still playing soccer on the ragged field down in the *baixa* and wanted to see if Peter remembered the victory dance.

Karol has moved south to São Paulo to become an airline attendant, pursuing her dream to travel and speak English.

Katia continues to manage the Pousada Colonial as efficiently as ever.

Robson and **Shirley** have a new son and continue to run their store down in the *baixa*.

Zeca is married and has become a professor of English in a language institute in Maceió.

Skyler is a junior in high school in Missoula and has just won several slopestyle ski competitions flipping on skis.

Molly is a junior at Macalester College, double majoring in media and cuture/international studies and interning at the Minnesota AIDS Project. She's preparing for a junior year abroad to be spent on a sailboat off New Zealand.

Peter sold the new book proposal that he began developing in Brazil, and that book, *Astoria*, published a few months before our return, is selling better than any before.

I decided, on leaving Brazil, to continue with the dance company, but after several gratifying years, I am finding I have come to the end of that chapter, at least as it was written. I feel sure my next adventure will be a full one and will include more travel. I continue to grapple with balance, but I am lucky to find joy in so many people and in doing so many things.

Portuguese Vocabulary:

água de coco: coconut water

atabaque: drum played by *capoeiristas*

baixa: below; often refers to the geographically lower part of a town, which can also be the business center, or downtown, in port towns where shops cluster around harbors

berimbau: the one-stringed instrument played by *capoeiristas*

cafezinho: demitasse cups of strong, sweetened black coffee

caipirinha: a popular drink made from *cachaça* (sugar cane alcohol) and usually limes

capoeira: a Brazilian martial art/dance form

capoeirista: a practitioner of capoeira

carnaval: a multi-day pre-Lent festival

empregada: a house cleaner and cook who comes in during the day

equip som car: a car equipped with massive sound speakers

Eskyloh: Portuguese pronunciation of Skyler's name

favela: urban slum

feijoada: celebratory Brazilian bean stew

fica: to make out

forró (pronounced *foho*): type of music and social dance found in Northeastern Brazil

frevo: a form of music and dance originating in Pernambuco, Brazil; the form it took most often in Penedo was of a small marching brass band

futebol: field soccer

futsal: small-court soccer

graviola: the green spiky fruit known in English as soursop

lancha: a passenger ferry shaped like a long tube that's not quite high enough to stand up in

lanchonete: lunch spot with cafeteria-style home cooking

maracujá: passion fruit

Mela-Mela: the flour and food-coloring fight that takes place in Neópolis during *carnaval*

obrigado(a): thank you; the -*o* ending is used by males and the -*a* by females

pandeiro: a tambourine-like instrument played by *capoeiristas*

pousada: a bed-and-breakfast

praça: a plaza

real (reais): Brazilian currency (singular and plural)

roda: the circle made by *capoeiristas* within which two players spar

sim: yes

tchau: bye

tudo bem: all is well

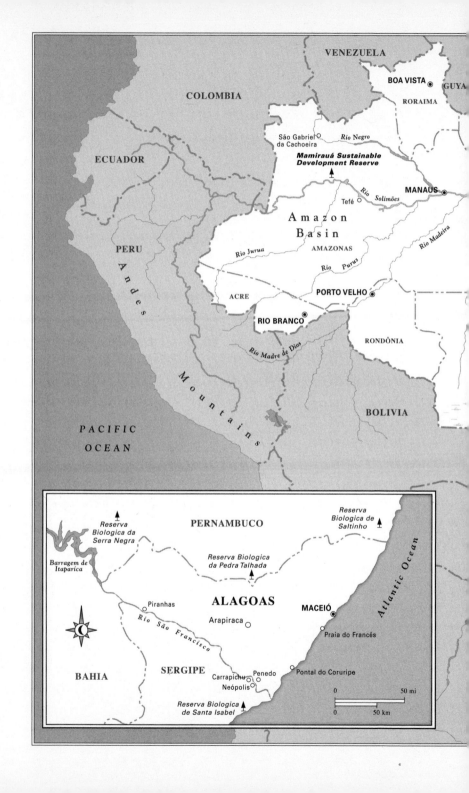

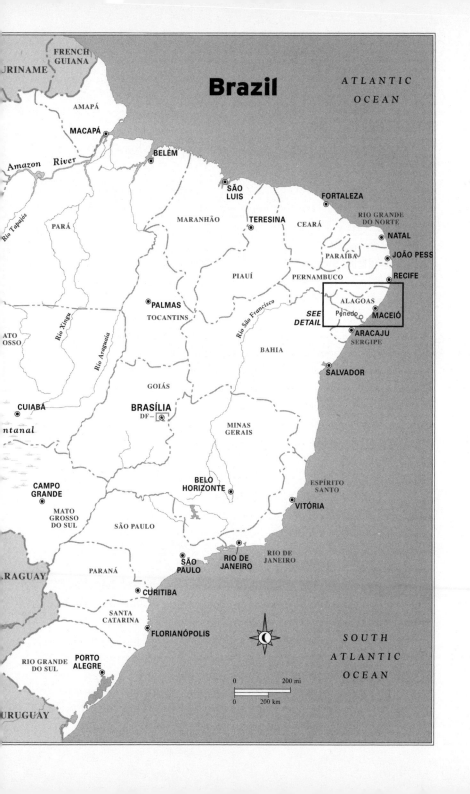

Acknowledgments

I WOULD LIKE TO THANK my writing coaches, Peter Stark and Caroline Patterson, and my many readers along the way: Jane Ragsdale, Noel Ragsdale, Elke Govertson, Jen Ellis, Karen Sandstrom, Caroline Lonski, John Brown, Brian Gerke, Joy Harris, Jennifer Weltz, Lisa Hendricks, and Molly Stark-Ragsdale. I am grateful for the encouragement of friends: Rosalie Cates, Martha Newell, Tom Duffield, Paul Elliott, and Stephanie Daley-Watson. Thank you to Whitney Dreier at *Outside Magazine Online* for her interest in trying out some of this material for the nascent column *Raising Rippers*. Thank you to The Break Espresso for offering a warm place to work and keeping me fueled with generras. I want to thank Barrett Briske for her eagle eye as a copyeditor and her rigorous effort to grapple with all the Portuguese language references. I give special thanks to my developmental editor Anne Horowitz for her thoroughness and insight, humor and tact (how am I doing with the dangling modifiers?), and to my executive editor Laura Mazer for her clarity of vision and enthusiasm. I am most grateful to my agent Judy Klein for her astute guidance, her belief in this book, and her willingness to stick with me.

Most of all, I want to thank the people of Penedo for their incredible kindness, generosity, and friendship: Katia for her ongoing support and Suzy for taking us into the Pousada Colonial; Giovanni for his friendship and instruction in Brazilian culture and language; Elizia for her enthusiastic open arms; Iracema for holding my hand through the challenges of my children's schooling; Mario and Valmir for their quiet bolstering of Molly and Skyler at school; Karol, Leila, Keyla, Ana Licia, Sara, and Larissa for being such wonderful friends to Molly; Victor, Ricardo, Breno, Paulinho, Pedro, and Giovanni for being such great friends to Skyler; Fernando for pulling Molly and me into dance; Aniete, Gel, and Shirley, Aunt Laura, and our landlady Ilda for their support in our home and guidance through Penedo's daily mysteries; Bentinho, Fabio, Azul, Taciana, and the many capoeiristas, and the soccer players Lu, Manuel, Junior, Frankie, and Dalan, all of whom gave us a community; and, finally, two open-hearted, wonderful families—that of Maria and her children, Victor, Karol, Italo, and Junior, and that of Zeca and his parents, Valter and Vilma, sister Rafaella, and uncle Robson, aunt Shirley, and their children Julia and Mateus. We are eternally grateful for your friendship. My ultimate thanks go to my adventurous parents for setting me on this path; to my two sisters, Noel and Dana Ragsdale, world travelers in their own rights; and to my children, Molly and Skyler, and husband, Peter, for their tremendous courage and willingness to step into the unknown. I feel so blessed to have such a family.

About the Author

AMY RAGSDALE is a writer and choreographer based out of Missoula, Montana, who was born in New York City and raised in Madison, Wisconsin; Asia; and North Africa. She earned a BA in Art History from Harvard College and an MALS from Wesleyan. Her articles on travel and dance have appeared in *High Desert Journal, Mamalode,* and *Outside Magazine Online,* where she initiated the column *Raising Rippers.*

Ragsdale's dance career included performing with Impulse in Boston, Fred Benjamin, Laughing Stone, and Ze'eva Cohen dance companies in New York, and as a guest with Bill T. Jones and Douglas Dunn. She moved to Missoula to head the dance program at the University of Montana. She has also taught contemporary dance in Spain, Indonesia, Martinique, Mozambique, and Brazil. Her choreographic work has been performed throughout the Northwest, in New York, and televised on CNN's *World News.* She is the founder of Headwaters Dance Co., the recipient of the University of Montana's Distinguished Teaching Award, and a 2009 Governor's Arts Award for the State of Montana.

She is married to writer Peter Stark. They have two fabulous children, an ancient imperious cat, and a relentlessly enthusiastic puppy.